Founders and the Constitution

In Their Own Words

We the People

Article 1

Volume 1

In Their Own Words
Volume 1

A program of **The Bill of Rights Institute**
200 North Glebe Road, Suite 1050
Arlington, Virginia 22203
www.BillofRightsInstitute.org

Founded in 1999, the Bill of Rights Institute's mission is to educate high school students and teachers about our country's Founding principles through programs that teach the words and ideas of the Founders; the liberties and freedoms guaranteed in our Founding documents; and how America's Founding principles affect and shape a free society. The Bill of Rights Institute is an educational non-profit organization, classified by the Internal Revenue Service as a 501(c)(3) organization, a public charity, and is supported by more than 3,000 individual and foundation donors.

Instructional Design
Stephen M. Klugewicz, Ph.D.
Claire McCaffery Griffin

Graphic Concepts/Production Assistant
Carolyn Davids

Contributors
Claire McCaffery Griffin
Brett Helm
Logan Murray
Tami Nutt

Editors
Stephen M. Klugewicz, Ph.D.
Claire McCaffery Griffin
Logan Murray

Co-authors/Academic Advisors
Stephen M. Klugewicz, Ph.D.
David Marion, Ph.D.
Robert M.S. McDonald, Ph.D.
Craig Yirush, Ph.D.

Production, Design, and Illustration: settingPace, LLC, Cincinnati, Ohio
Illustrations: Copyright © Paul Brinkdopke. Used by permission.

ISBN
Volume 1: 1-932785-14-0
Volume 2: 1-932785-15-9
Both Volumes: 1-932785-16-7

❧ TABLE OF CONTENTS—VOLUME 1 ❧

In 1760, what was to become the United States of America consisted of a small group of colonies strung out along the eastern seaboard of North America. Yet, in the next twenty-five years, the American colonists would challenge the political control of Britain, declare independence, wage a bloody war, and lay the foundations for a trans-continental, federal republican state. In these crucial years, the colonies would be led by a new generation of politicians, men who combined practical political skills with a sophisticated grasp of political ideas.

By Craig Yirush, Ph.D.

Thematic Essays:

For nearly 250 years, the existence of slavery deprived African Americans of independent lives and individual liberty. It also compromised the republican dreams of European Americans, who otherwise achieved unprecedented success in the creation of political institutions and social relationships based on citizens' equal rights and ever-expanding opportunity.

By Robert M.S. McDonald, Ph.D.

Religious toleration was a practical necessity in eighteenth-century America, where many creeds of Christianity flourished. The Founders realized that coercion of religious belief was both unjust and unwise, as it would serve merely to incite civil discord, thereby endangering the independence and political liberty they held so dear.

By Stephen M. Klugewicz, Ph.D.

The federal arrangement that was crafted by the delegates at the Constitutional Convention of 1787 was an ingenious response to the demand for both effective government on the one side, and rights-sensitive government on the other. The American federal system has long been recognized as one of the principal models of a modern democratic system of government.

By David E. Marion, Ph.D.

The relationship between republican government and commerce was one of the central problems that confronted the Founders in the late eighteenth century. Although the new Constitution laid the groundwork for an extended commercial republic, it did not end the debates among the Founders over the legitimacy of commerce.

By Craig Yirush, Ph.D.

Founders:

ACKNOWLEDGEMENTS

The National Endowment for the Humanities made *Founders and the Constitution: In Their Own Words* a reality by providing a generous grant through its *We the People* program.

The Bill of Rights Institute is also grateful to the Shelby Cullom Davis Foundation for providing seed funding to begin the development of *Founders and the Constitution* instructional material.

We are also grateful to the Bodman Foundation for providing a generous grant to assist in the development and marketing of this program.

Any views, findings, conclusions, or recommendations expressed in this publication do not necessarily represent those of the National Endowment for the Humanities, the Shelby Cullom Davis Foundation, or the Bodman Foundation.

Academic Advisory Council

Dr. William Damon
Professor and Director
Stanford Center on Adolescence,
Stanford University

Richard A. Epstein
Professor of Law
University of Chicago Law School

Dr. William Galston
Institute for Philosophy and
Public Policy
University of Maryland

A.E. Dick Howard
School of Law
University of Virginia

Alex M. Johnson, Jr.
Dean and William S. Pattee
Professor of Law
University of Minnesota
Law School

Dr. Charles R. Kesler
Department of Government
Claremont McKenna College

Dr. Sanford Levinson
School of Law
University of Texas

Dr. Stephen Macedo
Department of Politics
Princeton University

Dr. Pauline Maier
Department of History
Massachusetts Institute of
Technology

Dr. John Majewski
Department of History
University of California,
Santa Barbara

Dr. David Marion
Center for Leadership in the
Public Interest
Hampden Sydney College

Rodney Smolla
School of Law
University of Richmond

Eugene Volokh
School of Law
University of California,
Los Angeles

Dr. Keith Whittington
Department of Politics
Princeton University

Dr. Gordon Wood
Department of History
Brown University

Todd Zywicki
School of Law
George Mason University
Bill of Rights Institute
Academic Advisor

Field Testers

Terry Boggs
Freedom High School
Orlando, Florida

Lori Dumerer
R.L. Turner High School
Dallas, Texas

Scott Heinecke
Jesse Bethel High School
Vallejo, California

George Kropp
Calvert Hall College High School
Baltimore, Maryland

Ruth M. Lewis
Richwoods High School
Peoria, Illinois

Sr. Rita McCauley, C.S.J.
St. Francis Preparatory School
Fresh Meadows, New York

Gary Medland
Brandon High School
Ortonville, Michigan

Beth Sharp
St. Thomas Aquinas High School
Ft. Lauderdale, Florida

Michael H. Taylor
Turner Ashby High School
Bridgewater, Virginia

Rod Tillman
Stevens Point Area Senior High
Stevens Point, Wisconsin

PREFACE

"And for the support of this declaration, with a firm reliance on the protection of Divine Providence, we mutually pledge to each other our lives, our fortunes, and our sacred honor." With these words, the fifty-six signers of the Declaration of Independence took the momentous step of establishing an independent nation.

The story of America's Founding Fathers is truly a remarkable one. By defying the greatest empire on earth, these men made a courageous sacrifice to form a constitutional republic so that we may live free today. The Bill of Rights Institute developed the *Founders and the Constitution: In Their Own Words* educational resource to help you share these stories with your students so they may understand the unique role that our Founders played in securing our liberties and shaping American government.

Divided into two volumes, each of the twenty-four lessons is dedicated to a specific Founder, outlining his accomplishments and contributions to the Constitution. Each chapter includes a biographical essay on the Founder, a lesson plan, a primary-source activity, a bibliography of the Founder's works, and a list of print and Internet resources for further reading. To enhance your students' learning experience, each unit comes with a classroom poster that portrays the Founder and includes a famous quotation by the Founder.

Each volume of *Founders and the Constitution* also includes an introductory essay about the Founding Era as well as four thematic essays that shed light on important topics of the period, such as liberty, freedom of religion, and limited government. Concluding each volume is a list of additional classroom activities that may be used in conjunction with one or more of the units.

Founders and the Constitution provides instructional material that can be taught as a stand-alone lesson or used to supplement existing American History or Civics textbooks. By focusing on the Founders and original documents, *Founders and the Constitution* ties into state standards and curriculum content requirements for both U.S. History and Government classes.

By reintroducing the next generation to the lives and contributions of the Founding Fathers, the *Founders and the Constitution* program can help the next generation realize how remarkable America truly is.

—*Victoria Hughes,* President

INTRODUCTORY ESSAY:
EXPLAINING THE FOUNDING

In 1760, what was to become the United States of America consisted of a small group of colonies strung out along the eastern seaboard of North America. Although they had experienced significant economic and demographic growth in the eighteenth century and had just helped Britain defeat France and take control of most of North America, they remained politically and economically dependent upon London. Yet, in the next twenty-five years, they would challenge the political control of Britain, declare independence, wage a bloody war, and lay the foundations for a trans-continental, federal republican state. In these crucial years, the colonies would be led by a new generation of politicians, men who combined practical political skills with a firm grasp of political ideas. In order to better understand these extraordinary events, the Founders who made them possible, and the new Constitution that they created, it is necessary first to understand the political ideas that influenced colonial Americans in the crucial years before the Revolution.

THE COMMON LAW AND THE RIGHTS OF ENGLISHMEN

The political theory of the American colonists in the seventeenth and eighteenth centuries was deeply influenced by English common law and its idea of rights. In a guide for religious dissenters written in the late seventeenth century, William Penn, the founder of Pennsylvania, offered one the best contemporary summaries of this common-law view of rights. According to Penn, all Englishmen had three central rights or privileges by common law: those of life, liberty, and property. For Penn, these English rights meant that every subject was "to be freed in Person & Estate from Arbitrary Violence and Oppression." In the widely used language of the day, these rights of "Liberty and Property" were an Englishman's "Birthright."

In Penn's view, the English system of government preserved liberty and limited arbitrary power by allowing the subjects to express their *consent* to the laws that bound them through two institutions:

"Parliaments and Juries." "By the first," Penn argued, "the subject has a share by his chosen Representatives in the Legislative (or Law making) Power." Penn felt that the granting of consent through Parliament was important because it ensured that "no new Laws bind the People of England, but such as are by common consent agreed on in that great Council."

In Penn's view, juries were an equally important means of limiting arbitrary power. By serving on juries, Penn argued, every freeman "has a share in the *Executive* part of the Law, no Causes being tried, nor any man adjudged to loose [*sic*] Life, member or Estate, but upon the *Verdict of his Peers* or Equals." For Penn, "These two grand Pillars of English Liberty" were "the *Fundamental vital Priviledges* [*sic*]" of Englishmen.

The other aspect of their government that seventeenth-century Englishmen celebrated was a system that was ruled by laws and not by men. As Penn rather colorfully put it: "In France, and other Nations, the meer [*sic*] Will of the Prince is Law, his Word takes off any mans Head, imposeth Taxes, or seizes a mans Estate, when, how and as often as he lists; and if one be accussed [*sic*], or but so much as suspected of any Crime, he may either presently Execute him, or banish, or Imprison him at pleasure." By contrast, "*In England,*" Penn argued, "the Law is both the measure and the bound of every Subject's Duty and Allegiance, each man having a fixed Fundamental-Right born with him, as to Freedom of his Person and Property in his Estate, which he cannot be deprived of, but either by his Consent, or some Crime, for which the Law has impos'd such a penalty or forfeiture."

This common law view of politics understood political power as fundamentally *limited* by Englishmen's rights and privileges. As a result, it held that English kings were bound to rule according to known laws and by respecting the inherent rights of their subjects. It also enshrined the concept of consent as the major means to the end of protecting these rights. According to Penn and his contemporaries, this system of government—protecting as it did the "unparallel'd

Priviledge [*sic*] of Liberty and Property"—had made the English nation "more free and happy than any other People in the World."

The Founders imbibed this view of English rights through the legal training that was common for elites in the eighteenth-century Anglo-American world. This legal education also made them aware of the history of England in the seventeenth century, a time when the Stuart kings had repeatedly threatened their subjects' rights. In response, many Englishmen drew on the common law to argue that all political power, even that of a monarch, should be limited by law. Colonial Americans in the eighteenth century viewed the defeat of the Stuarts and the subsequent triumph of Parliament (which was seen as the representative of subjects' rights) in the Glorious Revolution of 1688 as a key moment in English history. They believed that it had enshrined in England's unwritten constitution the rule of law and the sanctity of subjects' rights. This awareness of English history instilled in the Founders a strong fear of arbitrary power and a consequent desire to create a constitutional form of government that limited the possibility of rulers violating the fundamental liberties of the people.

The seriousness with which the colonists took these ideas can be seen in their strong opposition to Parliament's attempt to tax or legislate for them without their consent in the 1760s and 1770s. After the Revolution, when the colonists formed their own governments, they wrote constitutions that included many of the legal guarantees that Englishmen had fought for in the seventeenth century as a means of limiting governmental power. As a consequence, both the state and federal constitutions typically contained bills of rights that enshrined core English legal rights as fundamental law.

NATURAL RIGHTS

The seventeenth century witnessed a revolution in European political thought, one that was to prove profoundly influential on the political ideas of the American Founders. Beginning with the Dutch writer Hugo Grotius in the early 1600s, several important European thinkers began to construct a new understanding of political theory that argued that all men by *nature* had equal rights, and that governments were formed for the sole purpose of protecting these natural rights.

> The political theory of the American colonists in the seventeenth and eighteenth centuries was deeply influenced by English common law and its idea of rights.

The leading proponent of this theory in the English-speaking world was John Locke (1632–1704). Deeply involved in the opposition to the Stuart kings in the 1670s and 1680s, Locke wrote a book on political theory to justify armed resistance to Charles II and his brother James. "To understand political power right," Locke wrote, "and derive it from its original, we must consider, what state all men are naturally in, and that is, a state of perfect freedom to order their actions, and dispose of their possessions and persons, as they think fit, within the bounds of the law of nature, without asking leave, or depending upon the will of any other man." For Locke, the state of nature was "a state also of equality, wherein all the power and jurisdiction is reciprocal, no one having more than another."

Although this pregovernmental state of nature was a state of perfect freedom, Locke contended that it also lacked an impartial judge or umpire to regulate disputes among men. As a result, men in this state of nature gathered together and consented to create a government in order that their natural rights would be better secured. Locke further argued that, because it was the people who had created the government, the people had a right to resist its authority if it violated their rights. They could then join together and exercise their collective or popular sovereignty to create a new government of their own devising. This revolutionary political theory meant that ultimate political authority belonged to the people and not to the king.

This idea of natural rights became a central component of political theory in the American colonies in the eighteenth century, appearing in numerous political pamphlets, newspapers, and sermons. Its emphasis on individual freedom and government by consent combined powerfully with the older idea of common law rights to shape the political theory of the Founders. When faced with the claims of the British Parliament in the 1760s and 1770s to legislate for them without their consent, American patriots invoked both the common law and Lockean natural rights theory to argue that they had a right to resist Britain.

Thomas Jefferson offers the best example of the impact that these political ideas had on the founding. As he so eloquently argued in the Declaration of Independence: "We hold these truths to be self-evident, that all men are created equal, that they are endowed by their Creator with certain unalienable Rights, that among these are Life, Liberty and the pursuit of Happiness. That to secure these rights, Governments are instituted among Men, deriving their just powers from the consent of the governed, That whenever any Form of Government becomes destructive of these ends, it is the Right of the People to alter or abolish it, and to institute new Government, laying its foundations on such principles and organizing its powers in such form, as to them shall seem most likely to effect their Safety and Happiness."

This idea of natural rights also influenced the course of political events in the crucial years after 1776. All the state governments put this new political theory into practice, basing their authority on the people, and establishing written constitutions that protected natural rights. As George Mason, the principal author of the influential Virginia Bill of Rights (1776), stated in the document's first section: "All men are by nature equally free and independent, and have certain inherent rights, of which, when they enter into a state of society, they cannot, by any compact, deprive or divest their posterity; namely, the enjoyment of life and liberty, with the means of acquiring and possessing property, and pursuing and obtaining happiness and safety." The radical implications of this insistence on equal natural rights would slowly become apparent in postrevolutionary American society as previously downtrodden groups began to invoke these ideals to challenge slavery, argue for a wider franchise, end female legal inequality, and fully separate church and state.

In 1780, under the influence of John Adams, Massachusetts created a mechanism by which the people themselves could exercise their sovereign power to constitute governments: a special convention convened solely for the purpose of writing a constitution, followed by a process of ratification. This American innovation allowed the ideas of philosophers like Locke to be put into practice. In particular, it made the people's natural rights secure by enshrining them in a constitution which was not changeable by ordinary legislation. This method was to influence the authors of the new federal Constitution in 1787.

> *Natural rights became a central component of political theory in the American colonies . . . , appearing in numerous political pamphlets, newspapers, and sermons.*

RELIGIOUS TOLERATION AND THE SEPARATION OF CHURCH AND STATE

A related development in seventeenth-century European political theory was the emergence of arguments for religious toleration and the separation of church and state. As a result of the bloody religious wars between Catholics and Protestants that followed the Reformation, a few thinkers in both England and Europe argued that governments should not attempt to force individuals to conform to one form of worship. Rather, they insisted that such coercion was both unjust and dangerous. It was unjust because true faith required voluntary belief; it was dangerous because the attempts to enforce religious beliefs in Europe had led not to religious uniformity, but to civil war. These thinkers further argued that if governments ceased to enforce religious belief, the result would be civil peace and prosperity.

Once again the English philosopher John Locke played a major role in the development of these new ideas. Building on the work of earlier writers, Locke published in 1689 *A Letter Concerning Toleration,* in which he contended that there was a natural right of conscience that no government could infringe. As he put it: "The care of Souls cannot belong to the Civil Magistrate, because his Power consists only in outward force; but true and saving Religion consists in the inward perswasion [*sic*] of the Mind, without which nothing can be acceptable to God. And such is the nature of the Understanding, that it cannot be compell'd to the belief of any thing by outward force. Confiscation of Estate, Imprisonment, Torments, nothing of that nature can have any such Efficacy as to make Men change the inward Judgment that they have formed of things."

These ideas about the rights of conscience and religious toleration resonated powerfully in the English colonies in America. Although the Puritans in the seventeenth century had originally attempted to set up an intolerant commonwealth where unorthodox religious belief would be prohibited, dissenters like Roger Williams challenged them and argued that true faith could not be the product of coercion. Forced to flee by the Puritans, Williams established the colony of Rhode Island, which offered religious toleration to all and had no state-supported church. As the Puritan Cotton Mather sarcastically remarked,

Rhode Island contained "everything in the world but Roman Catholics and real Christians." In addition, Maryland, founded in the 1630s, and Pennsylvania, founded in the 1680s, both provided an extraordinary degree of religious freedom by the standard of the time.

In the eighteenth century, as these arguments for religious toleration spread throughout the English-speaking Protestant world, the American colonies, becoming ever more religiously pluralistic, proved particularly receptive to them. As a result, the idea that the government should not enforce religious belief had become an important element of American political theory by the late eighteenth century. After the Revolution, it was enshrined as a formal right in many of the state constitutions, as well as most famously in the First Amendment to the federal Constitution.

> *By reading the classics, the American Founders were introduced to an alternate political vision, one that legitimated republicanism.*

COLONIAL SELF-GOVERNMENT

The political thinking of the Founders in the late eighteenth century was also deeply influenced by the long experience of colonial self-government. Since their founding in the early seventeenth century, most of the English colonies in the Americas (unlike the French and Spanish colonies) had governed themselves to a large extent in local assemblies that were modeled on the English Parliament. In these colonial assemblies they exercised their English common law right to consent to all laws that bound them.

The existence of these strong local governments in each colony also explains in part the speed with which the Founders were able to create viable independent republican governments in the years after 1776. This long-standing practice of self-government also helped to create an indigenous political class in the American colonies with the requisite experience for the difficult task of nation building.

In addition to the various charters and royal instructions that governed the English colonies, Americans also wrote their own Founding documents. These settler covenants were an early type of written constitution and they provided an important model for the Founders in the late eighteenth century as they sought to craft a new constitutional system based on popular consent.

CLASSICAL REPUBLICANISM

Not all the intellectual influences on the Founders originated in the seventeenth century. Because many of the Founders received a classical education in colonial colleges in the eighteenth century, they were heavily influenced by the writings of the great political thinkers and historians of ancient Greece and Rome.

Antiquity shaped the Founders' political thought in several important ways. First, it introduced them to the idea of republicanism, or government by the people. Ancient political thinkers from Aristotle to Cicero had praised republican self-government as the best political system. This classical political thought was important for the Founders as it gave them grounds to dissent from the heavily monarchical political culture of eighteenth-century England, where even the common law jurists who defended subjects' rights against royal power believed strongly in monarchy. By reading the classics, the American Founders were introduced to an alternate political vision, one that legitimized republicanism.

The second legacy of this classical idea of republicanism was the emphasis that it put on the moral foundations of liberty. Though ancient writers believed that a republic was the best form of government, they were intensely aware of its fragility. In particular, they argued that because the people governed themselves, republics required for their very survival a high degree of civic virtue in their citizenry. Citizens had to be able to put the good of the whole (the *res publica*) ahead of their own private interests. If they failed to do this, the republic would fall prey to men of power and ambition, and liberty would ultimately be lost.

As a result of this need for an exceptionally virtuous citizenry, ancient writers also taught that republics had to be small. Only in a small and relatively homogeneous society, they argued, would the necessary degree of civic virtue be forthcoming. In part, it was this classical teaching about the weakness of large republics that animated the contentious debate over the proposed federal Constitution in the 1780s.

In addition to their reading of ancient authors, the Founders also encountered republican ideas in the political theory of a group of eighteenth-century English writers called the "radical Whigs." These writers kept alive the republican legacy of the English Civil War at a time when most Englishmen believed that their constitutional monarchy was the best form of government in the world. Crucially for the Founding, these radical Whigs combined classical republican thought with the newer Lockean ideas of natural rights and popular sovereignty. They thus became an important conduit for a modern type of republicanism to enter American political thought, one that combined the ancient concern with a virtuous citizenry and the modern insistence on the importance of individual rights.

These radical Whigs also provided the Founders with an important critique of the eighteenth-century British constitution. Instead of seeing it as the best form of government possible, the radical Whigs argued that it was both corrupt and tyrannical. In order to reform it, they called for a written constitution and a formal separation of the executive branch from the legislature. This classically inspired radical Whig constitutionalism was an important influence on the development of American republicanism in the late eighteenth century.

CONCLUSION

Drawing on all these intellectual traditions, the Founders were able to create a new kind of republicanism in America based on equal rights, consent, popular sovereignty, and the separation of church and state. Having set this broad context for the Founding, we now turn to a more detailed examination of important aspects of the Founders' political theory, followed by detailed biographical studies of the Founders themselves.

Craig Yirush, Ph.D.
University of California, Los Angeles

Suggestions for Further Reading

Bailyn, Bernard. *The Ideological Origins of the American Revolution.* Cambridge, Mass.: Harvard University Press, 1967.

Lutz, Donald. *Colonial Origins of the American Constitution: A Documentary History.* Indianapolis, Ind.: Liberty Fund, 1998.

Reid, John Phillip. *The Constitutional History of the American Revolution.* Abridged Edition. Madison: The University of Wisconsin Press, 1995.

Rossiter, Clinton. *Seedtime of the Republic: The Origins of the American Tradition of Political Liberty.* New York: Harcourt Brace, 1953.

Zuckert, Michael. *Natural Rights and the New Republicanism.* Princeton, N.J.: Princeton University Press, 1994.

SLAVERY

For nearly 250 years, the existence of slavery deprived African Americans of independent lives and individual liberty. It also compromised the republican dreams of white Americans, who otherwise achieved unprecedented success in the creation of political institutions and social relationships based on citizens' equal rights and ever-expanding opportunity. Thomas Jefferson, who in 1787 described slavery as an "abomination" and predicted that it "must have an end," had faith that "there is a superior bench reserved in heaven for those who hasten it." He later avowed that "there is not a man on earth who would sacrifice more than I would to relieve us from this heavy reproach in any *practicable* way." Although Jefferson made several proposals to curb slavery's growth or reduce its political or economic influence, a workable plan to eradicate slavery eluded him. Others also failed to end slavery until finally, after the loss of more than 600,000 American lives in the Civil War, the United States abolished it through the 1865 ratification of the Thirteenth Amendment to the Constitution.

American slavery and American freedom took root at the same place and at the same time. In 1619—the same year that colonial Virginia's House of Burgesses convened in Jamestown and became the New World's first representative assembly— about 20 enslaved Africans arrived at Jamestown and were sold by Dutch slave traders. The number of slaves in Virginia remained small for several decades, however, until the first dominant labor system—indentured servitude—fell out of favor after 1670. Until then indentured servants, typically young and landless white Englishmen and Englishwomen in search of opportunity, arrived by the thousands. In exchange for passage to Virginia, they agreed to labor in planters' tobacco fields for terms usually ranging from four to seven years. Planters normally agreed to give them, after their indentures expired, land on which they could establish their own tobacco farms. In the first few decades of settlement, as demand for the crop

boomed, such arrangements usually worked in the planters' favor. Life expectancy in Virginia was short and few servants outlasted their terms of indenture. By the mid-1600s, however, as the survival rate of indentured servants increased, more earned their freedom and began to compete with their former masters. The supply of tobacco rose more quickly than demand and, as prices decreased, tensions between planters and former servants grew.

These tensions exploded in 1676, when Nathaniel Bacon led a group composed primarily of former indentured servants in a rebellion against Virginia's government. The rebels, upset by the reluctance of Governor William Berkeley and the gentry-dominated House of Burgesses to aid their efforts to expand onto American Indians' lands, lashed out at both the Indians and the government. After several months the rebellion dissipated, but so, at about the same time, did the practice of voluntary servitude.

In its place developed a system of race-based slavery. With both black and white Virginians living longer, it made better economic sense to own slaves, who would never gain their freedom and compete with masters, than to rent the labor of indentured servants, who would. A few early slaves had gained their freedom, established plantations, acquired servants, and enjoyed liberties shared by white freemen, but beginning in the 1660s Virginia's legislature passed laws banning interracial marriage; it also stripped African Americans of the rights to own property and carry guns, and it curtailed their freedom of movement. In 1650 only about 300 blacks worked Virginia's tobacco fields, yet by 1680 there were 3,000 and, by the start of the eighteenth century, nearly 10,000.

Slavery surged not only in Virginia but also in Pennsylvania, where people abducted from Africa and their descendants harvested wheat and oats, and in South Carolina, where by the 1730s rice planters had imported slaves in such quantity that they accounted for two-thirds of the population.

The sugar-based economies of Britain's Caribbean colonies required so much labor that, on some islands, enslaved individuals outnumbered freemen by more than ten to one. Even in the New England colonies, where staple-crop agriculture never took root, the presence of slaves was common and considered unremarkable by most.

Historian Edmund S. Morgan has suggested that the prevalence of slavery in these colonies may have, paradoxically, heightened the sensitivity of white Americans to attacks against their own freedom. Thus, during the crisis preceding the War for Independence Americans frequently cast unpopular British legislation—which taxed them without the consent of their assemblies, curtailed the expansion of their settlements, deprived them of the right to jury trials, and placed them under the watchful eyes of red-coated soldiers—as evidence of an imperial conspiracy to "enslave" them. American patriots who spoke in such terms did not imagine that they would be forced to toil in tobacco fields; instead, they feared that British officials would deny to them some of the same individual and civil rights that they had denied to enslaved African Americans. George Mason, collaborating with George Washington, warned in the Fairfax Resolves of 1774 that the British Parliament pursued a "regular, systematic plan" to "fix the shackles of slavery upon us."

As American revolutionaries reflected on the injustice of British usurpations of their freedom and began to universalize the individual rights that they had previously tied to their status as Englishmen, they grew increasingly conscious of the inherent injustice of African-American slavery. Many remained skeptical that blacks possessed the same intellectual capabilities as whites, but few refused to count Africans as members of the human family or possessors of individual rights. When Jefferson affirmed in the Declaration of Independence "that all men are created equal," he did not mean all *white* men. In fact, he attempted to turn the Declaration into a platform from which Americans would denounce the trans-Atlantic slave trade. This he blamed on Britain and its king who, Jefferson wrote, "has waged cruel war against human nature itself, violating it's [sic] most sacred rights of life and liberty in the persons of a distant people who never offended him, captivating & carrying them into slavery in another hemisphere."

> In 1650 only about 300 African Americans worked Virginia's tobacco fields, yet by 1680 there were 3,000; by the start of the eighteenth century, there were nearly 10,000.

The king was wrong, he asserted, "to keep open a market where MEN should be bought & sold." Delegates to the Continental Congress from South Carolina and Georgia, however, vehemently opposed the inclusion of these lines in the Declaration of Independence. Representatives of other states agreed to delete them. Thus began, at the moment of America's birth, the practice of prioritizing American unity over black Americans' liberty.

Pragmatism confronted principle not only on the floor of Congress but also on the plantations of many prominent revolutionaries. When Jefferson penned his stirring defense of individual liberty, he owned 200 enslaved individuals. Washington, the commander-in-chief of the Continental Army and future first president, was one of the largest slaveholders in Virginia. James Madison—who, like Jefferson and Washington, considered himself an opponent of slavery—was also a slaveholder. So was Mason, whose Virginia Declaration of Rights stands as one of the revolutionary era's most resounding statements on behalf of human freedom. Had these revolutionaries attempted to free their slaves, they would have courted financial ruin. Alongside their land-holdings, slaves constituted the principal asset against which they borrowed. The existence of slavery, moreover, precluded a free market of agricultural labor; they could never afford to pay free people—who could always move west to obtain their own farms, anyway—to till their fields.

Perhaps the most powerful objection to emancipation, however, emerged from the same set of principles that compelled the American revolutionaries to question the justice of slavery. Although Jefferson, Washington, Madison, and Mason considered human bondage a clear violation of individual rights, they trembled when they considered the ways in which emancipation might thwart their republican experiments. Not unlike many nonslaveholders, they considered especially fragile the society that they had helped to create. In the absence of aristocratic selfishness and force, revolutionary American governments relied on virtue and voluntarism. Virtue they understood as a manly trait; the word, in fact, derives from the Latin noun *vir*, which means "man." They considered men to be independent and self-sufficient, made free and responsible by habits borne of necessity. Virtuous citizens made good citizens, the Founders thought. The use of political power for the purpose of exploitation promised the virtuous little and possessed the potential to cost them much. Voluntarism was virtue unleashed: the civic-minded, selfless desire to ask little of one's community but, because of one's sense of permanence within it, to give much to it. The Founders, conscious of the degree to which involuntary servitude had rendered slaves dependent and given them cause to resent white society, questioned their qualifications for citizenship. It was dangerous to continue to enslave them, but perilous to emancipate them. Jefferson compared it to holding a wolf by the ears.

These conundrums seemed to preclude an easy fix. Too aware of the injustice of slavery to expect much forgiveness from slaves, in the first decades of the nineteenth century a number of Founders embarked on impractical schemes to purchase the freedom of slaves and "repatriate" them from America to Africa. In the interim, debate about the continued importation of slaves from Africa stirred delegates to the Constitutional Convention. South Carolina's Charles Pinckney vehemently opposed prohibitions on the slave trade, arguing that the matter was best decided by individual states. The delegates compromised, agreeing that the Constitution would prohibit for twenty years any restrictions on the arrival of newly enslaved Africans. As president, Jefferson availed himself of the opportunity afforded by the Constitution when he prohibited the continued importation of Africans into America in 1808. Yet he had already failed in a 1784 attempt to halt the spread of slavery into the U.S. government's western territory, which stretched from the Great Lakes south toward the Gulf of Mexico (the compromise Northwest Ordinance of 1787 drew the line at the Ohio River), and in his efforts to institute in Virginia a plan for gradual emancipation (similar to those that passed in Northern states, except that it provided for the education and subsequent deportation of freed African Americans). Of all the Founders, Benjamin Franklin probably took the most unequivocal public stand against involuntary servitude when, in 1790, he signed a strongly worded antislavery petition submitted to Congress by the Pennsylvania Abolition Society. This, too, accomplished little.

The revolutionary spirit of the postwar decade, combined with the desire of many Upper South plantation owners to shift from labor-intensive tobacco to wheat, created opportunities to reduce the prevalence of slavery in America—especially in the North. Those opportunities not seized upon—especially in the South—would not soon return.

Eli Whitney's invention of the cotton gin in 1793 widened the regional divide. By rendering more efficient the processing of cotton fiber—which in the first half of the nineteenth century possessed a greater value than all other U.S. exports combined—Whitney's machine triggered a resurgence of Southern slavery. Meanwhile, the wealth that cotton exports brought to America fueled a booming Northern industrial economy that relied on free labor and created a well-educated middle class of urban professionals and social activists. These individuals kept alive the Founders' desire to rid America of slavery, but they also provoked the development of Southern proslavery thought. At best, Southerners of the revolutionary generation had viewed slavery as a necessary evil; by the 1830s, however, slaveholders began to describe it as a positive good. African Americans were civilized Christians, they argued, but their African ancestors were not. In addition, the argument continued, slaves benefited from the paternalistic care of masters who, unlike the Northern employers of "wage slaves," cared for their subordinates from the cradle to the grave. This new view combined with an older critique of calls for emancipation: since slaves were the property of their masters, any attempt to force their release would be a violation of masters' property rights.

Regional positions grew more intractable as the North and South vied for control of the West. Proposals to admit into statehood Missouri, Texas, California, Kansas, and Nebraska resulted in controversy as Northerners and Southerners sparred to maintain parity in the Senate. The 1860 election to the presidency of Abraham Lincoln, a Republican who opposed the inclusion of additional slave states, sparked secession and the Civil War.

"I tremble for my country when I reflect that God is just," Jefferson had prophetically remarked, for "his justice cannot sleep for ever." Americans paid dearly for the sin of slavery. Efforts by

> "I tremble for my country when I reflect that God is just," Jefferson had prophetically remarked, for "his justice cannot sleep for ever." Americans paid dearly for the sin of slavery.

members of the founding generation failed to identify moderate means to abolish the practice, and hundreds of thousands died because millions had been deprived of the ability to truly live.

Robert M. S. McDonald, Ph.D.
United States Military Academy

Suggestions for Further Reading

Bailyn, Bernard. *The Ideological Origins of the American Revolution.* Cambridge, Mass.: Harvard University Press, reprint, 1992.

Freehling, William W. *The Road to Disunion: Secessionists at Bay, 1776–1754.* New York: Oxford University Press, 1990.

Jordan, Winthrop D. *White Over Black: American Attitudes toward the Negro, 1550–1812.* Chapel Hill, N.C.: University of North Carolina Press, 1968.

Miller, John Chester. *The Wolf by the Ears: Thomas Jefferson and Slavery.* Charlottesville: University of Virginia Press, reprint, 1991.

Morgan, Edmund S. *American Slavery—American Freedom: The Ordeal of Colonial Virginia.* New York: W.W. Norton, 1975.

Tise, Larry E. *Proslavery: A History of the Defense of Slavery in America, 1701–1840.* Athens: University of Georgia Press, 1987.

FREEDOM OF RELIGION

A sound understanding of the United States requires an appreciation of the historical commitment of the American people to certain fundamental liberties. High on the list of these liberties is freedom of religion. The image of brave seventeenth-century English Puritans making the difficult journey across the Atlantic to American shores in pursuit of the freedom to live according to their faith is a powerful part of the American myth. Less remembered, however, is the fact that the commonwealth established by the Puritans was as intolerant as Anglican England, from which they had fled. Indeed, the road to achieving full religious liberty in the United States was long and arduous. By the time of the writing of the United States Constitution in 1787, Americans were committed to the principle of religious tolerance (or, to use the term of the time, "toleration") and the idea of separation of church and state, but only to a limited degree. It would be another five decades before all states granted broad religious liberty to their citizens and provided for the complete separation of church and state.

Modern ideas about freedom of religion were developed in the wake of the Protestant Reformation of the sixteenth century, which shattered the unity of Christendom and plunged Europe into political and religious conflict. Though some European states remained religiously homogeneous, either retaining the traditional faith of Roman Catholicism or adopting some brand of Protestantism, religious division within many countries led to discord and bloodshed. In England, the church established in the mid-sixteenth century by King Henry VIII (who reigned from 1509 to 1547) faced stiff resistance, first from the many Catholics who refused to abandon the faith of their ancestors, and then from the Puritans who opposed the rule of bishops and wanted to purify the church so that it included only the elect.

Henry VIII's successors, Elizabeth I (1558–1603) and James I (1603–1625), successfully quelled opposition to the Church of England (the Anglican Church), largely through harsh persecution of dissenters. In 1642, however, England was engulfed by religious civil war, from which the Puritans emerged victorious. The Puritan Commonwealth established by Oliver Cromwell ruthlessly persecuted Anglicans and Catholics. But Puritan rule was short-lived. An Anglican monarch, Charles II, was restored to the throne in 1660. This "settlement" of the religious crisis, however, was threatened by the accession of a Catholic, James II, to the throne in 1685. Anxious Protestants conspired and invited a foreigner, William of Orange, to assume the kingship of England. William invaded England, drove James into exile, assumed the throne, and reestablished the Church of England as the national church.

In this contentious atmosphere some English political thinkers, such as John Locke, began to advocate a policy of religious toleration. Locke's ideas reflected a key assumption of Enlightenment thought—that religious belief, like political theory, is a matter of opinion, not absolute truth. "The business of laws," Locke wrote in his *Letter on Toleration* (1689), "is not to provide for the truth of opinions, but for the safety and security of the commonwealth and of every particular man's goods and person." Public security was in no way dependent on a uniformity of religious belief among the citizenry. "If a Jew do not believe the New Testament to be the Word of God," Locke stated, "he does not thereby alter anything in men's civil rights." Rather, intolerance led to "discord and war," and Locke warned that "no peace and security" could be "preserved amongst men so long as this opinion prevails . . . that religion is to be propagated by force of arms." Religious belief, in Locke's view, was a matter of individual choice, a matter for society, not for government.

Locke's views on religious liberty had a profound influence on American thinking in the next century. Other writings, however, particularly the Bible, had at least as great an impact on American political theory. Indeed, the American experiment in religious toleration began years before the publication of

Locke's treatise, though the early history of Puritan Massachusetts Bay was hardly indicative of the course that toleration would take in America. Established by John Winthrop in 1630, Massachusetts was a repressive place where church and state were one and where religious dissent was ruthlessly stamped out. Dissenters had few options: they could be silent, suffer persecution, or leave the colony. Roger Williams, a freethinking preacher, was forced to choose this last option, leaving Massachusetts in 1636 to establish the colony of Rhode Island.

In Rhode Island, Williams instituted toleration for all people, and his new colony quickly became a refuge for persecuted groups like Quakers and Baptists. Williams's case for toleration was at least as radical as Locke's. Basing his arguments on the Bible, Williams insisted that the Jews, Muslims, and atheists were also deserving of religious liberty. The only "sword" to be used in fighting their opinions was scripture itself. Intolerance was an offense to God. "An enforced uniformity of religion throughout a nation or civil state," Williams wrote in *The Bloudy Tenent of Persecution* (1644), "denies the principles of Christianity." Williams argued that forced belief was not only a violation of God's law but also an unwise policy. "Enforced uniformity (sooner or later) is the greatest occasion of civil war, ravishing of conscience, persecution of Christ Jesus in his servants, and of the hypocrisy and destruction of millions of souls."

Two years before the founding of Rhode Island, Cecil Calvert founded the colony of Maryland and proclaimed toleration for all Christians. Calvert himself was a Catholic, but he knew that the viability of his colony depended on luring enough Protestant settlers to make it an economic success. A policy of toleration, he hoped, would serve this purpose. In setting up Pennsylvania in the 1680s, William Penn, a Quaker, followed a similar course, making his colony a haven not only for his fellow coreligionists, but, like Rhode Island, a refuge for people of all religious sects.

Pennsylvania and Rhode Island would preserve uninterrupted their traditions of religious liberty, but in Maryland, freedom of religion would be curtailed for Catholics once Protestants came to power in the last decade of the seventeenth century. Still, the idea that some degree of religious liberty was a healthful policy for government became

> Locke warned that "no peace and security" could be "preserved amongst men so long as this opinion prevails . . . that religion is to be propagated by force of arms."

firmly rooted in America by the eighteenth century. Americans learned from the example of seventeenth-century England that religious persecution was ultimately detrimental to the political, social, and economic welfare of the nation. In America, where the Christian sects were more numerous than in England, the repercussions of religious intolerance would be especially adverse to the nation's prospects. Americans' devotion to religious freedom, then, was a product of necessity and experience as well as reason.

The crisis of empire during the 1760s and 1770s served to strengthen the American commitment to religious liberty. It was not only the intrusive economic measures passed by Parliament during these years that alarmed Americans. Patriot leaders also warned of the danger of the Anglican Church's interference in American religious affairs. There was much talk that the British government would install a bishop in America who would become the instrument of tyranny. This idea that political and religious liberty went hand in hand was reflected in the New York Constitution of 1776, which explicitly connected "civil tyranny" with "spiritual oppression and intolerance."

Nearly all the state constitutions written during the American independence movement reflected a commitment to some degree of religious liberty. The Massachusetts Constitution of 1780 promised that "no subject shall be hurt, molested, or restrained, in his person, liberty, or estate, for worshipping God in the manner and season most agreeable to the dictates of his own conscience." The Virginia Declaration of Rights of 1776, authored by George Mason, proclaimed "That Religion or the duty which we owe to our Creator and the manner of discharging it, can be directed only by reason and conviction, not by force or violence." Mason's ideas mirrored Locke's belief that government should not intrude upon the concerns of society.

But many states limited religious liberty to Christians in general, or to Protestants in particular. The North Carolina Constitution of 1776 decreed "That no person, who shall deny the being of God or the truth of the Protestant religion . . . shall be capable of holding any office or place of trust or profit in the civil department within this State." Similarly, the New Jersey Constitution of the same year declared that "there shall be no establishment of any one religious sect in this Province, in preference to another," but promised Protestants alone full civil rights. Thanks largely to the efforts of Charles Carroll of Carrollton, a Roman Catholic, Maryland's Revolutionary Constitution was more liberal in its guarantee of religious liberty to "all persons, professing the Christian religion."

The Protestant majority in America was indeed particularly concerned about the Catholic minority in its midst. Catholics constituted the largest non-Protestant creed in the country, and it was believed that Catholicism demanded loyalty to the pope above devotion to country. The connection between Catholicism and absolutism was deeply ingrained in the American Protestant mind and was a legacy of the Reformation, which Protestants saw as a period of liberation from the ignorance, superstition, and tyranny of the Roman Catholic Church. During the crisis with England, a wave of religious hysteria swept over American Protestants, who worried that the pope would personally lead the Catholics of Canada in a military assault on American forces. "Much more is to be dreaded from the growth of Popery in America," patriot leader Samuel Adams asserted in 1768, "than from Stamp-Acts or any other acts destructive of men's civil rights." This bigotry caused Roman Catholics to become outspoken proponents of religious toleration and the separation of church and state. In a country dominated by Protestants, this was the only realistic course for them.

All thirteen states at the time of American independence, then, acknowledged to some degree in their constitutions the principle of religious liberty. Most also provided for some degree of separation of church and state. Several states went so far as to prohibit clergymen from holding state office, a restriction in the Georgia Constitution of 1777 that the Reverend John Witherspoon of New Jersey would famously protest. But few states provided for a complete separation of church and state, for it was believed that the government should give some support to religion in general. Though a substantial number of American elites in the late eighteenth century were not church-going Christians, nearly all believed in the God of the Old Testament, and all recognized the practical value of Christianity as a check on antisocial behavior. Many of the state constitutions written

Thomas Jefferson asserted that the First Amendment created "a wall of separation between church and state." What Jefferson meant by this term is a subject of great debate.

in the era of independence, therefore, required that government give some support to Christianity. Though the Massachusetts Constitution guaranteed that "no subordination of any one sect or denomination to another shall ever be established by law," it also permitted the legislature to levy taxes "for the support and maintenance of public protestant teachers of piety, religion and morality." Similarly, the Maryland Constitution of 1776 permitted the legislature to "lay a general and equal tax for the support of the Christian religion."

There were, however, calls for complete religious disestablishment at the state level. In Virginia, James Madison and Thomas Jefferson were two of the most prominent advocates of a strict separation of church and state. Their ideas about religious liberty were clearly influenced by John Locke and fellow Virginian George Mason. In 1785, the Virginia legislature considered a bill that would provide for public funding of Christian instruction. The measure was backed by several prominent statesmen, including Patrick Henry. But James Madison, then a member of the legislature, took the lead in opposing the bill, reminding Virginians that "torrents of blood have been spilt in the old world, by vain attempts of the secular arm, to extinguish Religious discord, by proscribing all difference in Religious opinion." The bill was defeated, and the following year, Jefferson introduced "A Bill for Establishing Religious Freedom," which attempted to enshrine in law the idea "that no man shall be compelled to frequent or support any religious Worship place or Ministry whatsoever." The bill passed with minor changes.

By the time of the Constitutional Convention of 1787, there was a broad consensus regarding the proper relationship between the national government and religion: first, that the government ought not to give support to any religious sect; second, that the government ought not to require a religious test for office; third, that the government ought not to interfere with private religious practice; and fourth, that the government ought not to interfere with the right of the states to do as they wished in regard to religious establishment and religious liberty. These points of consensus were reflected in both the body of the United States Constitution and in the First Amendment, which was ratified in 1791 as part of the Bill of Rights. Article VI of the Constitution explicitly stated that "no religious test shall ever be required as a qualification to any office or public trust under the United States." The First Amendment declared that "Congress shall make no law respecting an establishment of religion, or prohibiting the free exercise thereof."

The right of the states to set their own policy in regard to religion was implicitly acknowledged in Article I of the Constitution, which stipulated that to be eligible to vote in elections for the United States House of Representatives, "the elector in each State shall have the qualifications requisite for electors of the most numerous branch of the State Legislature." Several states at the time mandated a religious test as a requirement for the franchise, and the Constitution therefore tacitly approved such tests. In addition, the First Amendment's prohibition against religious establishment applied explicitly to the national Congress alone. Indeed, it was not until after the American Civil War, in the incorporation cases, that the United States Supreme Court ruled that some of the restrictions placed on the federal government by the amendments also applied to the state governments.

By 1800, then, there was a broad consensus among Americans that religious freedom was essential to political liberty and the well-being of the nation. During the next two centuries, the definition of freedom of religion would be broadened, as states abandoned religious tests and achieved complete disestablishment and as state and federal courts ruled that various subtle forms of government encouragement of religion were unconstitutional. Shortly after the dawn of the nineteenth century, in a letter to a Baptist congregation in Danbury, Connecticut, Thomas Jefferson asserted that the First Amendment created "a wall of separation between church and state." What Jefferson meant by this term is a subject of great debate. But there is no doubt that his words have become part of the American political creed and a rallying cry for those who seek to expand the definition of religious liberty, even to mean that religion should be removed from public life altogether.

Stephen M. Klugewicz, Ph.D.
Bill of Rights Institute

Suggestions for Further Reading

Berns, Walter. *The First Amendment and the Future of American Democracy.* New York: Basic Books, 1976.

Dreisbach, Daniel. *Thomas Jefferson and the Wall of Separation between Church and State.* New York: New York University Press, 2003.

Levy, Leonard W. *The Establishment Clause: Religion and the First Amendment.* New York: MacMillan, 1989.

Novak, Michael. *On Two Wings: Humble Faith and Common Sense at the American Founding.* San Francisco: Encounter Books, 2003.

FEDERALISM

By the time the delegates to the Constitutional Convention had gathered in Philadelphia in 1787, the American people had been accustomed for more than one hundred and fifty years to having most of their affairs managed first within the colonies and then in independent states. It was not surprising that the Articles of Confederation, the initial constitutional system for "The United States of America," affirmed in its first article the general "sovereignty, freedom and independence" of the states. Beyond historical precedence, the commitment to state sovereignty drew support from sixteenth- and seventeenth-century theorists such as Jean Jacques Rousseau who argued that the habits and virtues needed by a self-governing people can be cultivated only in small republics. In short, history and theory seemed to be on the side of a confederation of small American republics or states.

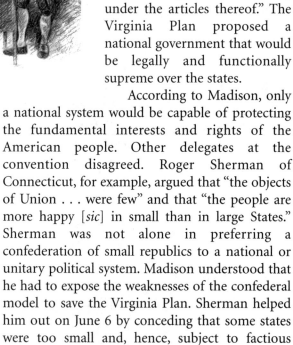

If the American people were inclined to favor state sovereignty, they also were interested in comfortable preservation—that is, in the enjoyment of both "safety and happiness," to borrow from the Declaration of Independence. By the mid-1780s, it was clear to many Americans that state sovereignty created obstacles to comfortable preservation, not the least being the impediments to a smooth-functioning commercial system. Concerns about the effects on the country of competing fiscal and commercial policies in the different states led to the Annapolis Convention of 1786. While the delegates to this convention did not come up with a specific plan for fixing the commercial system, they petitioned the confederation congress to arrange for a constitutional convention that would reconsider the Articles of Confederation with the aim of improving interstate commerce.

James Madison, one of seven delegates chosen to represent Virginia at the Constitutional Convention of 1787, prepared a document on the history of confederacies during the months preceding the meeting. Events such as Shays's Rebellion in Massachusetts and disputes over the commercial use of the Potomac River, along with his study of history, convinced him that a system based on state sovereignty was destined to fail. Madison worked with other members of the Virginia delegation on a plan for a basically national, rather than confederal, system of government. In addition to provisions for separate legislative, executive, and judicial branches, the "Virginia Plan" would have empowered Congress "to negative all laws passed by the several States, contravening in the opinion of the National Legislature the articles of Union; and to call forth the force of the Union against any member of the Union failing to fulfill its duty under the articles thereof." The Virginia Plan proposed a national government that would be legally and functionally supreme over the states.

According to Madison, only a national system would be capable of protecting the fundamental interests and rights of the American people. Other delegates at the convention disagreed. Roger Sherman of Connecticut, for example, argued that "the objects of Union . . . were few" and that "the people are more happy [sic] in small than in large States." Sherman was not alone in preferring a confederation of small republics to a national or unitary political system. Madison understood that he had to expose the weaknesses of the confederal model to save the Virginia Plan. Sherman helped him out on June 6 by conceding that some states were too small and, hence, subject to factious violence. Madison seized upon this argument. He responded that "faction & oppression" had "prevailed in the largest as well as the smallest" states, although less in the former than the latter.

The teaching for Madison was clear: large republics are more likely to provide "security for private rights, and the steady dispensation of Justice," than small republics. This argument hit home with the delegates. Madison convinced them that what they wanted most from government, that is, protection for rights or republican liberty, could best be achieved in a national system. Small republics, he argued, were actually bad for republican liberty, being hotbeds of factious division and violence. He summed up his position bluntly: "The only remedy is to enlarge the sphere, & thereby divide the community into so great a number of interests & parties, that in the 1st. place a majority will not be likely at the same moment to have a common interest separate from that of the whole or of the minority; and in the 2d. place, that in case they shd. have such an interest, they may not be apt to unite in the pursuit of it." Here was the outline of the famous defense of the large republic that appears in Madison's *Federalist Paper No. 10.*

In the end, the delegates at the Constitutional Convention settled on a plan that combined national and confederal elements. To quote *Federalist Paper No. 39:* the proposed system "in strictness" was "neither national nor a federal Constitution, but a composition of both." Madison's June 6 speech, however, insured that the new "compound" republic would have a national as opposed to a confederal tilt. This innovative governmental model, what came to be called the "federal" model, represented one of America's great contributions to the science of politics according to Madison. The model's national elements were evident not only in the creation of separate executive and judicial departments as well as proportional representation in the House of Representatives, but in the supremacy clause that affirmed that the Constitution as well as national laws enacted under its authority would constitute the supreme law of the land. The confederal elements appeared in the provision for equal state representation in the United States Senate (a feature especially desired by the small states) and state participation in the ratification of amendments. The addition of the 10th Amendment in 1791 provided added protection for state interests ("The powers not delegated to the United States by the Constitution, nor prohibited by it to the States, are reserved to the States respectively, or to the people").

The defenders of the confederal model continued their attacks on the new system during the ratification debates that followed the convention. Patrick Henry of Virginia, for example, accused the delegates to the Federal Convention of violating their authorization by proposing to establish a "consolidated" government based on the consent of the people, rather than the states. For Henry, the new constitutional system would endanger the rights and privileges of the people along with the "sovereignty" of the states. Richard Henry Lee, one of the Anti-Federalists, shared Henry's fear that a large republic would not be hospitable to liberty and natural rights. Like many other opponents of the Constitution, Lee also argued that republican liberty can be preserved only by a virtuous citizenry and that only small republics are capable of nurturing civic and moral virtues.

The fact that the document that issued from the Federal Convention did not include a bill of rights seemed to lend support to the charge by Patrick Henry and others that the proposed governmental system would promote neither the happiness nor the liberty of the people. In fact, several delegates to the convention, including George Mason of Virginia and Eldridge Gerry of Massachusetts, were sufficiently troubled by the absence of a bill of rights that they departed without adding their signatures to the document. Gerry also worried that the new government would not adequately represent the people and that its powers were not well defined. When it was clear that the opponents of the plan would not accept the argument that the framework set out by the delegates provided for a limited government of enumerated powers that would be incapable of emasculating natural rights and liberties, an agreement was reached during the ratification period to add amendments that would guarantee, among other things, freedom of speech and religion, trial by one's peers, and protection against unreasonable searches and seizures.

The federal system or compound republic crafted by the Framers was an ingenious response to the demand for both effective or competent government on the one side, and rights-sensitive government on the other. The decision to divide power among (federalism) and within (checks and balances) several governments positioned the American people to enjoy the benefits of a large republic (e.g., strong defense against foreign encroachments, national system of commerce, etc.) while still retaining significant control over their day-to-day affairs within the states. The states, and not the national government, were entrusted with the "police powers," that is, the

> *Madison convinced them that what they wanted most from government, that is, protection for rights or republican liberty, could best be achieved in a national system.*

authority to protect the health, morals, safety and welfare of the people. It is worth noting that Madison was quite content to entrust the police powers to the states—he never desired that the United States have a unitary system of government.

Ratification of the Constitution in 1791 hardly put an end to the debate between the advocates of state sovereignty or small republicanism and the proponents of national sovereignty and the large republic. The concerns of James Madison and Patrick Henry, for example, are never far from the surface of contemporary debates about the power of the federal government to impose regulations on the states under the Constitution's commerce clause or the Fourteenth Amendment. There is considerable evidence, however, that the tension between these positions not only adds vitality to the constitutional system, but has been critically important to the advancement of both national security and equality in the enjoyment of fundamental rights. The federal arrangement that was crafted by the delegates at the Federal Convention of 1787 has long been recognized as one of the principal models of a modern democratic system of government.

David E. Marion, Ph.D.
Hampden-Sydney College

Suggestions for Further Reading

Diamond, Martin. *The Founding of the Democratic Republic.* Itasca, IL: F.E. Peacock, 1981.

Frohnen, Bruce (ed.). *The American Republic: Primary Sources.* Indianapolis: Liberty Fund, 2002.

Kurland, Philip B. and Ralph Lerner (eds.). *The Founders' Constitution.* Indianapolis: Liberty Fund, 1987.

McDonald, Forrest. *E Pluribus Unum.* Indianapolis: Liberty Fund, 1979.

Storing, Herbert J. *What the Anti-Federalists Were For.* Chicago: The University of Chicago Press, 1981.

COMMERCE

Although the modern United States is the preeminent example of a nation dedicated to free enterprise and commercial activity, the relationship between republican government and commerce was one of the central problems that confronted the Founders in the late eighteenth century. In order to understand the Founders' attitudes toward commerce, we need to understand both the role that commercial activity played in the American colonies in the century before the Revolution, as well as the important arguments about the legitimacy of commercial societies that animated English and European thinkers in the two centuries before the American Founding.

The American colonies originated in part as commercial enterprises. From the first settlements in the early seventeenth century until the eve of the Revolution, British and European settlers saw America as a place where they could come and make a better life for themselves. By the mid-eighteenth century, the British colonies in America were prosperous places heavily engaged in production and trade. Although the population was still overwhelmingly rural, colonial farmers were increasingly engaged in commercial agriculture. In all regions, they produced more than was needed for subsistence, trading their surplus with other colonies as well as engaging in a growing transatlantic trade with Britain and Europe. The Southern colonies produced valuable staple crops for export (tobacco, rice, indigo, wheat); farmers in the Middle colonies had a flourishing agricultural economy which was also involved in trade with the wider world; and, by the eighteenth century, the New England colonies were building ships, selling timber, and trading produce with the British Caribbean sugar islands. As a result of these extensive Atlantic trading networks, all of the colonial economies grew enormously in the eighteenth century. In addition, the main colonial port cities—Boston, New York, Philadelphia, and Charles Town (Charleston)—grew in size and importance. This burgeoning commercial

society also had a large merchant class, with powerful and wealthy men like John Hancock in Boston involved in far-flung commercial ventures.

The pre-Revolutionary American colonies were also consumer societies that eagerly used their growing wealth to purchase goods from all over the world. And, as the Revolution approached, a growing number of white settlers not included in the political and economic elite were increasingly able to participate in this consumerism. Indeed, such was the widespread prosperity of these colonies that many modern historians have referred to them as the first middle class societies in the world.

All of this commercial activity, however, had a dark side. The Atlantic trade that the colonists engaged in with such profit was founded in part on the movement of African slaves to the New World. Once there, these slaves were responsible for producing the lucrative staple crops that the colonies sold to England and Europe in exchange for manufactured goods. In addition, the ever-expanding agricultural economy of the colonies depended on the removal of the Native American population from their lands.

Several strands of thought provided intellectual justification for the increasingly commercial world of the eighteenth-century British Atlantic. The long tradition of English common law stressed the importance of property rights, which it saw as central to liberty, and which it protected from arbitrary seizure by preventing governments from taking property without the subject's consent. By stressing the sanctity of person and property, the English common law provided a legal infrastructure which supported a commercial society.

Seventeenth-century English Puritanism also provided a justification of commercial activity. According to Puritanism, God wanted people to work hard and prosper. To do so was a sign that you were one of the "elect," destined to be "saved" and not "damned." This Puritan work ethic remained a powerful force in American life well past the Revolution.

The political theory of the English writer John Locke (1632–1704), and in particular his ideas about a natural right to liberty and property, also provided justification for a commercial society. Like the common law, it placed a value on the liberty of the person, including the liberty to engage in production and trade. In addition, Locke offered an elaborate theoretical defense of an individual's right to property. According to Locke, individuals were not given property rights by the state; rather, they generated a right to private property by their own labor. Locke defended commercial societies based on private property by arguing that they produced greater wealth for all than did those societies which eschewed private property and exchange. By making this case, Locke helped to legitimize commercial activity in the face of age-old denunciations that it was sinful. Building on these seventeenth-century ideas, English people on both sides of the Atlantic in the eighteenth century increasingly viewed themselves as free, Protestant, and deeply commercial.

By the time of the Revolution, the American Founders had also encountered the ideas of an influential group of eighteenth-century Enlightenment writers who offered a sophisticated defense of commercial societies. The French writer Montesquieu (1689–1755) argued that commerce "cures destructive prejudices" by fostering peaceful trade among peoples rather than war. Many Scottish writers in the eighteenth century made a similar defense of commerce. They argued that commercial societies constituted the highest stage of civilization and were the most conducive to human well-being, fostering political and religious liberty, peaceful relations among nations, higher standards of living, science, and the arts. The moral philosopher and economist Adam Smith (1723–1790), writing in the same year as the American Revolution, argued that self-interest was beneficent, and that those who sought private wealth were simultaneously benefiting society. All of these thinkers celebrated the modern commercial world in which they lived as superior to previous ages which, they argued, were characterized by feudal and aristocratic inequality, constant warfare, and religious fanaticism.

> *According to Puritanism, God wanted people to work hard and prosper. To do so was a sign that you were one of the "elect," destined to be "saved" and not "damned."*

However, the ideas that influenced the Founders were not all supportive of commerce. Christianity, even in its Puritan form, could be used to denounce moneymaking. In New England in the seventeenth century, the merchant Robert Keayne was put on trial on charges of usury. In the years after independence, this Christian critique combined in the Founders' thought with that of the republican thinkers of Greece and Rome who shared a similar skepticism about commerce. They argued that a society dedicated to commerce and self-interest would produce citizens overly concerned with private matters and insufficiently attentive to the public good. These classical republican thinkers were particularly concerned about the political effects of luxury, worrying that liberty would be lost if people were too focused on the pursuit of material gain. To the extent that republican thinkers defended property rights, they did so primarily as a means to the end of ensuring that there was an independent citizenry capable of acting for the public good. These classical ideas about the dangers of commerce to republican government influenced the Founders in the late eighteenth century. In particular, the ideas led some of them to be suspicious of the new institutions of commercial banking and public and private debt that supported the eighteenth-century commercial world.

The Revolution initially fostered these anticommercial sentiments in the colonial populace. In their attempts to harm the British economy, the colonies organized widespread nonimportation agreements in the 1760s and 1770s. Drawing on both the Christian and the classical republican critique of commerce, some colonists argued that this withdrawal from trade would also create a more virtuous citizenry, one less likely to succumb to luxury and self-interest. Writing his influential "Thoughts on Government" in 1776, a guide for lawmakers in the newly independent republican state governments, John Adams openly called for legal restrictions on consumption (called "sumptuary laws" in the eighteenth century), arguing that "the happiness of the people might be greatly promoted by them."

Following the Revolution, the experience of both the new state governments and that of the Continental Congress operating under the Articles of Confederation brought these questions about the relationship between republican governments and commercial activity to the fore. By ending the old British trading system, the Revolution also ushered in a debate about the commercial relations between the United States and the rest of the world.

The newly independent United States faced severe economic difficulties in the 1780s. The states found themselves with limited access to the lucrative British markets. They also owed money to those who had financed the war. But the Continental Congress lacked the legal power to compel the state governments to agree on a common commercial policy. It also lacked the authority to requisition the taxes necessary to pay off the Revolutionary War debt from the state governments. Robert Morris, who served as Congress' superintendent of finance from 1781–1783, was reduced to pleading with the state governors to send money to the national government.

> *Although the new Constitution laid the groundwork for an extended commercial republic, it did not end the debates among the Founders over the legitimacy of commerce.*

The war had also left the individual states with large debts to repay. In order to pay these debts off, many states raised taxes and issued paper money that rapidly depreciated. In addition, many of the states began to interfere with the free movements of goods within the United States.

The drafting of the new Constitution in Philadelphia in 1787 set out to address the economic problems of the 1780s by creating a national government that would have the authority to impose taxes, regulate foreign trade, and, most importantly, create a common commercial policy between the various state governments. In the *Federalist Papers,* James Madison and Alexander Hamilton, the most prominent defenders of the new Constitution, argued forcefully that the federal government needed these expanded powers in order to create a large free trading area within the continental United States. They, along with their coauthor John Jay, also argued for a vigorous commercial policy to open up markets for foreign trade.

In making these arguments, the framers were heavily influenced by the Enlightenment defense of commerce discussed above. The Framers further argued that republican government, by allowing both political and economic freedom, would foster virtuous behavior in its citizens. Freed from the burden of supporting monarchs and aristocrats, ordinary people in a republic would have the incentive to be industrious and productive, secure in the knowledge that they would be able to reap the benefits of their labor.

Although the new Constitution laid the groundwork for an extended commercial republic, it did not end the debates among the Founders over the legitimacy of commerce. In the 1790s, the Federalists argued for a government-led program of commercial expansion, involving investments in infrastructure as well as the creation of a national banking system. However, the Democratic-Republican Party under Thomas Jefferson was much more divided on the merits of commercial republicanism. One strand of Jeffersonian thought was skeptical of extensive commercial activity, preferring instead a society of independent yeoman farmers whose landed status would give them a secure material base for republican citizenship. In making this argument, the Jeffersonians echoed the republican thinkers of antiquity who valued landed property over commercial property because it alone enabled the virtuous citizen to act in the public interest. This aspect of Jeffersonian thought was also skeptical of manufacturing and wage labor, fearing that a populace engaged in such pursuits would not be able to obtain the independence required of republican citizens. Finally, Jeffersonians were very concerned about the modern institutions of banking and public and private debt, fearing that they would enable powerful men to undermine republican government by setting up an aristocracy of money.

However, Jeffersonian thought also had a strong laissez-faire element, one that became increasingly important as the eighteenth century came to a close. Although still preferring commercial agriculture over manufacturing, Jeffersonians were ardently in favor of free labor, free trade, and free markets. On this view, commerce was a liberating, even equalizing force, allowing the common people to benefit from the fruits of their own labor. In addition, this Jeffersonian policy of laissez-faire was very skeptical of the Federalist plans for extensive state-directed commerce, preferring instead to let individuals make their own economic decisions. This element of the Jeffersonian attitude toward commerce expressed the powerful desire of the American populace for material improvement, a desire which had deep roots in the colonial past.

Jefferson's election in 1800 did not end these debates about the propriety of commercial activity. Most Americans agreed that republican liberty included the right to own property and to enjoy the fruits of one's labor. However, as Jefferson's "empire of liberty" expanded west, this vision of free men and free labor clashed with the institution of slavery as it became an increasingly profitable form of commercial activity, and one that was sometimes defended as an expression of the American commitment to private property. Along with the relationship between slavery and free labor, the question of the place of manufacturing in a republican society, the role of banks, the issue of free trade, and the desirability of state intervention in the economy remained pressing questions in the increasingly commercial United States well into the nineteenth century.

Craig Yirush, Ph.D.
University of California, Los Angeles

Suggestions for Further Reading

Appleby, Joyce. *Capitalism and a New Social Order: The Republican Vision of the 1790s.* New York: New York University Press, 1984.

Heyrman, Christine. *Commerce and Culture: The Maritime Communities of Colonial Massachusetts, 1690–1750.* New York: W. W. Norton & Co., 1984.

Innes, Stephen. *Creating the Commonwealth: The Economic Culture of Puritan New England.* New York: W. W. Norton & Co., 1995.

Lerner, Ralph. "Commerce and Character." In *The Thinking Revolutionary: Principle and Practice in the New Republic.* Ithaca, N.Y. : Cornell University Press, 1987.

McCoy, Drew R. *The Elusive Republic: Political Economy in Jeffersonian America.* New York: W. W. Norton & Co., 1982.

Nelson, John R. *Liberty and Property: Political Economy and Policymaking in the New Nation, 1789–1812.* Baltimore, Md.: Johns Hopkins University Press, 1987.

Founders

CHARLES CARROLL
(1737–1832)

I do hereby recommend to the present and future generations the principles of that important document as the best earthly inheritance their ancestors could bequeath to them.

—*Charles Carroll of Carrollton on the Declaration of Independence, 1826*

Introduction

Charles Carroll is primarily remembered today for his political leadership in Maryland during the Revolutionary era. A wealthy planter, Carroll became a major figure in the patriot movement in 1773 when he penned the First Citizen letters, attacking the governor's unilateral imposition of a fee as an unjust tax upon the people. A member of the Continental Congress, Carroll signed the Declaration of Independence. He also helped to write Maryland's Constitution of 1776. After American independence was achieved, he served in the United States Senate and the Maryland legislature.

Carroll's role as a champion of religious liberty is less well known. Like many American Catholics at the time, he favored the separation of church and state and the free exercise of religion, at least for Christians. These principles were a logical consequence of the minority status of Catholics in Maryland and the nation. In nearly every American colony, Catholics suffered legal disabilities of some kind. Catholics in Maryland, for example, were denied the vote and the right to hold office. In his First Citizen letters, Carroll defended his right—and by extension, the right of his co-religionists—to participate in public affairs. He successfully fought to have religious liberty for all Christians, including Catholics, guaranteed by the Maryland Constitution of 1776.

In his later years, Carroll became famous among his countrymen as the last surviving signer of the Declaration of Independence. By the time of his death in 1832, American independence was assured, but the battle for tolerance in the United States for Catholics and other religious minorities was unfinished.

Relevant Thematic Essay for Charles Carroll

- Freedom of Religion

In His Own Words:
CHARLES CARROLL
ON RELIGIOUS LIBERTY

Overview

In this lesson, students will learn about Charles Carroll. They should first read as background homework **Handout A—Charles Carroll (1737–1832)** and answer the **Reading Comprehension Questions.** After discussing the answers to these questions in class, the teacher should have the students answer the **Critical Thinking Questions** as a class. Next, the teacher should introduce the students to the primary source activity, **Handout C—In His Own Words: Charles Carroll on Religious Liberty,** in which Carroll defends his right as a Catholic to participate in public affairs. As a preface, there is **Handout B—Vocabulary and Context Questions,** which will help the students understand the document.

There are **Follow-Up Homework Options** that ask the students to consider whether a group's religious beliefs can pose a threat to a free society. **Extensions** provides opportunity for thought as students are asked to research the extent of religious tolerance in the earliest state constitutions, the history of religious liberty in their own state, or the extent of religious freedom in another country.

Objectives

Students will:

- appreciate Carroll's role as a leader of the American opposition to British tyranny
- explain Carroll's objections to the governor's fee proclamation
- understand the reasons for Carroll's championing of religious tolerance
- analyze what Carroll stood to gain and lose by supporting American independence

Standards
  CCE (9–12): IIA1, IIC1, IIIA1, IIIA2
  NCHS (5–12): Era III, Standards 3A, 3B
  NCSS: Strands 2, 5, 6, and 10

Materials
Student Handouts
- Handout A—Charles Carroll (1737–1832)
- Handout B—Vocabulary and Context Questions
- Handout C—In His Own Words: Charles Carroll on Religious Liberty

Additional Teacher Resource
- Answer Key

Recommended Time
  One 45-minute class period. Additional time as needed for homework.

LESSON PLAN

I. Background Homework

Ask students to read **Handout A—Charles Carroll (1737–1832)** and answer the Reading Comprehension Questions.

II. Warm-Up [10 minutes]

A. Review answers to homework questions.

B. Conduct a whole-class discussion to answer the Critical Thinking Questions.

C. Ask a student to summarize the historical significance of Charles Carroll.

Charles Carroll was a wealthy Maryland planter and a leader of the Revolution. He became famous in the colony in 1773 when he wrote the First Citizen letters. In these essays, Carroll criticized as illegal a fee that the governor had imposed on the people. He also defended his right as a Catholic to participate in public life in Maryland. As a member of the Continental Congress in 1776, Carroll signed the Declaration of Independence, the only Catholic to do so. In that same year, he helped write a new constitution for Maryland, successfully including as part of that document a clause that guaranteed religious liberty for Christians. After the Revolutionary War, Carroll served in the Maryland legislature and United States Senate. He was the last signer of the Declaration to die.

III. Context [5 minutes]

A. Be sure that the students understand that there was one united Christian Church (called "Catholic," meaning "universal") until the Protestant Reformation of the sixteenth century. At that time, the Christian Church began to splinter. The term "Protestant" refers in a general way to all non-Catholic Christians (those who "protested" against the Church). The term "Catholic" refers to individuals who remained loyal to the Pope in Rome.

B. Discrimination against Catholics was a long-standing policy in post-Reformation England. Prior to American independence in 1776, most colonies discriminated in some way against Catholics, usually by the denial of the right to vote and hold office. Many of the state constitutions written after independence guaranteed Christians full political rights, though some states, such as Massachusetts and North Carolina, continued to deny Catholics certain rights and privileges until well into the nineteenth century.

IV. In His Own Words [25 minutes]

A. Distribute **Handout B—Vocabulary and Context Questions.** Be sure that the students understand the vocabulary and the "who, what, where, and when" of the document.

B. Explain to the class that in eighteenth-century America, newspapers were often read publicly to crowds on the street—much as people gather around televisions in stores today when a major news event occurs. Tell the students that they are about to listen to the excerpts from the Antilon-First Citizen letters read by members of the class.

C. Choose two students who are good speakers. Distribute **Handout C—In His Own Words: Charles Carroll on Religious Liberty** to these students. Assign one of the students the task of representing Daniel Dulany (Antilon) and the other the role of Charles Carroll (the First Citizen). Allow these students a few minutes to review their assigned parts.

LESSON PLAN

D. As the speakers prepare, pair up the remaining students. Tell them that each pair will listen carefully to the dialogue between Dulany and Carroll and then compose a one-paragraph summary of the exchange.

E. Have the two speakers stand in front of the class and read the dialogue.

F. When the speakers are finished, have the pairs of students write their paragraphs. Then have the pairs exchange their paragraphs, so that each pair has the work of another group. Give the groups a minute or two to read the paragraphs they now have.

G. Have the speakers read the dialogue again. Each pair should now check to see if the paragraph they are reading summarizes well the exchange between Carroll and Dulany.

H. Ask the student-listeners to read the paragraph they have in front of them, if they believe it is a good summary of the dialogue.

V. Wrap-Up Discussion [5 minutes]

Ask the students to consider how Marylanders of Carroll's day might have reacted to his dialogue with Dulany.
Answers will vary.

VI. Follow-Up Homework Options

Students could compose a short essay (three to five paragraphs) in which they consider the following questions:

A. When, if ever, can a group's religious beliefs pose a threat to a free society?

B. Should limits be placed on the freedom to practice religion in order to protect society?

VII. Extensions

A. Students could research the history of religious liberty in their state.

B. Students could research the extent of religious liberty currently allowed in other countries.

C. Using the links below, students could research the extent of religious tolerance found in the earliest state constitutions, most of which were written at the time of the American Revolution. (Note that the present-day constitutions of Massachusetts and Rhode Island date to 1776 and 1843, respectively, though both have been amended.)
   <http://www.yale.edu/lawweb/avalon/states/stateco.htm>
   <http://www.state.ma.us/legis/const.htm>
   <http://www.state.ri.us/rihist/riconst.htm>

Resources

Print

Hanley, Thomas O'Brien. *Charles Carroll of Carrollton: The Making of a Revolutionary Gentleman.* Chicago: Loyola University Press, 1982.

Hanley, Thomas O'Brien. *Revolutionary Statesman: Charles Carroll and the War.* Chicago: Loyola University Press, 1983.

Hoffman, Ronald. *Dear Papa, Dear Charley: The Peregrinations of a Revolutionary Aristocrat, as Told by Charles Carroll of Carrollton and His Father, Charles Carroll of Annapolis.* Chapel Hill: University of North Carolina Press, 2000.

Hoffman, Ronald. *Princes of Ireland, Planters of Maryland: A Carroll Saga, 1500–1782.* Chapel Hill: University of North Carolina Press, 2000.

Onuf, Peter S., ed. *Maryland and the Empire, 1773: The Antilon-First Citizen Letters.* Baltimore: Johns Hopkins University Press, 1974.

Internet

The Carroll House. National Park Service. <**http://www.cr.nps.gov/nr/travel/baltimore/b28.htm**>.

The Charles Carroll House of Annapolis. Historic Annapolis Foundation. <**http://www.charlescarrollhouse.com/**>.

"Charles Carroll of Carrollton." New Advent Catholic Encyclopedia. <**http://www.newadvent.org/cathen/03379c.htm**>.

"Charles Carroll of Carrollton, 1737–1832." Biographical Directory of the United States Congress. <**http://bioguide.congress.gov/scripts/biodisplay.pl?index=C000185**>.

"Charles Carroll of Carrollton." Signers of the Declaration of Independence. USHistory.org. <**http://www.ushistory.org/declaration/signers/carroll.htm**>.

Selected Works by Charles Carroll
- *First Citizen Letters* (1773)
- *Address on the Fiftieth Anniversary of the Declaration of Independence* (1826)

CHARLES CARROLL (1737–1832)

Government was instituted for the general good, but officers entrusted with its powers, have most commonly perverted them to the selfish views of avarice and ambition.

—*Charles Carroll, 1773*

The boisterous patrons of the small Maryland tavern fell suddenly silent as the small, well-dressed man appeared in the entrance. Charles Carroll of Carrollton paused as the gazes of so many fell upon him. Suddenly, one man called out, "There is the First Citizen!" The crowd rose as one to its feet and burst into applause. Carroll politely doffed his hat and bowed slightly in return. Carroll had been using the pen name "First Citizen" in a series of newspaper essays defending the liberties of Marylanders against the colonial government. By this spring of 1773, the prosperous plantation owner had indeed become the first among equals in the eyes of his fellow Marylanders.

Background

Charles Carroll was born on September 19, 1737, to a Catholic family in Annapolis, Maryland. His grandfather had moved there from Great Britain to escape religious persecution. Charles' father owned hundreds of slaves and prospered as a tobacco planter. He expected young Charles to take over the family business once he had proved himself "a worthy heir." Charles was sent to London and Paris, where he received an extensive Catholic education. When he returned to Maryland in 1765, he helped his father manage a forty-thousand-acre estate on which two hundred eighty-five slaves toiled.

As a Catholic, Carroll knew that he was at a disadvantage in America. When his grandfather came to Maryland, the governing family, the Baltimores, practiced religious tolerance. However, Maryland became a royal colony in 1691 and, therefore, subject to English law. The Church of England became the official church, and Catholics felt the consequences. They could not practice law or vote. They were prohibited from serving in government. They were also forced to pay taxes to the Anglican Church. Despite these severe restrictions, Carroll remained in his homeland.

The Revolutionary

The year 1772 marked the beginning of Carroll's twenty-eight-year role as revolutionary spokesman and civil servant. He became involved in politics when the governor of Maryland fixed government officials' public service fees at a high rate. At the time, citizens had to pay officials directly for certain public services. The proceeds from these fees were used to pay the officials' salaries. Daniel Dulany, a high-ranking Maryland official, defended the governor's act in a series of articles published in the *Maryland Gazette.* Carroll quickly responded.

Writing under the name "First Citizen," Carroll argued that the fees were taxes. He contended that only the Maryland Assembly, not the governor, had the right to levy taxes. "In a land of freedom," Carroll argued, "this arbitrary [unpredictable] exertion of prerogative [power] will not, must not, be endured." The identity of the First Citizen soon became known to all. Dulany responded with both argument and personal attack. He questioned Carroll's right as a Catholic to become involved in public affairs. Carroll defended the right of Catholics to speak out on political issues.

Carroll believed that the restrictions placed on Catholics in Maryland were motivated by a desire for power on the part of the Protestant majority. Religious belief was merely an excuse to deny political influence to men like Carroll. "Designing and selfish men," Carroll complained in the year following his First Citizen letters, "invented religious tests to exclude from posts of profit and trust their weaker or more conscientious fellow subjects, thus to secure to themselves all the emoluments [benefits] of Government."

The battle on paper between a powerful government official and a Catholic landowner captivated the reading public. As First Citizen, Carroll earned a reputation for intelligence and character. Soon he was elected to serve on local committees that supported revolutionary ideals.

In October 1774, Carroll was again in the spotlight. The local merchant ship *Peggy Stewart* had arrived in Annapolis with a shipment of goods, including tea leaves. With Lexington and Concord only six months away, times were tense. The English monopoly on tea and oppressive British trade policies had driven most merchants to sign a nonimportation agreement in protest. When the colonists learned of the shipment, they were outraged. They threatened the lives of the owner and crew.

The vessel's owner called upon the influential Carroll for advice. It was immediately clear to Carroll that an apology or exportation of the tea would not satisfy the crowd. He offered a drastic solution: burn the tea along with the entire ship. Doubtful but desperate, the owner agreed. Crisis was averted.

Diplomacy and the Declaration

As the colonies plunged deeper into conflict with the British, Carroll worked tirelessly for independence. The citizens of Maryland elected him to serve on the first Committee of Safety in Annapolis. He also served in the Provincial Congress in 1775. The following year, he was chosen to represent Maryland in the Continental Congress.

The Congress chose Carroll, along with Benjamin Franklin and Samuel Chase, to serve on a mission to gain Canada's support for the Revolution. Carroll was picked because he spoke French and was Catholic, like many Canadians. Though the delegation returned home empty-handed, Carroll became recognized as an important player in the national political arena.

In the spring of 1776, Carroll returned home and learned that Congress would soon vote on a resolution to separate from Great Britain. He also found out that the Maryland delegates in Congress had been instructed by the colonial assembly to oppose independence.

Carroll immediately returned to Annapolis to argue the merits of independence. He reminded the delegates of England's tyranny. After much debate, the Maryland legislature joined in support of separation. In July, Carroll returned to the Continental Congress. Though he missed the vote for independence on July 4, he "most willingly" signed the Declaration of Independence on August 2. Carroll was the only Catholic to put his name to that document.

It was reported that after Carroll signed his name, a spectator commented, "There go a few millions." If Britain won the war, Carroll would certainly lose his family estate and perhaps even his life. Victory, however, could bring both political and religious liberty. Like all who supported the Revolution, Carroll was willing to sacrifice everything he had for independence and liberty.

© The Bill of Rights Institute

In Service to State and Nation

During the American Revolution, Carroll immersed himself in public duties. In 1776, he was elected to the Maryland Convention, the body that governed the state during the war. The convention appointed Carroll to the committee responsible for creating a state constitution. Carroll succeeded in enshrining religious liberty in the Declaration of Rights attached to the document. The final version of the Declaration asserted that "all persons professing the Christian religion are equally entitled to protection in their religious liberty." Catholics thereby became equal citizens under Maryland law, having earned the right to vote and hold office.

After independence, Carroll continued to serve in the Maryland legislature. Following the adoption of the new Constitution in 1789, Carroll also served as a United States senator. In 1792, however, Maryland disallowed simultaneous service in both the national and state legislatures. Carroll therefore resigned from the national legislature in order to continue serving his state. He retired from the Maryland Senate in 1800.

Retirement

Even in retirement, Carroll continued to make public appearances. On July 4, 1826, the fiftieth anniversary of the signing of the Declaration of Independence, Carroll composed a short address to honor the occasion. "I do hereby recommend," he announced, "to the present and future generations the principles of that important document as the best earthly inheritance their ancestors could bequeath to them."

Carroll's stature grew in his later years; he became famous among his countrymen as the last surviving signer of the Declaration of Independence. On November 14, 1832, at the age of ninety-five, Carroll died, quietly closing a chapter on the Founding generation.

Reading Comprehension Questions

1. What two topics did Carroll address in his First Citizen letters?
2. What did Carroll think was the reason that Catholics were denied rights in Maryland?
3. Why did Carroll become even more famous during the last few years of his life?

Critical Thinking Questions

4. What did Charles Carroll stand to lose by supporting the American Revolution? What did he stand to gain?
5. Imagine that you are Charles Carroll in 1832. Compose a one-paragraph newspaper article in which you reflect on the changes in Maryland between 1765 and 1832.

VOCABULARY AND CONTEXT QUESTIONS

Excerpts from the Antilon-First Citizen Letters

1. **Vocabulary:** *Use context clues to determine the meaning or significance of each of these words and write their definitions:*

    a. disabled/disabilities

    b. resolve

    c. speculative

    d. approbation

    e. papist

    f. knaves

    g. sects/denominations

    h. malice

    i. basest

2. **Context:** *Answer the following questions.*

    a. When were these documents written?

    b. Where were these documents written?

    c. Who wrote these documents?

    d. What type of document are these?

    e. What were the purposes of these documents?

    f. Who was the audience for these documents?

IN HIS OWN WORDS:
CHARLES CARROLL ON RELIGIOUS LIBERTY

Excerpts from the Antilon-First Citizen Letters

Between January 7 and July 1, 1773, Charles Carroll and Daniel Dulany, a Maryland government official, conducted a debate in the form of a series of letters published in Maryland newspapers. At issue was the governor's proclamation setting government officials' public service fees at a high rate. Dulany defended the governor's act in a series of articles published in the Maryland Gazette. *Dulany called himself "Antilon," which combines "anti" ("against") and an old English word meaning "unfair taxes."*

Charles Carroll quickly responded. Writing under the name "First Citizen," Carroll argued that the fees were taxes. He contended that only the Maryland Assembly, not the governor, had the right to levy taxes. Dulany replied with both argument and personal attack. He questioned Carroll's right as a Catholic to become involved in public affairs.

Below are excerpts from the third and fourth letters written by Dulany and Carroll.

Antilon's Third Letter
Who is he [Carroll]? He has no share in the legislature, as a member of any branch; he is incapable of being a member; he is disabled from giving a vote in the choice of representatives, by the laws and constitution of the country, on account of his principles, which are distrusted by those laws. He is disabled by an express resolve from interfering in the election of members, on the same account. He is not a protestant.

First Citizen's Third Letter
What my speculative notions of religion may be, this is neither the place, nor time to declare; my political principles ought only to be questioned on the present occasion; surely they are constitutional, and have met, I hope, with the approbation of my countrymen.

Antilon's Fourth Letter
We are . . . put upon our guard by our laws, and constitution, which have laid him under disabilities, because he is a papist, and his religious principles are suspected to have so great influence, as to make it unsafe to permit his interference, in any degree, when the interests of the established religion, or the civil government, may be concerned.

First Citizen's Fourth Letter
I am as averse to having a religion crammed down people's throats, as proclamation. There are my political principles, in which I glory. . . . Knaves, and bigots of all sects and denominations I hate, and I despise. . . . [Catholics] cannot . . . enjoy any place of profit, or trust, while they continue papists; but do these disabilities extend so far, as to preclude them from thinking and writing on matters merely of a political nature? . . .

He will not allow me freedom of thought or speech. . . . That you have talents admirably well adapted to the works of darkness, malice to attempt the blackest, and meanness to stoop to the basest, is too true.

Source: From Peter S. Onuf, ed., *Maryland and the Empire, 1773: The Antilon-First Citizen Letters* (Baltimore: Johns Hopkins University Press, 1974), 122, 125–126, 188, 226–227.

BENJAMIN FRANKLIN
(1706–1790)

W e must all hang together, or assuredly we shall all hang separately.

—Benjamin Franklin, at the signing of the Declaration of Independence, 1776

Introduction

Although he was the old sage of the American Revolution and the Founding generation, Benjamin Franklin's considerable work in the areas of journalism, science, and invention often obscure his many contributions to the creation of the Constitution and protection of American freedoms. His stature was second only to George Washington in lending credibility to the new federal government, and his wisdom helped ensure the structural stability of what is now the oldest written constitution still in force in the world.

Franklin's Albany Plan of 1754 was the first formal proposal for a union of the English colonies. Though it failed to gain the requisite support, it signaled the colonies' desire to be more independent of the mother country. Also, the Albany Plan's federal system of government in some ways foreshadowed the political system created by the Constitution three decades later.

Franklin was also an early opponent of slavery who feared that the institution would corrode the cords of friendship among the new American states. Despite his abhorrence of the slave system, however, Franklin was willing to compromise on the issue at the Constitutional Convention, and he remained optimistic about the young nation's prospects.

Relevant Thematic Essays for Benjamin Franklin
- Slavery
- Republican Government (Volume 2)

In His Own Words:
BENJAMIN FRANKLIN
AND THE ALBANY PLAN OF UNION

Overview

In this lesson, students will learn about Benjamin Franklin. They should first read as homework **Handout A—Benjamin Franklin (1706–1790)** and answer the **Reading Comprehension Questions.** After discussing the answers to these questions in class, the teacher should have the students answer the **Critical Thinking Questions** as a class. Next, the teacher should introduce the students to the primary source activity, **Handout C—In His Own Words: Benjamin Franklin and the Albany Plan of Union,** in which sections of Franklin's Albany Plan are compared to similar sections of the Constitution. As a preface, there is **Handout B—Vocabulary and Context Questions,** which will help the students understand the document.

The students will be divided into five groups, each of which will analyze one set of comparisons. The students will then come together as a large group and discuss their answers. There are **Follow-Up Homework Options,** which ask the students to create a British official's report on the Albany Plan or to create a debate between pro- and anti-Albany Plan delegates. **Extensions** asks students to consider Franklin's claim that the passage of the Albany Plan would have averted the American Revolution.

Objectives

Students will:

- appreciate Franklin's contributions to his community and country
- understand the purpose of the Albany Congress
- analyze the basic components of the Albany Plan
- understand Franklin's views on the Articles of Confederation and the Constitution
- explain Franklin's role in the Constitutional Convention
- explain Franklin's efforts to oppose slavery

Standards
CCE (9–12): IC2, IIB1, IIIA2
NCHS (5–12): Era III, Standard 3A; Era IV, Standard 3B
NCSS: Strands 2, 5, 6, and 10

Materials
Student Handouts
- Handout A—Benjamin Franklin (1706–1790)
- Handout B—Vocabulary and Context Questions
- Handout C—In His Own Words: Benjamin Franklin and the Albany Plan of Union

Additional Teacher Resource
- Answer Key

Recommended Time
One 45-minute class period. Additional time as needed for homework.

LESSON PLAN

I. **Background Homework**
Ask students to read **Handout A—Benjamin Franklin (1706–1790)** and answer Reading Comprehension Questions 1–3.

II. **Warm-Up [10 minutes]**
   A. Review answers to homework questions.
   B. Conduct a whole-class discussion to answer Reading Comprehension Question 3 and the Critical Thinking Questions.
   C. Ask a student to summarize the historical significance of Benjamin Franklin.

   Benjamin Franklin was one of the most famous Americans of his era. He was a businessman, inventor, philanthropist, and statesman. His Albany Plan was the first formal proposal for a union of the colonies. Franklin became a champion of American rights during the crisis with England, and after independence, he joined the call for revising the Articles of Confederation. At the Constitutional Convention, Franklin took a moderate position on most issues. Though he favored a stronger central government, he also insisted on safeguards against tyranny. Franklin was also an early opponent of slavery. His last public act was to recommend that Congress adopt a plan to extinguish slavery.

III. **Context [10 minutes]**
   A. Review the challenges that faced the American colonists in the 1750s. Point out that the colonies were facing trouble with Indian tribes as well as with the French, who were seeking to strengthen and expand their North American empire. Emphasize that the colonies lacked any formal system for cooperation and usually dealt independently with Indian attacks, French encroachments, and British meddling.

   B. Franklin's Albany Plan of Union called for the creation of a colonial assembly, a "Grand Council," and an executive, named the "President-General." In several ways this form of government was similar to the Congress and the office of president later created by the United States Constitution.

IV. **In His Own Words [15 minutes]**
   A. Distribute **Handout B—Vocabulary and Context Questions.**
   B. Distribute **Handout C—In His Own Words: Benjamin Franklin and the Albany Plan of Union.** Be sure that the students understand the vocabulary and the "who, what, where, and when" of the document.
   C. Divide the class into five groups, assigning to each group one of the sets of comparisons in **Handout C.** Have each group list the similarities and differences between the relevant sections of the Albany Plan and the Constitution.

LESSON PLAN

V. Wrap-Up Discussion [10 minutes]

Have the students come together as a large group and share their answers to **Handout C.**

VI. Follow-Up Homework Options

A. Have the students assume the role of a British official who has the duty of supervising the American colonies in 1754. Then have them compose this official's report on the Albany Plan to the king. The report should be in the form of a two- to three-paragraph essay, and it should explain why the official thinks the Albany Plan is either a good or a bad idea.

B. Have the students create a debate between two delegates at the Albany Congress, one who supports Franklin's plan and another who opposes it. The debate should be no longer than one page in length and should be in the form of a script or dialogue.

VII. Extensions

Franklin reflected many years later on the consequences of the rejection of the Albany Plan:

Remark, February 9, 1789.

On Reflection, it now seems probable, that if the foregoing Plan or some thing like it, had been adopted and carried into Execution, the subsequent Separation of the Colonies from the Mother Country might not so soon have happened, nor the Mischiefs suffered on both sides have occurred, perhaps during another Century. For the Colonies, if so united, would have really been, as they then thought themselves, sufficient to their own Defence, and being trusted with it, as by the Plan, an Army from Britain, for that purpose would have been unnessessary: The Pretences for framing the Stamp-Act would not then have existed, nor the other Projects for drawing a Revenue from America to Britain by Acts of Parliament, which were the Cause of the Breach, and attended with such terrible Expence of Blood and Treasure: so that the different Parts of the Empire might still have remained in Peace and Union. But the Fate of the Plan was singular. For tho' after many Days thorough Discussion of all its Parts in Congress it was unanimously agreed to, and Copies ordered to be sent to the Assembly of each Province for Concurrence, and one to the Ministry in England for the Approbation of the Crown. The Crown disapprov'd it, as having plac'd too much Weight in the democratic Part of the Constitution; and every Assembly as having allow'd too much to Prerogative. So it was totally rejected.

Source: *The U.S. Constitution Online.* <**http://www.usconstitution.net/albany.html**>.

Suggestions:

A. Ask the students to decide if they agree or disagree with Franklin's idea that "the subsequent Separation of the Colonies from the Mother Country might not so soon have happened" if the Albany Plan had passed.

B. Ask the students to discuss how the Albany Plan could have been modified in order for it to pass.

Resources

Print

Brands, H. W. *The First American: The Life and Times of Benjamin Franklin.* New York: Doubleday, 2000.

Morgan, Edmund S. *Benjamin Franklin.* New Haven, Conn.: Yale University Press, 2002.

Shaw, Peter, ed. *The Autobiography and Other Writings by Benjamin Franklin.* New York: Bantam Books, 1989.

Srodes, James. *Franklin: The Essential Founding Father.* Washington, D.C.: Regnery Publishing, 2002.

Van Doren, Carl. *Benjamin Franklin.* Reprint. New York: Penguin, 2001.

Internet

"The Albany Plan of Union, 1754." The Avalon Project at Yale University Law School. <**http://www.yale.edu/lawweb/avalon/amerdoc/albany.htm**>.

"Benjamin Franklin, Queries and Remarks respecting Alterations in the Constitution of Pennsylvania." The Founders' Constitution. <**http://press-pubs.uchicago.edu/founders/documents/v1ch12s25.html**>.

"Benjamin Franklin, 1706–1790." Colonial Hall. <**http://www.colonialhall.com/franklin/franklin.asp**>.

Poor Richard's Almanack. <**http://www.sage-advice.com/Benjamin_Franklin.htm**>.

"Proposals Relating to the Education of Youth in Pensilvania." University Archives and Records Center, University of Pennsylvania. <**http://www.archives.upenn.edu/primdocs/1749proposals.html**>.

Selected Works by Benjamin Franklin
- *Poor Richard's Almanack* (1733–1758)
- *Autobiography* (1771–1788)
- *Rules by Which a Great Empire May Be Reduced to a Small One* (1773)

BENJAMIN FRANKLIN (1706–1790)

Our Constitution is in actual operation;
everything appears to promise that it will last;
but in this world nothing is certain but death and taxes.

—Benjamin Franklin, Letter to M. Leroy, 1789

Although his voice was weak, it could be clearly heard throughout Convention Hall in Philadelphia. The delegates had temporarily ceased their bickering as Benjamin Franklin, at eighty-one years the oldest member of the group, read one of his proposals. With the exception of George Washington, Franklin was probably the most esteemed member of the remarkable group of statesmen who filled Convention Hall that hot summer of 1787. Franklin had repeatedly called for harmony in the proceedings. This newest proposal, like his previous ones, sought to forge a compromise among the delegates.

A Public Servant

Franklin was a prominent American capitalist. But an important part of his life's work was the promotion of the common good. His cardinal teaching was that "the most acceptable Service of God is doing Good to Man." Franklin sought to promote public virtues through his many writings, such as *Poor Richard's Almanack.* He formed a secret society, the Junto, to promote beneficial ideas. In 1743, he helped to create the American Philosophical Society to advance the cause of science in the New World. He also played a major role in building the first fire department, the first public library, and the first hospital in Philadelphia.

Franklin also worked to improve his community through scientific invention. An example of his selflessness was his refusal to accept patent protection for his famous stove. "That as we enjoy great advantages from the inventions of others," Franklin asserted, "we should be glad of an opportunity to serve others by any invention of ours, and this we should do freely and generously." His fellow citizens repeatedly called upon Franklin to serve in public. He served as deputy postmaster of Philadelphia and deputy postmaster general of the colonies. He was a clerk for and later a member of the Pennsylvania Assembly. After American independence, he established the U.S. Post Office. "I shall never ask, never refuse, nor ever resign an office," Franklin once declared.

The Albany Plan

In 1754, the prospect of war with the French led several of the royal governors to call for a congress of all the colonies. One purpose of the meeting was to plan war operations against the French. Another purpose was to prepare some plan of confederation among the colonies. Only seven colonies sent commissioners to this congress, which met in Albany, New York. Reception among the American colonists and the colonial newspapers was generally unfavorable. But Franklin's own *Pennsylvania Gazette* ran a political cartoon with the motto "Join, or Die!"

At Albany, Franklin drafted and introduced the first formal proposal for a permanent union of the thirteen colonies. This became known as the Albany Plan. It was similar to the decentralized system of government that would later emerge under the Articles of Confederation. There would be a union of the colonies under a single central government, though each colony would preserve its local independence.

Public opinion, however, was not yet ready for a centralized colonial government. Though the Albany Congress did adopt Franklin's plan, the colonial assemblies rejected it because it encroached on their powers. The British government also disapproved of the plan, fearing it would give the colonies too much independence.

Defender of American Rights

Between 1757 and 1775, Franklin resided in England as an agent for several colonies. During the Stamp Act crisis of 1765 he became famous in London as a defender of American rights. The British later branded Franklin a traitor. He escaped probable imprisonment by returning to Philadelphia in May 1775. There he was received as a hero of the American cause and was immediately nominated to be a member of the Second Continental Congress. Thirteen months later, he served on the committee that drafted the Declaration of Independence. He then served as president of Pennsylvania's constitutional convention.

Not long afterward, the aged statesman set sail once again for Europe as a diplomat for the newly established United States of America. Franklin succeeded in gaining French support for the American Revolution. As commissioner to France from 1779–1785, Franklin, along with John Jay and John Adams, negotiated the Treaty of Paris (1783) that ended the War for Independence.

Sage of the Constitutional Convention

Franklin arrived back in the United States in 1785. Believing the Articles of Confederation to be too weak, he joined in the call for a Constitutional Convention. He was chosen to represent the state of Pennsylvania at the Constitutional Convention that met in Philadelphia in the summer of 1787. At 81, Franklin was the oldest member of the convention. He attended almost every session, though his age and illness sometimes made it necessary for others to speak for him.

Franklin's prestige reassured his countrymen about the meeting in Philadelphia, and his presence promoted harmony in the proceedings. Franklin made several successful proposals at the Convention. His ideas often reflected his sympathy with the common people. For example, he favored giving the lower house of Congress the sole power to propose money and tax bills. Franklin believed that the lower house would reflect the "public spirit of our common people." He also successfully opposed property requirements for voting and financial tests for holders of federal office.

Though he favored a stronger central government, Franklin also worried about the possibility of tyranny. He therefore desired a clear listing of the powers of the federal government. He also supported an executive council instead of a single president. When this idea failed, Franklin seconded Virginian George Mason's call for an advisory council to the president. He believed that the president should be limited to only one term in office, so that no one man should gain too much power. He also opposed giving the executive absolute veto power over the Congress. Franklin's proposals met with some success. A cabinet was established, and Congress was given the power to override presidential vetoes by a two-thirds vote.

© The Bill of Rights Institute

On September 17, the convention met for the last time. Fellow Pennsylvanian James Wilson delivered a speech on behalf of Franklin in support of the Constitution. Passage of the plan, Franklin asserted in the speech, "will astonish our enemies, who are waiting with confidence to hear . . . that our States are on the point of separation, only to meet hereafter for the purpose of cutting one another's throats." The new Constitution was ratified into law by the states on June 21, 1788.

Franklin was concerned, however, that the issue of slavery could someday result in the states "cutting one another's throats." Franklin had been an opponent of slavery as early as the 1730s. At the convention, he made the case that all free black men be counted as citizens. Such a course, Franklin believed, would have the "excellent effect of inducing the colonies to discourage slavery and to encourage the increase of their free inhabitants." In 1787, Franklin was elected first president of the Pennsylvania Society for Promoting the Abolition of Slavery. His final public act was signing a petition to Congress recommending dissolution of the slave system.

Franklin was optimistic about America's future. As the convention delegates signed the Constitution, he pointed to the sun carved into the president's chair, and reflected: "I have often . . . in the course of this session . . . looked at that . . . without being able to tell whether it was rising or setting; but now at length I have the happiness to know that it is a rising and not a setting sun." As he exited Convention Hall upon the completion of the Constitution, a woman came up to him and asked what the delegates had created. Franklin responded, "A republic, if you can keep it." Franklin died two and one-half years later, still optimistic that the republic he helped to shape would endure.

Reading Comprehension Questions

1. List three ways in which Franklin improved the lives of those in his community.

2. What was the Albany Congress?

3. List five proposals that Franklin made at the Constitutional Convention.

Critical Thinking Questions

4. How do you think the other delegates at the Constitutional Convention viewed Franklin?

5. What did Franklin mean when he told the woman outside Convention Hall that the delegates had created "a republic, if you can keep it"?

VOCABULARY AND CONTEXT QUESTIONS

Excerpts from the Albany Plan of Union (1754) and the United States Constitution (1788)

1. **Vocabulary:** *Use context clues to determine the meaning or significance of each of these words and write their definitions:*

    a. tranquility

    b. posterity

    c. ordain

    d. delegated

    e. respective

    f. vested

    g. assent

    h. requisite

    i. originated

    j. approbation

    k. concur

    l. consent

    m. consuls

    n. levy

    o. duties

    p. imposts

    q. excises

2. **Context:** *Answer the following questions.*

    a. When was this document written?

    b. Where was this document written?

    c. Who wrote this document?

    d. What type of document is this?

    e. What was the purpose of this document?

    f. Who was the audience for this document?

IN HIS OWN WORDS: BENJAMIN FRANKLIN AND THE ALBANY PLAN OF UNION

Excerpts from the Albany Plan of Union (1754) and the United States Constitution (1788)

Directions: *Compare the selected portions of the Albany Plan to the corresponding excerpts from the Constitution. List the ways in which the sections are similar and then the ways in which they are different.*

1: Preamble and Federal System

Albany Plan

(Preamble): It is proposed that humble application be made for an act of Parliament of Great Britain, by virtue of which one general government may be formed in America, including all the said colonies, within and under which government each colony may retain its present constitution, except in the particulars wherein a change may be directed by the said act, as hereafter follows.

Constitution

(Preamble): We, the people of the United States, in order to form a more perfect Union, establish justice, insure domestic tranquility, provide for the common defense, promote the general welfare, and secure the blessings of liberty to ourselves and our posterity, do ordain and establish this Constitution for the United States of America.

(Tenth Amendment): The powers not delegated to the United States by the Constitution, nor prohibited by it to the States, are reserved to the States respectively, or to the people.

2: Branches of Government

Albany Plan

(1): [It is proposed] that the said general government be administered by a President-General, to be appointed and supported by the crown; and a Grand Council, to be chosen by the representatives of the people of the several Colonies met in their respective assemblies.

(4): There shall be a new election of the members of the Grand Council every three years.

Constitution

(Article II, Section 1, Clause 1): The Executive power shall be vested in a President of the United States of America.

(Article I, Section 1): All legislative powers herein granted shall be vested in a Congress of the United States, which shall consist of a Senate and House of Representatives.

(Article I, Section 2, Clause 1): The House of Representatives shall be composed of members chosen every second year by the people of the several States.

(Article I, Section 3, Clause 1): The Senate of the United States shall be composed of two Senators from each State, chosen by the legislature thereof, for six years.

3: Legislative Process

Albany Plan

(6): The Grand Council shall meet once in every year, and oftener if occasion require.

(9): [It is proposed] that the assent of the President-General be requisite to all acts of the Grand Council, and that it be his office and duty to cause them to be carried into execution.

Constitution

(Article I, Section 4, Clause 2): The Congress shall assemble at least once in every year.

(Article I, Section 7, Clause 2): Every bill which shall have passed the House of Representatives and the Senate, shall, before it become a law, be presented to the president of the United States; if he approve, he shall sign it, but if not, he shall return it, with his objections, to that house in which it shall have originated, who shall enter the objections at large on their journal, and proceed to reconsider it. If after such reconsideration, two thirds of that house shall agree to pass the bill, it shall be sent, together with the objections, to the other house, by which it shall likewise be reconsidered, and if approved by two-thirds of that house, it shall become a law.

(Article II, Section 3): [The President] shall take care that the Laws be faithfully executed.

4: Military Powers

Albany Plan

(10): [It is proposed] that the President-General, with the advice of the Grand Council, hold or direct all Indian treaties, in which the general interest of the Colonies may be concerned; and make peace or declare war with Indian nations.

(23): [It is proposed] that all military commission officers, whether for land or sea service, to act under this general constitution, shall be nominated by the President-General; but the approbation of the Grand Council is to be obtained, before they receive their commissions.

Constitution

(Article I, Section 8, Clause 11): [The Congress shall have the power] to declare war.

(Article II, Section 2, Clause 1): The President shall be Commander-in-Chief of the Army and Navy of the United States, and of the militia of the several States, when called into the actual service of the United States.

(Article II, Section 2, Clause 2): He shall have power, by and with the advice and consent of the Senate, to make treaties, provided two-thirds of the Senators present concur; and he shall nominate, and by and with the advice and consent of the Senate, shall appoint ambassadors, other public ministers and consuls, judges of the Supreme Court, and all other officers of the United States.

5: Power of Taxation

Albany Plan

(16): That for these purposes [the President-General and the Grand Council] have power to make laws, and lay and levy such general duties, imposts, or taxes, as to them shall appear most equal and just (considering the ability and other circumstances of the inhabitants in the several Colonies), and such as may be collected with the least inconvenience to the people; rather discouraging luxury, than loading industry with unnecessary burdens.

Constitution

(Article I, Section 8, Clause 1): The Congress shall have the power to lay and collect taxes, duties, imposts and excises, to pay the debts and provide for the common defence and general welfare of the United States; but all duties, imposts and excises shall be uniform throughout the United States.

Sources: "The Albany Plan of Union, 1754." The Avalon Project at Yale University Law School.
<http://www.yale.edu/lawweb/avalon/amerdoc/albany.htm>.

"Constitution of the United States." The Bill of Rights Institute.
<http://www.billofrightsinstitute.org/sections.php?op=viewarticle&artid=44>.

ELBRIDGE GERRY
(1744–1814)

S omething must be done or we shall disappoint not only America but the whole world.

—*Elbridge Gerry,*
at the Constitutional Convention, 1787

Introduction

Elbridge Gerry is remembered today for his controversial attempt as governor to draw congressional districts in Massachusetts to the advantage of his party. Indeed, "gerrymandering" is a common political tactic today and undeniably part of Gerry's legacy. But Gerry was more than a cunning politician. He was also a leader of the American independence movement, an important critic of the Constitution, and a wartime vice president of the United States.

Cantankerous and obstinate, Gerry seemed to shift his political views according to circumstances. His unpredictable nature often frustrated even his allies. At the Constitutional Convention, he first played the role of moderate and mediator but ended up a critic of the final document. Gerry feared that the central government set up by the Constitution would become dangerously powerful. He was one of three delegates who stayed until the end of the convention but who refused to sign the Constitution.

Once the document was ratified, however, Gerry accepted a seat in the new Congress and even began to sympathize with the Federalist Party, which favored a strong central government. But after being criticized by the Federalists for his role in the "X, Y, Z Affair" that strained the relationship between France and the United States during the administration of John Adams, Gerry embraced the rival Democratic-Republicans. As a member of this party, Gerry served as governor of Massachusetts and as vice president under James Madison during the War of 1812. He died while serving in the latter office, a public servant until the end of his life.

Relevant Thematic Essays for Elbridge Gerry
- Federalism
- Limited Government (Volume 2)

By His Own Hand: ELBRIDGE GERRY
AND GERRYMANDERING

Overview

In this lesson, students will learn about Elbridge Gerry. They should first read as background homework **Handout A—Elbridge Gerry (1744–1814)** and answer the **Reading Comprehension Questions.** After discussing these questions in class, the teacher should have the students answer the **Critical Thinking Questions** as a class. Next, the teacher should introduce the students to the primary source activity, **Handout B—By His Own Hand: Elbridge Gerry and Gerrymandering,** in which the students will draw congressional districts to one political party's advantage.

There are **Follow-Up Homework Options** that ask the students to consider how gerrymandering can be used to discriminate against certain ethnic and religious groups. **Extensions** provides opportunities for reflection on historical and contemporary controversies; students are asked to research Supreme Court cases that deal with gerrymandering as well as their state's most recent experience with reapportionment.

Objectives

Students will:

- appreciate Gerry's role as a leader of the American opposition to British tyranny
- analyze the reasons for Gerry's opposition to the Constitution
- understand how Gerry drew congressional districts in Massachusetts to favor the Federalist Party
- apply Gerry's redistricting tactics (gerrymandering) in a hypothetical scenario

Standards

CCE (9–12): IIA1, IIC1, IIIA1, IIIA2
NCHS (5–12): Era III, Standards 3A, 3B
NCSS: Strands 2, 5, 6, and 10

Materials
Student Handouts

- Handout A—Elbridge Gerry (1744–1814)
- Handout B—By His Own Hand: Elbridge Gerry and Gerrymandering

Additional Teacher Resource

- Answer Key

Recommended Time

One 45-minute class period. Additional time as needed for homework.

LESSON PLAN

I. **Background Homework**

Ask students to read **Handout A—Elbridge Gerry (1744–1814)** and answer the Reading Comprehension Questions.

II. **Warm-Up** [10 minutes]
   A. Review answers to homework questions.
   B. Conduct a whole-class discussion to answer the Critical Thinking Questions.
   C. Ask a student to summarize the historical significance of Elbridge Gerry.

   Elbridge Gerry was a Massachusetts merchant who became a leader of the American independence movement. As a member of the Continental Congress he signed the Declaration of Independence and Articles of Confederation. He represented Massachusetts at the Constitutional Convention in Philadelphia, where he chaired the committee that forged the Great Compromise that resolved the dispute about representation in the Senate and House of Representatives. He was one of three delegates who stayed until the end of the convention but who refused to sign the final document. Gerry feared that the national government as designed by the Constitution was too powerful. In 1797, John Adams chose Gerry as one of a three-member delegation to negotiate with the French government. In France he became involved in the divisive "X, Y, Z Affair." In 1810, Gerry became governor of Massachusetts and approved a controversial redistricting plan. The plan created new, irregularly shaped congressional voting districts designed to give his party an advantage in the elections for state senate, a tactic called "gerrymandering."

III. **Context** [5 minutes]

Briefly review Article I, Section 2, Clause 3 of the Constitution (as amended by Section 2 of the Fourteenth Amendment), which explains how representatives are to be apportioned among the states every ten years according to the national census. Point out to the students that the Constitution leaves the method of electing representatives to each individual state. The states were left to decide whether their allotted number of representatives would be chosen at large (by a state-wide election) or by districts. Today, after reapportionment, states usually undertake redistricting, the process of redrawing district lines for each office so that all districts have nearly identical voter population. This process is often influenced by political considerations, as the party in power in the state legislature and in the governor's office ordinarily attempts to draw district boundary lines to its advantage.

Be sure to show the students the original political cartoon of 1812 that depicts Gerry's salamander-shaped district: <**http://www.boondocksnet.com/cartoons/mcc253.html**>.

IV. **By His Own Hand** [25 minutes]
   A. Divide the class into an even number of groups. Each group should be composed of three to five students.
   B. Tell the class that each group will have the task of drawing Massachusetts' congressional districts so as to favor a particular political party. Assign half the groups the task of favoring the Federalist Party and the other half the job of favoring the Republican Party.

LESSON PLAN

C. Distribute **Handout B—By His Own Hand: Elbridge Gerry and Gerrymandering.**
Tell the students that this map depicts the political affiliation of the population of
the Commonwealth of Massachusetts around 1810. (This is a fictional map, not
based on actual statistics.) Each *F* represents a group of voters likely to vote for
Federalists; each *R* represents a group of voters who are inclined to vote for
Republicans. Each letter represents an equal number of people.

D. There are fifty letters on the map—twenty-five representing Federalist voters and
twenty-five representing Republican voters. Students must create ten congressional
districts of five letters each. For the purposes of this activity, districts must be
contiguous (that is, there cannot be separate "islands" that comprise one district).

E. Each district will favor one party. The job of each group is to make as many
districts as possible favor its assigned party. They must make at least six districts
favor their party. HINT: Tell the students that they might want to concentrate the
opposition in a small number of districts.

F. Have each group present its map to the class and discuss the tactics it used to draw
district boundary lines so as to favor one party. (It may be easier to make an
overhead of the Massachusetts map and let each group draw its finished map on
the surface on which the map is projected.)

V. Wrap-Up Discussion [5 minutes]

After the presentations and discussion, ask the students these questions: Is it realistic
to think that a state legislature could put aside political considerations when drawing
congressional districts? If not, can you think of a fair and impartial way for a state to
draw district boundaries? Should independent commissions be created to oversee
redistricting?

Answers will vary.

VI. Follow-Up Homework Options

Have the students answer this question in one to two paragraphs:

• How could gerrymandering be used to discriminate against certain ethnic and
religious groups?

VII. Extensions

A. Ask the students to research one or more of the following Supreme Court cases
that deal with redistricting, and then write a one-paragraph summary of the
Court's decision:

• *Baker* v. *Carr* (1962)
• *Reynolds* v. *Sims* (1964)
• *Lucas* v. *Colorado* (1964)
• *Davis* v. *Bandemer* (1986)
• *Shaw* v. *Reno* (1993)
• *Abrams* v. *Johnson* (1997)
• *Easley* v. *Cromartie* (2001)

B. Ask the students to research your state's most recent experience with
reapportionment. They should be ready to tell the class whether your state gained
or lost representatives after the 2000 census (reapportionment) and whether there
was any controversy about redistricting.

Elbridge Gerry   47

LESSON PLAN

Resources

Print

Allen, William B., and Gordon Lloyd. *The Essential Anti-Federalist.* Lanham, MD.: Rowman and Littlefield, 2002.

Austin, James T. *The Life of Elbridge Gerry.* 2 vols. New York: Da Capo Press, 1970.

Billias, George Athan. *Elbridge Gerry: Founding Father and Republican Statesman.* New York: McGraw-Hill, 1976.

Gardiner, C. Harvey. *A Study in Dissent: The Warren-Gerry Correspondence, 1776–1792.* Carbondale: Southern Illinois University Press, 1968.

Storing, Herbert J. *What the Anti-Federalists Were For.* Chicago: The University of Chicago Press, 1981.

Internet

"The Constitutional Convention." TeachingAmericanHistory.org. <**http://www.teachingamericanhistory.org/convention/**>.

"Elbridge Gerry." National Archives and Records Administration. <**http://www.archives.gov/national_archives_experience/constitution_founding_fathers_massachusetts.html**>.

"Elbridge Gerry (1813–1814)." Reprinted from *Vice Presidents of the United States, 1789–1993.* Government Printing Office. <**http://www.senate.gov/artandhistory/history/resources/pdf/elbridge_gerry.pdf**>.

"Elbridge Gerry's Reasons for Not Signing the Constitution." The Library of Congress. A Century of Lawmaking for a New Nation: U.S. Congressional Debates and Documents, 1774–1875. <**http://memory.loc.gov/learn/features/timeline/newnatn/usconst/egerry.html**>.

"The Gerry-mander": Political Cartoon by Elkanah Tisdale (1812). Political Cartoons and Cartoonists. <**http://www.boondocksnet.com/cartoons/mcc253.html**>.

Selected Works by Elbridge Gerry
- *Objections to Signing the National Constitution* (1787)

ELBRIDGE GERRY (1744–1814)

It must be admitted that a free people are the proper guardians of their rights and liberties; that the greatest men may err, and that their errors are sometimes of the greatest magnitude.

—*Elbridge Gerry, 1787*

The delegates were exhausted. For four long, hot months in Philadelphia, representatives of twelve of the American states had discussed, debated, and negotiated as they hammered out a new constitution for the country. It was now the 15th day of September 1787, and the delegates were putting the finishing touches on the document. As the day's proceedings came to a close, Virginia delegates Edmund Randolph and George Mason voiced their objections to the Constitution. Then Elbridge Gerry of Massachusetts stood to speak. There was a murmur among the delegates. Gerry was a difficult man who had seemingly objected during the proceedings to every proposal that he did not put forth. What would he say now? Gerry announced that he would withhold his signature from the document. He listed several flaws in the Constitution, which he said that he could overlook if the rights of the citizens were made secure under this proposed government. But these rights were not guaranteed, Gerry warned. He argued that the Congress as designed was too powerful, and he called for a second convention to revise the document. Several delegates groaned and muttered in frustration as Gerry returned to his seat.

Background

The son of a wealthy shipping magnate, Elbridge Gerry was born in Marblehead, Massachusetts, in 1744. After graduating from Harvard in 1762, he joined the family business. He soon came to see firsthand how British economic policy hurt American merchants. Gerry began to sympathize with the American patriot movement, which openly opposed British policy toward the colonies. In 1770, he supported a successful boycott of British tea. Gerry soon became well known among Marblehead's citizens, who sent him to the colonial legislature two years later. There Gerry met Samuel Adams, the well-respected patriot leader from Boston, Massachusetts.

Revolution and Declaration

Adams recruited Gerry for the patriot movement. In 1774, Gerry became convinced that the colonies needed to declare independence. Marblehead's citizens appointed Gerry to Massachusetts' Committee of Correspondence. This committee mustered support and spread information for the patriot cause. The colonists soon realized that war with the mother country was likely. In the Massachusetts legislature, Gerry helped Adams and John Hancock oversee military preparations. He used his shipping connections to import gunpowder and other military supplies. He also loaned money—interest free—to the cause.

Gerry was selected to attend the Continental Congress in 1775. There he worked tirelessly to convince delegates to declare independence. In the process, he won the respect of fellow delegates like John Adams, cousin of Samuel Adams. The future president declared, "If every Man here was a Gerry, the Liberties of America would be safe against the Gates of Earth and Hell."

But Gerry was also a stubborn and difficult man. He lacked a sense of humor and seemed to enjoy arguing. He often irritated even his allies, including John Adams, who complained that Gerry's "obstinacy . . . will risk great things to secure small ones." In 1779, Gerry stormed out of the Continental Congress in a rage after a dispute about payments for suppliers of the Continental Army. He would not return for three years.

Constitutional Convention

During his service in the Continental Congress, Gerry had signed the Declaration of Independence and the Articles of Confederation. After the Revolutionary War, Gerry served from 1783–1785 in the new Congress created by the Articles. In 1786, he left Congress and served in the Massachusetts legislature. The following year, the citizens of Massachusetts chose Gerry as a delegate to the national convention in Philadelphia that had been called to revise the Articles of Confederation.

At the convention, Gerry at first adopted a moderate stance between nationalists, who favored a strong central government, and states' rights advocates. He chaired the committee that forged the Great Compromise. This agreement provided for equal representation of the states in the Senate and proportional representation in the House of Representatives. But Gerry again was combative and, in the words of a fellow delegate, "objected to everything he did not propose."

Soon, Gerry began to fear that the national government was being given too much power. He worried that Congress in particular would be able to trample on the rights of the people and of the states. Gerry suggested that provisions be added to the Constitution limiting Congress' authority. Two of these passed—namely, the prohibitions against ex post facto laws and bills of attainder. Gerry also insisted, along with George Mason, that a bill of rights be added to the document. The convention voted down this idea.

On September 15, 1787, as the Philadelphia Convention drew to a close, Gerry announced that he could not sign the Constitution. He believed it would create an all-powerful central government. He sent the Massachusetts legislature a letter outlining his reasons for this decision. Gerry and the Virginians George Mason and Edmund Randolph were the only delegates who stayed until the end of the convention but did not sign the Constitution.

Despite his refusal to approve the document, Gerry did not speak against it. He believed the Constitution was necessary to prevent the union of the states from falling apart. During the ratification debates in Massachusetts, he argued that the state should approve the Constitution only on the condition that amendments would be added as soon as possible. Massachusetts ratified the Constitution but also attached a list of recommended amendments.

Congressman, Peace Commissioner, Governor, and Vice President

Once the Constitution was approved in 1788, Gerry supported the new government. He was elected to the United States House of Representatives the following year. To the surprise of many, he supported Secretary of the Treasury Alexander Hamilton's plan to create a national bank. This measure strengthened the federal government. Gerry left Congress and returned home in 1793 to care for his sick wife and children.

In 1797, John Adams chose Gerry as one of a three-member delegation to negotiate with the French government. Tensions between the United States and Napoleonic France were high. France was at war with much of Europe at the time. Napoleon refused to allow American ships to travel to European ports. Private ships licensed by the French government attacked and sank many American merchant ships. Adams hoped that Gerry, along with Charles Cotesworth Pinckney and John Marshall, could resolve the situation.

© The Bill of Rights Institute

Tensions increased when three French officials—who became known as "X, Y, and Z" among American officials in order to guard their identity—demanded a bribe from the Americans before they would open negotiations. The American delegation was outraged. Pinckney and Marshall immediately left for the United States. But Gerry, hoping to continue the negotiations and avert a war between the two countries, stayed behind. Members of the Federalist Party in Congress criticized Gerry for his action, especially his alleged partiality to France. Finally, President Adams ordered Gerry to return to the United States. The event became known as the "X, Y, Z Affair," and it tarnished Gerry's reputation.

Spurned by the anti-French Federalists, Gerry turned to the Democratic-Republican (or simply, Republican) Party. He was elected governor of Massachusetts in 1810 and 1811 under the banner of this party. At the end of his second term in office, Gerry approved a controversial redistricting plan. The plan created new, irregularly shaped congressional voting districts designed to give Republicans an advantage in the elections for state senate. Angry Federalists dubbed the tactic "gerrymandering," for the awkward, salamander-like shape of one of the districts. The term is still used today to describe the drawing of districts to favor one party.

Many Massachusetts voters resented the governor's attempt to gerrymander the state's districts. Gerry may have lost the 1812 gubernatorial race because of his political gamesmanship. His political career, however, was not over. That same year, President James Madison selected him to run as his vice president. Gerry accepted the offer.

Madison and Gerry were victorious in the election of 1812. By the time Gerry assumed his new post, the United States was at war with Great Britain. One of Gerry's duties as vice president was to preside over the Senate. That body, like the American public, was sharply divided between pro-war Republicans and anti-war Federalists. Gerry was already in poor health—one observer described him as an "old skeleton"—and the political battles took their toll on him. In November 1814, Gerry collapsed and died on his way to the Senate.

Reading Comprehension Questions

1. Which historical documents did Gerry sign?

2. What did Gerry think about the Constitution when the delegates at Philadelphia completed the final version of the document? What stance did he take during the ratification debates in Massachusetts?

3. How did the term "gerrymandering" evolve?

Critical Thinking Questions

4. Gerry sometimes failed to consider carefully the consequences of his actions. Give an example of an instance in which Gerry could have chosen to act differently and thereby avoid the negative consequences of his action.

5. Imagine that you are a boyhood friend of Elbridge Gerry and that you are about to introduce him to John Adams at the Continental Congress. What can you tell Adams privately about Gerry in regard to his politics and personality before the two meet?

BY HIS OWN HAND:
ELBRIDGE GERRY AND GERRYMANDERING

Fictional Map of Political Affiliations in Massachusetts around 1810

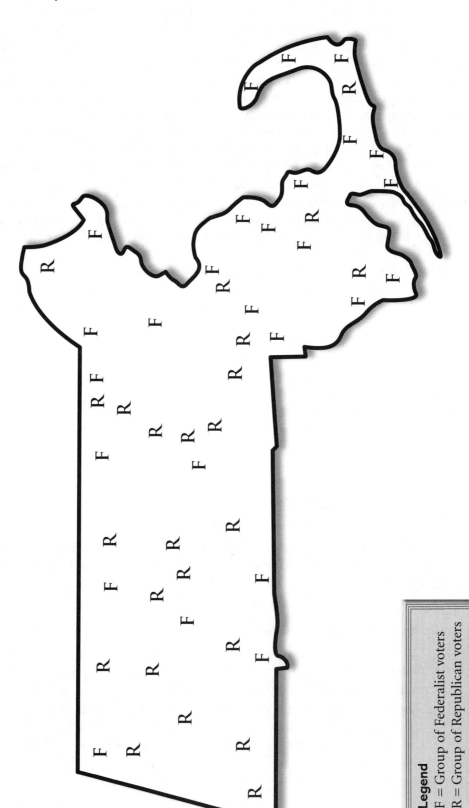

Legend
F = Group of Federalist voters
R = Group of Republican voters

PATRICK HENRY
(1736–1799)

Show me that age and country where the rights and liberties of the people were placed on the sole chance of their rulers being good men without a consequent loss of liberty! I say that the loss of that dearest privilege has ever followed, with absolute certainty, every such mad attempt.

—*Patrick Henry, 1788*

Introduction

Patrick Henry's fame rested largely on his oratorical skills, which he employed in the cause of liberty. Henry was one of the most persuasive speakers of his time. His oratory differed from that typical of the period in that Henry rarely made allusions to classical texts. Instead, imitating the revivalist preachers he had heard as a boy during the Great Awakening, he filled his speeches with Biblical allusions and Christian symbolism. Henry's persuasive speaking style converted the hearts of many. At the same time, however, his abrasive nature could alienate others. After battling Henry on revisions to the Virginia constitution, Thomas Jefferson became exasperated. "What we have to do I think," Jefferson suggested to James Madison, "is devoutly to pray for his death."

Henry was an articulate spokesman for American liberty during the crisis with Great Britain. After the United States won independence, he became a leading Anti-Federalist and opponent of the new Constitution. Henry feared that the new government would destroy individual rights and the authority of the states. His insistence that a bill of rights at least be attached to the document did much to make the first ten amendments to the Constitution a reality. Henry believed his duty was to guard zealously the rights of his people. He knew that future generations of Americans would judge his efforts, and he hoped that "they will see that I have done my utmost to preserve their liberty."

Relevant Thematic Essays for Patrick Henry

- Federalism
- Freedom of Religion
- Limited Government (Volume 2)

In His Own Words:
PATRICK HENRY
ON THE CONSTITUTION

Overview

In this lesson, students will learn about Patrick Henry. They should first read as background homework **Handout A—Patrick Henry (1736–1799)** and answer the **Reading Comprehension Questions**. After discussing the answers to these questions in class, the teacher should have the students answer the **Critical Thinking Questions** as a class. Next, the teacher should introduce the students to the primary source activity, **Handout C—In His Own Words: Patrick Henry on the Constitution,** in which Henry warns the members of the Virginia Ratifying Convention that the new Constitution will produce tyranny in the United States. As a preface, there is **Handout B—Context Questions,** which will help the students understand the document.

Students will be divided into five groups, each of which will paraphrase a section of the document in one to two sentences. They will then jigsaw into new groups, and each group will present a one-minute version of Henry's speech that retains the main ideas of the original. There are **Follow-Up Homework Options** that ask the students to compose a response to Henry's speech by a defender of the Constitution and to examine the use of fear and sarcasm in Henry's speeches. **Extensions** provides opportunity for thought as students are asked to compose a speech in the style of Henry about a contemporary issue which they have researched.

Objectives

Students will:
- explain why Henry is often called "The Orator of Liberty"
- understand Henry's role in the American independence movement
- explain Henry's objections to the Constitution
- analyze Henry's speaking style

Standards

CCE (9–12): IIA1, IIC1, IIIA1, IIIA2
NCHS (5–12): Era III, Standards 3A, 3B
NCSS: Strands 2, 5, 6, and 10

Materials
Student Handouts
- Handout A—Patrick Henry (1736–1799)
- Handout B—Context Questions
- Handout C—In His Own Words: Patrick Henry on the Constitution

Additional Teacher Resource
- Answer Key

Recommended Time
One 45-minute class period. Additional time as needed for homework.

LESSON PLAN

I. Background Homework
Ask students to read **Handout A—Patrick Henry (1736–1799)** and answer the Reading Comprehension Questions.

II. Warm-Up [10 minutes]
A. Review answers to homework questions.
B. Conduct a whole-class discussion to answer the Critical Thinking Questions.
C. Ask a student to summarize the historical significance of Patrick Henry.

> *Patrick Henry was one of the most radical leaders of the opposition to British tyranny. He became famous for his speech during the Parson's Cause of 1763 in which he denounced British misrule in Virginia. He also spoke out against the Stamp Act, claiming that only the Virginia legislature possessed the power to tax Virginia's citizens. During the American Revolution and soon after independence, Henry served in the state legislature and as governor of Virginia. He was a leading opponent of the proposed Constitution of 1787, which he feared would establish tyranny in the United States. Henry wanted a bill of rights added to the document, but he opposed as inadequate the twelve amendments sent to the states in 1789.*

III. Context [5 minutes]
Briefly review with students the main issues involved in the debate between Federalists and Anti-Federalists. (The Federalists believed that the confederation would break up if the Constitution was not ratified. Anti-Federalists feared that a stronger central government would endanger the rights of the people.)

IV. In His Own Words [25 minutes]
A. Distribute **Handout B—Context Questions.**
B. Divide the class into five equal groups. Give each group one of the pages of **Handout C—In His Own Words: Patrick Henry on the Constitution.** Be sure that the students understand the vocabulary and the "who, what, where, and when" of the document.
C. Each group will be given the job of paraphrasing its assigned passage in one to two sentences that convey Henry's main idea. Below each passage of Henry's speech are aids for understanding the document: vocabulary words and their definitions, a list of relevant sections of the Constitution, and clues to understanding the passage.
D. Once all groups believe that they understand their assigned passage, jigsaw into five new groups (regroup the students so that each new group contains at least one "expert" from each of the original groups).
E. Tell each student to imagine that he or she is Patrick Henry and has been given one minute to deliver a speech at the Virginia Ratifying Convention. Give each group the task of editing the entire five-paragraph speech so that when read aloud, it takes no longer than one minute. Students should edit the speech sentence by sentence; that is, they should delete entire sentences, leaving complete sentences. Remind the students that they should retain the five main ideas that comprise the speech.
F. Once the groups have edited the speech to one minute, have each group select its best speaker to deliver its version to the entire class. Remind the speakers that Henry used emotion when making his speeches.

LESSON PLAN

V. Wrap-Up Discussion [5 minutes]

After each speaker has given his or her group's speech, conduct a large-group discussion to determine which group did the best job of summarizing the five main points of Henry's speech. List these five main points on the board, making sure that the students understand them.

VI. Follow-Up Homework Options

A. Tell the students to imagine that they are delegates to the Virginia Ratifying Convention who favor the Constitution. Have each student compose a page-long response to Henry's speech that addresses each of Henry's five main points.

B. Using both **Handout A** and **Handout C,** have the students highlight phrases or sentences uttered by Henry in which he most successfully employs fear to arouse his listeners. Also have the students underline phrases or sentences in which Henry employs sarcasm to attack his opponents.

VII. Extensions

In his speech to the Virginia Ratifying Convention, Henry warned that some Americans wished to build a powerful empire at the expense of the people's liberty. Some people today, echoing Henry, have argued that recent presidents have sought to expand the influence of the United States at the expense of the freedom of Americans. Have the students find a news article or editorial in which someone—a news commentator, government official, political candidate, etc.—makes such an argument. Then have the students compose a one-paragraph speech about the issue in the style used by Patrick Henry.

Resources

Print

Beeman, Richard. *Patrick Henry: A Biography.* New York: McGraw-Hill, 1974.

Mayer, Henry. *A Son of Thunder: Patrick Henry and the American Republic.* Reprint. New York: Grove Press, 2001.

McCants, David A. *Patrick Henry: The Orator.* New York: Greenwood Press, 1990.

Meade, Robert Douthat. *Patrick Henry.* 2 vols. Philadelphia: Lippincott, 1957–1969.

Vaughan, David J. *Give Me Liberty: The Uncompromising Statesmanship of Patrick Henry.* Nashville, TN: Cumberland House, 1997.

Internet

Red Hill, Patrick Henry National Memorial. <**http://www.redhill.org/**>.

"Give Me Liberty or Give Me Death." The Avalon Project at Yale University Law School.
    <**http://www.yale.edu/lawweb/avalon/patrick.htm**>.

"Patrick Henry." U.S. History.org. <**http://www.ushistory.org/declaration/related/henry.htm**>.

"Patrick Henry." The American Revolution.org. <**http://theamericanrevolution.org/ipeople/phenry.asp**>.

"Meet the People: Patrick Henry." Colonial Williamsburg Foundation.
    <**http://www.history.org/Almanack/people/bios/biohen.cfm**>.

Selected Works by Patrick Henry

- "Give Me Liberty or Give Me Death": Speech of March 23, 1775, to the Second Continental Congress
- Speech of June 5, 1788, in the Virginia Ratifying Convention

PATRICK HENRY (1736–1799)

I know not what course others may take; but as for me, give me liberty or give me death.

—Patrick Henry, 1775

Patrick Henry's imposing figure and confident voice commanded his fellow delegates' attention. Standing six feet tall and possessing flashing blue eyes, the fifty-two-year-old, self-taught lawyer had already earned a reputation in the state as a powerful speaker. As Virginia's leaders gathered in 1788 to consider ratification of the Constitution, Henry's opposition echoed through the hall. He warned that approval of the document would create a too-powerful central government that would eventually degenerate into a tyranny. "Away with your president!" Henry thundered. "We shall have a king: the army will salute him monarch; your militia will leave you, and assist in making him king, and fight against you: and what have you to oppose this force? What will then become of you and your rights? Will not absolute despotism ensue?" Henry's words were passionate and powerful, so much so that one delegate confessed that he felt imaginary iron shackles close around his hands as Henry spoke his warning.

Background

By all accounts, Patrick Henry was not a hard worker. Thomas Jefferson once called him "the laziest man in reading I ever knew." Born in 1736 in Hanover County, Virginia, he was schooled mostly by his father, who expected him to be a farmer. Henry had little interest in either academics or farming. He was spellbound, however, by the revivalist Christian preachers who came to his town during the 1740s and 1750s. Their fiery oratory had a lasting effect on the young Henry.

When he was twenty-one years old, Henry and his brother became the owners of a general store that their father had established for them. But the brothers were poor businessmen. Within a year, the store had gone bankrupt. Henry married and tried his hand at farming and, for a second time, at storekeeping. Neither venture was successful. He then decided to teach himself the law. After studying for only a few weeks, Henry was admitted to the Virginia bar in 1760 at the age of twenty-three.

The Parson's Cause

Three years later, Henry argued a case that became known as the "Parson's Cause." In 1758, the Virginia House of Burgesses had passed the Two-Penny Act. This law had the effect of lowering drastically the salaries of the Virginia clergy, which were paid by wealthy Virginia planters. When the parsons protested to the king, the British government repealed the Two-Penny Act.

Several clergymen filed lawsuits to collect the money they had lost since the passage of the Two-Penny Act. They won their cases. In the Parson's Cause of 1763, Henry was hired by a group of planters to argue their side when a jury was deciding the amount of money owed to a parson. Henry took advantage of the opportunity to make an hour-long speech denouncing the king's repeal of the Two-Penny Act as "an instance of misrule" and perhaps tyranny. The king, he declared, should not interfere with Virginia's right to make its own laws.

Henry's bold speech caused some in the courtroom to whisper that the lawyer's words were treasonous. But Henry's words persuaded the jury, who awarded the parson a mere penny in damages. After court was adjourned, most observers, who resented the king's interference in Virginia's affairs, cheered Henry. Several men hoisted Henry onto their shoulders and carried him to a local tavern, where they celebrated the victory for American liberty with vast amounts of liquor. In the course of an hour, Henry had made a name for himself in Virginia.

Tyranny and Revolution

In 1765, Henry was elected to the Virginia House of Burgesses. There he added to his fame by opposing the Stamp Act of 1765. Passed by the British Parliament, this law in effect placed a tax on legal documents, newspapers, and playing cards produced in the colonies. Henry introduced a series of resolutions to the House, one of which asserted that "the General Assembly of this Colony have the only and sole exclusive Right & Power to lay . . . taxes upon the Inhabitants of this Colony." Again, Henry was not afraid of being labeled a traitor. "If this be treason," he thundered, "make the most of it!"

By the 1770s, Henry had emerged as one of the most radical leaders of the opposition to British tyranny. In 1774, he represented Virginia at the First Continental Congress. The following year, Henry attended the second Virginia Convention. At St. John's Church in Richmond, he urgently advised his fellow Virginians to take arms against the British. "Gentlemen may cry 'Peace! Peace!' but there is no peace," Henry intoned. "The war is actually begun!" He closed his speech with the now legendary words: "I know not what course others may take; but as for me, give me liberty or give me death."

Henry's call to arms succeeded in drowning out the voices of those reluctant to go to war. Governor Lord Dunmore so feared the discontented colonists that he ordered the removal of the gunpowder from the Williamsburg Magazine and had it loaded onto a British ship. In response, Henry threatened to use the Virginia militia to reclaim Virginia's property. In the end, the governor paid the colony for the powder.

In 1776, Virginia and the other colonies declared their independence from Great Britain. Henry served as the first governor of Virginia from 1776 to 1779. He then served in the Virginia House of Delegates from 1780 to 1784. As a member of the legislature, he championed a bill that would have required a tax for the general support of the Christian religion. But James Madison, also a member of the legislature, succeeded in defeating the proposal and winning passage of the Statute for Religious Freedom. This act provided for the separation of church and state in Virginia. In 1784, Henry was elected again to the governorship for a two-year term.

The Virginia Convention

In 1787, Henry received an invitation to participate in a convention whose purpose was to revise the Articles of Confederation. Saying he "smelled a rat," Henry refused to attend what became the Constitutional Convention. He feared that the meeting was a plot by the powerful to construct a strong central government of which they would be the masters.

When the new Constitution was sent to Virginia for ratification in 1788, Henry was one of its most outspoken critics. Deeming liberty the "direct end and foundation" of government, Henry warned that the new Constitution would create a "consolidated" government in which power would be concentrated in the hands of a few. The document did not provide for adequate checks and balances and therefore did not protect the people against evil rulers. Henry was concerned that the Constitution also gave the central government the power of direct taxation. It also created a standing army, which Henry feared a power-hungry president could use to awe the people into submission.

© The Bill of Rights Institute

Henry wondered aloud why the Constitution did not include a bill of rights. "Is it because it will consume too much paper?" he asked sarcastically. Henry believed that the absence of a bill of rights was part of the attempt by the few to amass power. The arguments of Henry and other Anti-Federalists compelled Madison, the leader of the Virginia Federalists (supporters of adoption of the Constitution), to promise the addition of a bill of rights to the Constitution once the document was approved. But Henry warned his Anti-Federalist allies that Madison's promise was an empty one. Henry's passionate appeals, however, failed to sway the convention. After twenty-five days of heated debate, on June 26, 1788, Virginia became the tenth state to ratify the Constitution.

A Respected Statesman

Henry refused to serve in the new government. "Some of its leading principles," he told a friend, "are subversive of those to which I am forever attached." But Henry did not give up the fight for liberty. He continued to call for a bill of rights, and his efforts forced Madison, who was a candidate for a congressional seat, to promise voters that he would work to add a bill of rights to the Constitution.

In 1789, the first Congress of the United States sent a list of twelve amendments to the states. Henry believed that these amendments did not adequately safeguard the rights of the people and the states. He therefore did not support them, instead calling for a new convention to revise the Constitution. Nevertheless, Virginia approved all twelve amendments, and ten of these were ratified by the required number of states and added to the Constitution in 1791. These ten amendments became known as the Bill of Rights.

Thwarted in his efforts to put together a second Constitutional convention, Henry returned to his plantation at Red Hill, Virginia. There he resumed his law practice. Unlike most former Anti-Federalists, Henry did not join the Republican Party formed by Thomas Jefferson and James Madison in the 1790s. He disliked both men and, as a devout Christian, was disgusted by the enthusiasm of many Republicans for the atheistic French Revolution.

Nor did Henry immediately ally himself with the new Federalist Party, which included most members of the Washington administration. In 1795 and 1796, Henry turned down offers from George Washington first to serve as secretary of state and then chief justice of the supreme court. President Washington, however, did persuade Henry to run for election for a seat in the Virginia legislature in 1799. Henry won the election but died before the legislature formally convened.

Reading Comprehension Questions

1. Why did Henry refuse to attend the Constitutional Convention in 1787?

2. What were Henry's objections to the Constitution?

3. Why did Henry, unlike most former Anti-Federalists, refuse to join the Republican Party?

Critical Thinking Questions

4. In what way are the arguments made by Henry in the Parson's Cause and in his resolutions against the Stamp Act similar?

5. Some have referred to Henry's "Give Me Liberty or Give Me Death" speech of 1775 as "the first shot" of the Revolutionary War. Why?

CONTEXT QUESTIONS

Excerpts from Patrick Henry's Speech of June 5, 1788, in the Virginia Ratifying Convention

Answer the following questions.

    a. When was this document written?

    b. Where was this document written?

    c. Who wrote this document?

    d. What type of document is this?

    e. What was the purpose of this document?

    f. Who was the audience for this document?

IN HIS OWN WORDS:
PATRICK HENRY ON THE CONSTITUTION

Excerpts from Patrick Henry's Speech of June 5, 1788, in the Virginia Ratifying Convention

Directions: *Each group should paraphrase its assigned passage in one to two sentences that convey Henry's main idea. Below each passage of Henry's speech are aids for understanding the document.*

1. Majority Rule

This, sir, is the language of democracy—that a majority of the community have a right to alter government when found to be oppressive. But how different is the genius of your new Constitution from this! How different from the sentiments of freemen that a contemptible minority can prevent the good of the majority! . . . If, sir, amendments are left to the twentieth, or tenth part of the people of America, your liberty is gone for ever. . . . It will be easily contrived to procure the opposition of the one-tenth of the people to any alteration, however judicious. . . .

Vocabulary:

    a. genius = nature
    b. contemptible = disgraceful
    c. contrived = arranged
    d. procure = obtain
    e. alteration = change
    f. judicious = sensible

Relevant Section(s) of the Constitution:

Article V: Amendment Process

Clues to Understanding the Passage:

The amendment process states that the approval of three fourths of the states is necessary for any proposed amendment to be enacted. In a union of thirteen states, an amendment would require the approval of ten states. The opposition of any four states—even those with small populations—would kill an amendment.

Source: Speech made on June 5, 1788, in the Virginia Ratifying Convention. The American Revolution.org. <**http://theamericanrevolution.org/ipeople/phenry/phenryspeech1.asp**>.

IN HIS OWN WORDS:
PATRICK HENRY ON THE CONSTITUTION

Excerpts from Patrick Henry's Speech of June 5, 1788, in the Virginia Ratifying Convention

2. A Standing Army

A standing army we shall have, also, to execute the execrable commands of tyranny; and how are you to punish them? Will you order them to be punished? Who shall obey these orders? Will your mace-bearer be a match for a disciplined regiment? In what situation are we to be? The clause before you gives . . . an exclusive power of legislation, in all cases whatsoever, for ten miles square, and over all places purchased for the erection of forts, magazines, arsenals, dockyards, etc. What resistance could be made? The attempt would be madness. . . .

Vocabulary:

a. execrable = repulsive
b. mace = a primitive weapon
c. regiment = a unit of soldiers in the army
d. arsenal = place where weapons are stored

Relevant Section(s) of the Constitution:

- Article I, Section 8, Clause 12: "[The Congress shall have the power] to raise and support armies."
- Article I, Section 8, Clause 17: "[The Congress shall have the power] to exercise exclusive legislation in all cases whatsoever, over . . . the seat of the government of the United States."

Clues to Understanding the Passage:

Americans traditionally feared a "standing army," a permanent force consisting of professional, paid soldiers. Instead, most Americans favored defending their country with militia, part-time citizen-soldiers.

Source: Speech made on June 5, 1788, in the Virginia Ratifying Convention. The American Revolution.org. <http://theamericanrevolution.org/ipeople/phenry/phenryspeech1.asp>.

IN HIS OWN WORDS:
PATRICK HENRY ON THE CONSTITUTION

Excerpts from Patrick Henry's Speech of June 5, 1788, in the Virginia Ratifying Convention

3. Liberty vs. Empire

If we admit this consolidated government, it will be because we like a great, splendid one. Some way or other we must be a great and mighty empire; we must have an army, and a navy, and a number of things. When the American spirit was in its youth, the language of America was different; liberty, sir, was then the primary object. . . . But now, sir, the American spirit, assisted by the ropes and chains of consolidation, is about to convert this country into a powerful and mighty empire. If you make the citizens of this country agree to become the subjects of one great consolidated empire of America, your government will not have sufficient energy to keep them together. Such a government is incompatible with the genius of republicanism. . . .

Vocabulary:

a. consolidated = powerful
b. splendid = magnificent
c. convert = change
d. sufficient = enough
e. incompatible = unable to coexist
f. genius = nature

Relevant Section(s) of the Constitution:

Henry is referring to many passages of the Constitution, and in particular to the following clauses:
- Article I, Section 8, Clause 12: "[The Congress shall have the power] to raise and support armies."
- Article I, Section 8, Clause 13: "[The Congress shall have the power] to provide and maintain a navy."

Clues to Understanding the Passage:

Opponents of the Constitution often charged that the document would create a consolidated government—one in which too much power would be concentrated in the central government and too little power would be given to the states. Henry voiced the concerns of many Americans that liberty and empire were incompatible. (Note that in the second sentence Henry is being sarcastic.)

Source: Speech made on June 5, 1788, in the Virginia Ratifying Convention. The American Revolution.org. <**http://theamericanrevolution.org/ipeople/phenry/phenryspeech1.asp**>.

IN HIS OWN WORDS:
PATRICK HENRY ON THE CONSTITUTION

Excerpts from Patrick Henry's Speech of June 5, 1788, in the Virginia Ratifying Convention

4. Good and Bad Rulers

This Constitution is said to have beautiful features; but when I come to examine these features, sir, they appear to me horribly frightful. . . . It is on a supposition that your American governors shall be honest that all the good qualities of this government are founded; but its defective and imperfect construction puts it in their power to perpetrate the worst of mischiefs should they be bad men; and, sir, would not all the world, blame our distracted folly in resting our rights upon the contingency of our rulers being good or bad? Show me that age and country where the rights and liberties of the people were placed on the sole chance of their rulers being good men without a consequent loss of liberty! I say that the loss of that dearest privilege has ever followed, with absolute certainty, every such mad attempt.

Vocabulary:
 a. supposition = assumption
 b. perpetrate = commit
 c. mischiefs = harm
 d. distracted folly = unthinking foolishness
 e. contingency = possibility
 f. consequent = resulting

Relevant Section(s) of the Constitution:

Henry is referring in general to the powers given to members of the legislative, executive, and judicial branches in Articles I, II, and III, respectively.

Clues to Understanding the Passage:

Opponents of the Constitution charged that the document did not include enough checks on the powers of those who held federal office.

Source: Speech made on June 5, 1788, in the Virginia Ratifying Convention. The American Revolution.org. <**http://theamericanrevolution.org/ipeople/phenry/phenryspeech1.asp**>.

IN HIS OWN WORDS:
PATRICK HENRY ON THE CONSTITUTION

Excerpts from Patrick Henry's Speech of June 5, 1788, in the Virginia Ratifying Convention

5. The President, a Tyrant

If your American chief be a man of ambition and abilities, how easy is it for him to render himself absolute! . . . If we make a king we may prescribe the rules by which he shall rule his people, and interpose such checks as shall prevent him from infringing them; but the president, in the field, at the head of his army, can prescribe the terms on which he shall reign master. . . . Can he not, at the head of his army, beat down every opposition? Away with your president! We shall have a king: the army will salute him monarch; your militia will leave you, and assist in making him king, and fight against you: and what have you to oppose this force? What will then become of you and your rights? Will not absolute despotism ensue?

Vocabulary:
   a.   ambition = determination to have fame or power
   b.   render = make
   c.   absolute = total
   d.   prescribe = set down
   e.   interpose = to put between
   f.   infringing = violating
   g.   reign = rule as
   h.   despotism = tyranny
   i.   ensue = follow, develop

Relevant Section(s) of the Constitution:

Henry is referring to the powers given to the president in Article II and particularly to the following passage:
   •   Article II, Section 2, Clause 1: "The President shall be Commander-in-Chief of the Army and Navy of the United States, and of the militia of the several States, when called into the actual service of the United States."

Clues to Understanding the Passage:

Many opponents of the Constitution feared that the president would become a king.

Source: Speech made on June 5, 1788, in the Virginia Ratifying Convention. The American Revolution.org. <http://theamericanrevolution.org/ipeople/phenry/phenryspeech1.asp>.

THOMAS JEFFERSON
(1743–1826)

May it [the Declaration of Independence] be to the world what I believe it will be, . . . the Signal of arousing men to burst the chains, under which monkish ignorance and superstition had persuaded them to bind themselves, and to assume the blessings and security of self government. . . . All eyes are opened, or opening to the rights of man.

—*Thomas Jefferson, 1826*

Introduction

Thomas Jefferson hoped that he would be remembered for three accomplishments: his founding of the University of Virginia, his crafting of the Virginia Statute for Religious Freedom, and his authorship of the Declaration of Independence. It is for the last that he has most endeared himself to succeeding generations as a champion of liberty and equality.

Jefferson indeed believed that these achievements were the high points of a life dedicated to the promotion of human freedom. Education, he held, freed the mind from ignorance. Tolerance freed the will from coercion. And the assertion of human liberty and equality freed the body from the chains of tyranny.

But Jefferson's actions sometimes contradicted his words. An opponent of centralized power, as president he completed the Louisiana Purchase and unhesitatingly employed the resources of the federal government to enforce the harsh and unpopular Embargo Act. A proponent of individual rights, he excused the atrocities committed by the French Revolutionaries during the Reign of Terror. A critic of slavery who outlawed the slave trade as president, he was the owner of more than 200 African Americans. The key to understanding Jefferson lies in the difficult task of reconciling these inconsistencies.

Relevant Thematic Essays for Thomas Jefferson
- Slavery
- Freedom of Religion
- Commerce
- Republican Government (Volume 2)
- Equality (Volume 2)
- Liberty (Volume 2)

In His Own Words:
THOMAS JEFFERSON
ON THE CONSTITUTION

Overview

In this lesson, students will learn about Thomas Jefferson. They should first read as background homework **Handout A—Thomas Jefferson (1743–1826)** and answer the **Reading Comprehension Questions.** After discussing the answers to these questions in class, the teacher should have the students answer the **Critical Thinking Questions** as a class. Next, the teacher should introduce the students to the primary source activity, **Handout C—In His Own Words: Thomas Jefferson on the Constitution,** in which Jefferson, in a letter to James Madison, gives his opinion of the newly written Constitution. As a preface, there is **Handout B—Vocabulary and Context Questions,** which will help the students understand the document.

Next, the students will complete **Handout D— Thomas Jefferson on the Constitution** which asks them to imagine Jefferson's reaction to certain sections of the final version of the Constitution. There are **Homework Options** that ask the students to reflect on the classroom discussions and group activity. **Extensions** provide opportunity for thought as students are asked to consider Jefferson's ideas about the nature of law as expressed in a letter written to James Madison after the Constitution had gone into effect.

Objectives

Students will:
- appreciate Jefferson's efforts to protect individual rights and human liberty
- evaluate the importance of Jefferson's contributions to the Founding
- understand Jefferson's views on the Constitution and a bill of rights
- explain the apparent contradictions between Jefferson's words and actions

Standards
CCE (9–12): IIA1, IIC1, IIIA1, IIIA2
NCHS (5–12): Era III, Standards 3A, 3B
NCSS: Strands 2, 5, 6, and 10

Materials
Student Handouts
- Handout A—Thomas Jefferson (1743–1826)
- Handout B—Vocabulary and Context Questions
- Handout C—In His Own Words: Thomas Jefferson on the Constitution (Letter to James Madison, December 20, 1787)
- Handout D—Analysis: Thomas Jefferson on the Constitution

Additional Teacher Resource
- Answer Key

Recommended Time
One 45-minute class period. Additional time as needed for homework.

LESSON PLAN

I. Background Homework

Ask students to read **Handout A—Thomas Jefferson (1743–1826)** and answer the Reading Comprehension Questions.

II. Warm-Up [10 minutes]

A. Review answers to homework questions.

B. Conduct a whole-class discussion to answer the Critical Thinking Questions.

C. Ask a student to summarize the historical significance of Thomas Jefferson.

Thomas Jefferson wrote the Declaration of Independence and the Virginia Statute for Religious Freedom, served as governor of Virginia, as the first U.S. secretary of state, and as the third president of the United States. He also founded the University of Virginia. Jefferson was known as a champion of American and individual liberty. He took a leading role in opposing British policy toward the colonies in the 1760s and 1770s. After independence, he pushed for the addition of a bill of rights to the Constitution. As a member of the Republican opposition in 1798, he wrote the Kentucky Resolutions, which declared that states had the right to disregard federal laws they found unconstitutional. As president, he purchased in 1803 the Louisiana Territory, which he believed would provide enough space so that Americans could live in liberty for "a thousand generations."

III. Context [5 minutes]

A. Briefly review with students the concept of natural rights and representative government. Write the following excerpt from the Declaration of Independence on the board or overhead:

We hold these truths to be self-evident, that all men are created equal, that they are endowed by their Creator with certain unalienable Rights, that among these are Life, Liberty and the pursuit of Happiness.—That to secure these rights, Governments are instituted among Men, deriving their just powers from the consent of the governed,— That whenever any Form of Government becomes destructive of these ends, it is the Right of the People to alter or to abolish it.

B. Help the students (as a large group) paraphrase the above excerpt. Answers will vary, but the paraphrasing should be similar to the following:

God gave all people the same rights. These rights cannot be taken away. The duty of government is to protect these rights. When the government fails to protect their rights, the people may change or get rid of the government.

Explain to the students that they will read and analyze Jefferson's thoughts on how well the finished Constitution protected the rights of the people.

IV. In His Own Words [20 minutes]

A. Distribute **Handout B—Vocabulary and Context Questions.**

B. Distribute **Handout C—In His Own Words: Thomas Jefferson on the Constitution.** Be sure that the students understand the vocabulary and the "who, what, where, and when" of the document. Have the students read the document together as a class.

C. Give the students **Handout D—Analysis: Thomas Jefferson on the Constitution.** Have the students fill in the chart, describing Jefferson's reaction to specific sections of the Constitution. Advanced students may dispense with **Handout D** and instead locate the clauses in the Constitution that are relevant to Jefferson's comments in his letter to Madison.

LESSON PLAN

V. Wrap-Up Discussion [10 minutes]

Have the students share their answers to **Handout D.** Ask them to consider whether Jefferson's disapproval of certain clauses of the Constitution is justified.
Answers will vary.

VI. Follow-Up Homework Options

A.   Have the students compose a bill of rights based on Jefferson's wishes as expressed in the letter to Madison.

B.   Have the students assume the role of Jefferson. Tell them Madison has responded to his letter. Congress is willing to incorporate all but one of his suggestions into the Constitution, and they want him to choose which one to disregard. Have the students explain in a short essay which suggestion they believe Jefferson would be willing to give up and why.

VII. Extensions

On September 6, 1789, six months after the new government of the Constitution had been instituted, Jefferson, who was still in France, wrote again to James Madison, reflecting on the idea of constitutions and laws as follows:

The question Whether one generation of men has a right to bind another, seems never to have been started either on this side or our side of the water. Yet it is a question of such consequences as not only to merit decision, but place also, among the fundamental principles of every government. . . . I set out on this ground, which I suppose to be self evident, 'that the earth belongs in usufruct to the living': that the dead have neither powers nor rights over it. The portion occupied by any individual ceases to be his when himself ceases to be, and reverts to the society. . . .

What is true of every member of the society individually, is true of them collectively. . . . No society can make a perpetual constitution, or even a perpetual law. The earth belongs always to the living generation. They may manage it then, and what proceeds from it, as they please, during their usufruct. . . . The constitution and the laws of their predecessors [are] extinguished then in their natural course with those who gave them being. . . . Every constitution then, and every law, naturally expires at the end of 19 years [Jefferson's calculation of a generation]. If it be enforced longer, it is an act of force, and not of right.

Source: Jefferson to Madison, September 6, 1789, in Merrill D. Peterson, ed. *Thomas Jefferson: Writings* (New York: Library of America, 1984), 444–451.

Suggestions:

A.   Students could make a list of what might happen if Jefferson's proposal to have laws expire every nineteen years were adopted in the present-day United States.

B.   Students could make a list of what would happen if their school adopted Jefferson's policy and re-wrote school rules every two years.

LESSON PLAN

Resources

Print

Ellis, Joseph J. *American Sphinx: The Character of Thomas Jefferson.* New York: Alfred A. Knopf, 1997.

Levy, Leonard. *Jefferson and Civil Liberties: The Darker Side.* Chicago: Ivan R. Dee, 1989.

Matthews, Richard K. *The Radical Politics of Thomas Jefferson.* Lawrence: The University Press of Kansas, 1984.

Mayer, David. *The Constitutional Thought of Thomas Jefferson.* Charlottesville: University of Virginia Press, 1995.

Yarbrough, Jean. *American Virtues: Thomas Jefferson on the Character of a Free People.* Lawrence: The University Press of Kansas, 1998.

Internet

"Jefferson's Story of the Declaration." U.S. History.org. <**http://www.ushistory.org/declaration/account/index.htm**>.

"Jefferson's Letter to the Danbury Baptists: The Draft and Recently Discovered Text." The Library of Congress. <**http://www.loc.gov/loc/lcib/9806/danpre.html**>.

Monticello, the Home of Thomas Jefferson. <**http://www.monticello.org/**>.

The Papers of Thomas Jefferson. The Avalon Project at Yale University Law School. <**http://www.yale.edu/lawweb/avalon/presiden/jeffpap.htm**>.

The Thomas Jefferson Papers at the Library of Congress. <**http://memory.loc.gov/ammem/mtjhtml/mtjhome.html**>.

Selected Works by Thomas Jefferson
- *A Summary View of the Rights of British America* (1774)
- *The Declaration of Independence* (1776)
- *Draft Constitution for Virginia* (1776)
- *Virginia Statute for Religious Freedom* (1777)
- *Notes on the State of Virginia* (1781)
- *The Kentucky Resolutions* (1798)
- *First Inaugural Address* (1801)

THOMAS JEFFERSON (1743–1826)

> I hold it that a little rebellion now and then is a good thing,
> and as necessary in the political world as storms in the physical. . . .
> An observation of this truth should render honest republican governors
> so mild in their punishment of rebellions, as not to discourage them too
> much. It is a medicine necessary for the sound health of government.
>
> —*Thomas Jefferson to James Madison, January 30, 1787*

No one else wanted the job. Some thought it a mere formality. Besides, there were more pressing matters. The members of the committee set up by the Continental Congress were happy to have Thomas Jefferson take on the task. As darkness descended upon the city of Philadelphia, the lanky Virginian lit a small candle, placed it on his writing desk, and picked up his quill pen. Bending over a piece of parchment, he carefully penned the first words of the Declaration of Independence: "When in the course of human events, . . ." With those words, a nation was born, and Jefferson's name was engraved upon the hearts of his countrymen for all time.

Background

Born on April 13, 1743, Thomas Jefferson was raised on a plantation in the Virginia wilderness. He began the study of books at an early age. Jefferson was admitted to the Virginia Bar in April 1767 and was later recognized as one of America's best legal minds. At age twenty-five, he was elected to the House of Burgesses, colonial Virginia's legislature.

Jefferson soon became known as a champion of American and individual liberty. He worked on the Virginia Committee of Correspondence to oppose British policies toward the colonies. He served in the Virginia House of Delegates from 1776 to 1779. In 1779, he was elected to the office of governor of Virginia. In his *Notes on the State of Virginia* of 1781, Jefferson expressed his ideas about religious freedom, universal education for white boys and girls, and the importance of property to a free people. He was also successful in pushing through the legislature a bill that established freedom of religion in the state.

The Declaration of Independence

Jefferson secured his place in history by writing the Declaration of Independence. A member of the Second Continental Congress in 1775, he was appointed to the committee in charge of drafting the Declaration. The other committee members chose Jefferson to write the document. After debate and amendment, *The Unanimous Declaration of the Thirteen United States of America* passed Congress on July 4, 1776.

In the Declaration, Jefferson listed King George III's violations of the rights of Americans. He accused the king of trying to establish "an absolute Tyranny over these States." Jefferson insisted that all men "are created equal" and that they possessed the rights to "life, liberty and the pursuit of happiness," which no one could take away. Jefferson's ideas about rights were not new. He was influenced by the writings of English thinkers Algernon Sidney and John Locke.

The Declaration's promises of equality and liberty did not apply to African Americans in the late 1700s. Indeed, many of the leaders of the Revolution owned slaves. Jefferson himself had mixed feelings about slavery. He warned that the institution might one day tear the Union apart. He condemned the slave trade and proposed a plan for ending it. But Jefferson owned more than 200 slaves who lived on and near his great plantation of Monticello, and he freed none of them while he lived. He did provide in his will for the emancipation of seven of his slaves, including Sally Hemings (the slave with whom Jefferson is alleged to have had a sexual relationship), her five children, and her nephew.

Jefferson and the Bill of Rights

Jefferson did not participate in the Constitutional Convention in Philadelphia. He was serving as a trade delegate and minister to France from 1784 to 1789. But he was concerned that the people's rights be protected. He therefore wrote to James Madison about a bill of rights while the convention was in session. Jefferson stated that a bill of rights was "necessary by way of supplement" to the rights already protected within the Constitution.

Jefferson supported many ideas that found their way into the final version of the Bill of Rights. He believed that "no freeman should be debarred the use of arms." He supported the free exercise of religion and opposed the government's support of any particular religion. Jefferson also supported the rights of people accused of crimes.

Leader of the Republican Opposition

In 1789, George Washington appointed Jefferson the first secretary of state. Jefferson and Secretary of the Treasury Alexander Hamilton soon became bitter adversaries. Hamilton favored a strong central government and supported Britain in foreign affairs. His success in creating a Bank of the United States was especially alarming to Jefferson. In an effort to block Hamilton's programs, Jefferson formed what became the nation's first political party, the Democratic-Republicans (often called simply, "Republicans"). The Federalist Party emerged in support of Hamilton's policies.

Jefferson resigned his post after three years in office. He ran for election for president against John Adams in 1796 but lost by three electoral votes. Under the original electoral system, Jefferson became vice-president. While in this office, he opposed many of the Federalists' policies. For example, Jefferson denounced the Alien and Sedition Acts, which were aimed at silencing Republican criticism of the government. Jefferson argued that these laws violated the principle of free speech. In 1798, he wrote the Kentucky Resolutions, which declared that states had the right to disregard federal laws they found unconstitutional.

America's Third President

Jefferson ran for election for president against John Adams again in 1800. The campaign was nasty. The Federalists accused the Virginian of being a "man of party," not a man of principle. But Jefferson was victorious, and he tried to make peace between the parties. In his inaugural address to the nation, he declared, "We are all federalists—we are all republicans." In the war between Britain and Napoleonic France, Jefferson accepted the wisdom of Washington's policy of neutrality in foreign affairs.

During his first term, Jefferson worked to reduce the size and power of the federal government. "That government is best which governs the least," he declared. To this end, Jefferson reduced the number of public employees, cut military spending, and lowered the national debt. But he put aside his concerns about government power in 1803 when he purchased the Louisiana Territory from Napoleon for $15 million. This land, Jefferson believed, was necessary for America's future development. It would provide enough space so that Americans could live as independent farmers for a "thousand generations."

Jefferson easily won re-election in 1804. His second term, however, was a time of foreign and domestic trouble. On the high seas, the British Navy forced American sailors into service on British vessels. This led Jefferson to sign the Embargo Act of 1807, which outlawed American trade with foreign countries. Jefferson dealt harshly with violators of the law. In doing so, he violated the civil liberties of many Americans. Jefferson hoped, however, that the policy would prevent the United States from being drawn into the Napoleonic Wars. The Embargo Act sank the economy into a depression. As a result, the United States was ill-prepared for the war with England that began in 1812.

A Fruitful Retirement

Jefferson retired to Monticello after his second term. The achievement of which he was most proud during these years was the founding of the University of Virginia in 1819. He designed and supervised the construction of the university and also hired its original faculty. Jefferson died on July 4, 1826, exactly fifty years after the adoption of the Declaration of Independence. A few hours before his death, he asked, "Is it the fourth?" These were his last words.

Reading Comprehension Questions

1. What was Jefferson's position on slavery?

2. What steps did Jefferson take as president to reduce the size of the federal government?

3. What individual freedoms did Jefferson champion?

Critical Thinking Questions

4. Did Jefferson's actions ever violate his principles?

5. Jefferson asked to be remembered for three accomplishments: his founding of the University of Virginia, his crafting of the Virginia Statute for Religious Freedom, and his authorship of the Declaration of Independence. Why do you think he chose these three things as his greatest achievements? What do they all have in common?

6. What did Jefferson mean when he declared in his presidential inaugural speech, "We are all federalists—we are all republicans"?

VOCABULARY AND CONTEXT QUESTIONS

Letter to James Madison, December 20, 1787

1. **Vocabulary:** *Use context clues to determine the meaning or significance of each of these words and write their definitions:*

   a. levy

   b. omission

   c. sophisms

   d. monopolies

   e. eternal

   f. unremitting

   g. *habeas corpus*

   h. entitled

   i. abandonment

   j. magistrate

2. **Context:** *Answer the following questions.*

   a. When was this document written?

   b. Where was this document written?

   c. Who wrote this document?

   d. What type of document is this?

   e. What was the purpose of this document?

   f. Who was the audience for this document?

In His Own Words:
Thomas Jefferson on the Constitution

Letter to James Madison, December 20, 1787

This is an excerpt from one letter in a long correspondence between Jefferson and Madison concerning the Constitution. Jefferson was in Paris at this time, acting as United States minister (ambassador) to France.

December 20, 1787

I like the organization of the government into Legislative, Judiciary, and Executive. I like the power given the Legislature to levy taxes; and for that reason solely approve of the greater house [the House of Representatives] being chosen by the people directly.... The people are not to be taxed but by representatives chosen immediately by themselves.... I am much pleased too with the substitution of the method of voting by persons [in the legislature], instead of that of voting by states: and I like the negative given to the Executive with a third of either house, though I should have liked it better had the Judiciary been associated for that purpose, or invested with a similar and separate power....

I will now add what I do not like. First the omission of a bill of rights providing clearly and without the aid of sophisms for freedom of religion, freedom of the press, protection against standing armies, restrictions against monopolies, the eternal and unremitting force of the habeas corpus laws, and trials by jury.... Let me add that a bill of rights is what the people are entitled to against every government on earth....

The second feature I dislike, and greatly dislike, is the abandonment in every instance of the necessity of rotation in office, and most particularly in the case of the President. Experience concurs with reason in concluding that the first magistrate will always be re-elected if the constitution permits it. He is then an officer for life.... The power of removing him from office every fourth year is a power which will not be exercised....

I have thus told you freely what I like and dislike.... I own that I am not a friend to a very energetic government. It is always oppressive.

Source: Jefferson to Madison, December 20, 1787, in Merrill D. Peterson, ed., *Thomas Jefferson: Writings* (New York: Library of America, 1984), 428–433.

ANALYSIS: THOMAS JEFFERSON ON THE CONSTITUTION

Directions: In the column on the right, briefly describe how Jefferson reacted to the section of the Constitution reproduced in the left column. Use Handout C as the basis for your answers.

	THE CONSTITUTION'S PROVISION	JEFFERSON'S REACTION
A	The government is separated into three branches: legislative **(Article 1)**, executive **(Article 2)**, and judicial **(Article 3)**.	
B	**Article 1, Section 2, Clause 1:** The House of Representatives shall be chosen . . . by the People of the several States. **Article 1, Section 7, Clause 1:** All Bills for raising Revenue shall originate in the House of Representatives.	
C	**Article 1, Section 7, Clause 2:** The Votes of both Houses shall be determined by [individual] Yeas and Nays.	
D	**Article 1, Section 7, Clause 2:** Every Bill which shall have passed the House of Representatives and the Senate, shall . . . be presented to the President of the United States; If he approve he shall sign it, but if not he shall return it, with his Objections to that House in which it shall have originated, who shall . . . proceed to reconsider it. If after such Reconsideration two thirds of that House shall agree to pass the Bill, it shall be sent . . . to the other House, . . . and if approved by two thirds of that House, it shall become a Law.	
E	**Article 1, Section 9, Clause 2:** The Privilege of the Writ of Habeas Corpus shall not be suspended, unless when in Cases of Rebellion or Invasion the public Safety may require it.	
F	**Article 3, Section 2, Clause 3:** The Trial of all Crimes, except in Cases of Impeachment, shall be by Jury.	
G	**Article 1, Section 8, Clauses 12 & 14:** [The Congress shall have Power] To raise and support Armies, but no Appropriation of Money to that Use shall be for a longer Term than two Years. . . . [and] To make Rules for the Government and Regulation of the land and naval Forces.	
H	**Article 2, Section 1, Clause 1:** [The President] shall hold his Office during the Term of four years.	

© The Bill of Rights Institute

RICHARD HENRY LEE
(1732–1794)

I know there are [those] among you who laugh at virtue, and with vain ostentatious display of words will deduce from vice, public good! But such men are much fitter to be Slaves in the corrupt, rotten despotisms of Europe, than to remain citizens of young and rising republics.

—*Richard Henry Lee, 1779*

Introduction

Richard Henry Lee in many ways personified the elite Virginia gentry. A planter and slaveholder, he was tall, handsome, and genteel in his manners. Raised in a conservative environment, Lee was nonetheless radical in his social and political views. As early as the 1750s, he denounced slavery as an evil, and he even favored the vote for women who owned property. Lee was also among the first to advocate separation from Great Britain, introducing the resolution in the Second Continental Congress that led to independence.

Though Lee was a planter, politics was his true calling. He reveled in backroom bargaining, and during the imperial crisis he learned how to utilize mob action to resist British tyranny. In denouncing British transgressions, Lee's oratory was said to rival that of his more renowned fellow Virginian, Patrick Henry. Lee was an ally and friend of Samuel Adams, who shared the Virginian's aversion to moneygrubbing and ostentatious displays of wealth. Like Adams, Lee neglected his financial affairs and often struggled to make ends meet. At one point in his life, he was forced to live on a diet of wild pigeons.

Lee believed that good government required virtue, defined as self-sacrifice for the public good. He rejected the idea held by some Founders that the proper design of governing institutions was all that was needed to protect liberty. Nevertheless, a poorly constructed government could destroy virtue and, as a consequence, liberty. This is why Lee opposed the Constitution of 1787, which in his opinion dangerously concentrated power in the federal government. Lee has sometimes been credited with authorship of the *Letters from the Federal Farmer to the Republican,* a series of newspaper essays published anonymously in Virginia in 1787–1788 by an opponent of the Constitution. Though this is still a matter of much debate among historians, the views of the Federal Farmer undoubtedly mirror Lee's own quite closely.

Relevant Thematic Essays for Richard Henry Lee
- Federalism
- Republican Government (Volume 2)

In His Own Words:
RICHARD HENRY LEE
ON THE CONSTITUTION

Overview

In this lesson, students will learn about Richard Henry Lee. They should first read as background homework **Handout A—Richard Henry Lee (1732–1794)** and answer the **Reading Comprehension Questions.** After discussing the answers to these questions in class, the teacher should have the students answer the **Critical Thinking Questions** as a class. Next, the teacher should introduce the students to the primary source activity, **Handout C—In His Own Words: Richard Henry Lee on the Constitution,** in which Lee lays out his objections to the newly written Constitution. As a preface, there is **Handout B—Vocabulary and Context Questions,** which will help the students understand the document.

There are **Follow-Up Homework Options** that ask the students to compose a *Federal Farmer* letter of their own, based on Lee's ideas. **Extensions** provides opportunity for thought as students are asked to consider how Lee might have reacted to later developments in United States history, had he lived long enough to observe them.

Objectives

Students will:

- understand Lee's views on the slave trade and slavery
- appreciate Lee's role as a leader of the American opposition to British tyranny
- explain the importance of virtue in Lee's political theory
- analyze the reasons for Lee's opposition to the Constitution

Standards

CCE (9–12): IIA1, IIC1, IIIA1, IIIA2
NCHS (5–12): Era III, Standards 3A, 3B
NCSS: Strands 2, 5, 6, and 10

Materials
Student Handouts

- Handout A—Richard Henry Lee (1732–1794)
- Handout B—Vocabulary and Context Questions
- Handout C—In His Own Words: Richard Henry Lee on the Constitution

Additional Teacher Resource

- Answer Key

Recommended Time

One 45-minute class period. Additional time as needed for homework.

LESSON PLAN

I. Background Homework

Ask students to read **Handout A—Richard Henry Lee (1732–1794)** and answer the Reading Comprehension Questions.

II. Warm-Up [10 minutes]

A. Review answers to homework questions.

B. Conduct a whole-class discussion to answer the Critical Thinking Questions.

C. Ask a student to summarize the historical significance of Richard Henry Lee.

Richard Henry Lee was a Virginia planter and one of the leaders of the opposition to British tyranny during the 1760s and 1770s. He was one of the first Americans to call for independence from Great Britain. As a member of the Second Continental Congress, Lee introduced the resolution that led to the drafting of the Declaration of Independence. He was also an outspoken opponent of the Constitution. In his Letters from the Federal Farmer to the Republican, *Lee voiced his concern that the Constitution lacked a bill of rights and gave too much power to the central government. Some of the* Federal Farmer *essays were published as a pamphlet, and thousands of copies were sold. Lee served as a senator in the first Congress under the new Constitution, where he was a leading supporter of the first ten amendments to the Constitution, which were ratified in 1791 and became known as the Bill of Rights.*

III. Context [5 minutes]

Briefly review with students the main issues involved in the debate between Federalists and Anti-Federalists. (The Federalists believed that the confederation would break up if the Constitution was not ratified. Anti-Federalists feared that a stronger central government would endanger the rights of the people.)

IV. In His Own Words [20 minutes]

A. Distribute **Handout B—Vocabulary and Context Questions.**

B. Distribute **Handout C—In His Own Words: Richard Henry Lee on the Constitution.** Be sure that the students understand the vocabulary and the "who, what, where, and when" of the document.

C. Tell the students that they will read together as a class ten brief excerpts from the *Federal Farmer*. Ask the students to consider whether each excerpt is (1) a statement of Lee's principles, or (2) a criticism of the proposed Constitution. The students should mark each excerpt with "principle" or "criticism" accordingly. Have a different student read each of the ten excerpts to the class. Then have a large-group discussion to determine how each excerpt should be labeled.

D. Ask the students to determine the main idea of each excerpt and write it down.

V. Wrap-Up Discussion [10 minutes]

Ask the students to imagine that they are in charge of the New York publishing firm that printed some of the *Federal Farmer* essays as a pamphlet. Tell the students that there is room for only five essays in the pamphlet. Which five of the ten excerpts would work best as topics for these essays?

LESSON PLAN

VI. Follow-Up Homework Options

Ask the students to choose one of the excerpts from the *Federal Farmer* letters and to compose their own paragraph-long *Federal Farmer* letter based on the idea expressed by Lee in the excerpt.

VII. Extensions

Ask the students: How might Richard Henry Lee have reacted to the following developments in American history, had he lived long enough to observe them?
- The United States Congress's banning of the importation of slaves (1808)
- The Civil War between the North and the South (1861–1865)
- The abolition of slavery by the Thirteenth Amendment (1865)

Resources

Print

Ballagh, James C. *The Letters of Richard Henry Lee.* 2 vols. New York: Macmillan Co., 1911–1914; Reprint: Cambridge, MA: Da Capo Press, 1970.

Chitwood, Oliver. *Richard Henry Lee, Statesman of the Revolution.* Morgantown: West Virginia University Library, 1967.

Maier, Pauline. *The Old Revolutionaries: Political Lives in the Age of Samuel Adams.* New York: W. W. Norton & Company, Reprint ed., 1990.

Matthews, John C. *Richard Henry Lee.* Williamsburg, VA: The Virginia Independence Bicentennial Commission, 1978.

McDonald, Forrest, ed. *Empire and Nation: Letters from a Farmer in Pennsylvania by John Dickinson; Letters from the Federal Farmer to the Republican by Richard Henry Lee.* Indianapolis: Liberty Fund, 1999.

Internet

"Letters from the Federal Farmer to the Republican." The Constitution Society. <**http://www.constitution.org/afp/fedfar00.htm**>.

"Resolution of Richard Henry Lee, June 7, 1776." The Avalon Project at Yale University Law School. <**http://www.yale.edu/lawweb/avalon/contcong/06-07-76.htm**>.

"Richard Henry Lee." The Atlantic Monthly. <**http://cdl.library.cornell.edu/cgi-bin/moa/moa-cgi?notisid=ABK2934-0066-4**>.

"Richard Henry Lee: Gentleman Radical." Fredericksburg.com. <**http://www.fredericksburg.com/News/FLS/2001/072001/07072001/324163**>.

Stratford Hall Plantation. <**http://www.stratfordhall.org/**>.

Selected Works by Richard Henry Lee
- *Letters from the Federal Farmer to the Republican* (1787–1788)

RICHARD HENRY LEE (1732–1794)

The happiness of America will be secured . . . as long as it continues virtuous, and when we cease to be virtuous we shall not deserve to be happy.

—*Richard Henry Lee, 1776*

The mob was led by a tall, thin man with reddish-brown hair and a hand wrapped in black silk. Richard Henry Lee was an unlikely leader of the raucous group of laborers, artisans, and sailors who were making their way through the streets of Leedstown, Virginia, on this cold winter night of 1766. An aristocratic planter, Lee usually personified the southern ideal of upper-class gentility and grace. He was a fixture of high society. But on this night, he walked next to violent men of the lower classes on a mission of intimidation. Their destination was the home of a merchant who was cooperating with the hated Stamp Act recently passed by the British Parliament. Lee hoped to convince this man to join other merchants in boycotting the stamps. A skilled politician, Lee knew that there were many tactics to be employed in the art of persuasion— including the threat of bodily harm.

A Life of Privilege

Richard Henry Lee was born in 1732 at Stratford Hall Plantation in Westmoreland County, Virginia. The Lees were one of the wealthiest and most powerful families in Virginia. The eldest of four sons, Lee was first taught by tutors and then sent to England to finish his education. Returning home in 1752, he purchased land from his brother in Westmoreland County and there built his plantation home, which he named "Chantilly." Lee studied law and was elected to the House of Burgesses at the age of twenty-five.

Opponent of Slavery

In the House of Burgesses, Lee became an outspoken opponent of the international slave trade. His first official act was to introduce a bill that proposed "to lay so heavy a duty on the importation of slaves as to put an end to that iniquitous and disgraceful traffic within the colony of Virginia." Though other slaveholders also opposed importation, few condemned the institution of slavery itself, as Lee did. Blacks, Lee declared, were "equally entitled to liberty and freedom by the great law of nature." He warned that slaves would rebel if they "observed their masters possessed of a liberty denied to them."

Nevertheless, Lee did not free any of his slaves. Indeed, he simply could not afford to do so. Lee earned much of his income by renting his slaves to other planters and by buying and selling them. "I do not see how I could in justice to my family refuse any advantages that might arise from the selling of them," Lee explained.

Political Activist and Patriot

Lee's radical nature was evident in his political views also. In the 1760s, he assumed a leading role in opposing British policies toward America. Lee founded the Westmoreland Association in opposition to the Stamp Act of 1765. This body organized boycotts of British goods and harassed royal officials who attempted to enforce the Stamp Act. Lee was one of the first Patriots to call for independence. He condemned the Townshend Acts of 1767 as "destructive of that mutual beneficial connection which every good subject would wish to see preserved."

Lee understood Virginia could not stand on her own in defiance of British policies. In 1773, he organized the Virginia Committee of Correspondence as a way to exchange information with Patriot leaders in other colonies. He also received regular information about events in England from his two brothers living in London.

In 1774, Lee was elected to represent Virginia at the First Continental Congress in Philadelphia. There he tried to persuade other members of the need for American independence. In the Congress, Lee played a vital role in uniting American opposition in the North and South. He became a good friend of Samuel Adams, one of the most prominent Patriot leaders in Boston.

Though the First Congress did not go so far as to declare American independence, Lee did not give up. In 1776, he was chosen a member of the Second Continental Congress. On June 7, Lee introduced a resolution that declared "that these United Colonies are, and of right ought to be, free and independent States." This led to the drafting of the Declaration of Independence. Lee's resolution was adopted by Congress on July 2, 1776.

Lee stayed in Congress through 1779, helping guide the nation through the first years of the Revolution. He then returned home to Virginia, where he served in the state legislature. In 1781, the Articles of Confederation, which set up a government for the new nation, went into effect. Lee at first turned down the offer to serve in the new Congress. He believed that he owed service to his state first. But in 1784, he accepted a seat in the national Congress and served as that body's president his first year as a member.

As a member of the Confederation Congress, Lee helped guide the Northwest Ordinance through Congress in 1787. This law organized the Ohio territory and provided for its entry into the Union. One of the provisions of the Northwest Ordinance declared that "there shall be neither slavery nor involuntary servitude in the said territory."

Anti-Federalist

During the 1780s, Lee became concerned that Americans were losing their republican virtue—defined as self-sacrifice for the public good—and their love of liberty. Instead, Lee worried, people were more concerned about amassing money and power. When some leading Americans called for revising the Articles of Confederation so as to strengthen the national government, Lee was alarmed. He feared that these men craved power for themselves at the expense of the people's liberty.

Lee therefore refused to take part in the Constitutional Convention of 1787. He also tried to persuade delegates to the convention not to alter the Articles. Despite his warnings, the delegates at Philadelphia designed an entirely new system of government. When the Constitution was sent to the states for approval, Lee became a leader of the opposition to ratification in Virginia.

In 1787 and 1788, an anonymous series of essays, the *Letters from the Federal Farmer to the Republican,* appeared in Virginia newspapers. The Federal Farmer laid out arguments against the Constitution. Some of the *Federal Farmer* essays were published as a pamphlet, and thousands of copies were sold. Some historians have claimed that Lee was the author of these letters, though this is a matter of much debate. Nevertheless, the views of the Federal Farmer mirror Lee's own quite closely.

In the essays, the Farmer criticized the Constitution's centralization of powers in the federal government and its lack of a bill of rights. He warned that the Constitution would destroy the states and create a "consolidated" government in which all power was dangerously concentrated in one place. The Farmer instead hoped to preserve a federal system, in which power was divided between the national and state governments. He hoped that a second convention could be organized to revise the Constitution.

Despite Lee's opposition, the Constitution was approved by the requisite nine states by the end of June 1788. Lee was disappointed. Hoping to protect the people's liberty, however, he accepted a Senate seat in the first Congress under the Constitution. He spent his time in Congress advocating laws and amendments that would limit the power of the new government. Lee was a leading supporter of the first ten amendments to the Constitution, which were ratified in 1791 and became known as the Bill of Rights.

Retirement

Poor health forced Lee to retire from public life and return to Chantilly in 1792. Lee was pessimistic about the prospects of the United States. He feared that desire for wealth and power had replaced republican virtue among many of his countrymen, especially in his own beloved Virginia. "The hasty, unpersevering, aristocratic genius of the south suits not my disposition," Lee wrote, "and is inconsistent with my ideas of what must constitute social happiness and security." He even once considered retiring to Massachusetts. But Lee never left Virginia. He died at Chantilly in 1794 at the age of sixty-two.

Reading Comprehension Questions

1. What was Lee's view of the slave trade and slavery?

2. What important resolution did Lee introduce as a member of the Second Continental Congress?

3. What did Lee argue in the *Letters from the Federal Farmer to the Republican*?

Critical Thinking Questions

4. Why do you think Lee kept his authorship of the *Letters from the Federal Farmer to the Republican* a secret? Why do you think he used the pseudonym "the Federal Farmer"?

5. Lee believed that those who serve in government must be virtuous or else liberty is endangered. Do you agree or disagree? Is it possible to design governmental institutions so as to protect the people against evil government officials?

VOCABULARY AND CONTEXT QUESTIONS

Letters from the Federal Farmer to the Republican

1. **Vocabulary:** *Use context clues to determine the meaning or significance of each of these words and write their definitions:*

   a. consolidated

   b. vicinage

   c. inalienable

   d. explicitly

   e. ascertained

   f. ambitious

   g. props

2. **Context:** *Answer the following questions.*

   a. When was this document written?

   b. Where was this document written?

   c. Who wrote this document?

   d. What type of document is this?

   e. What was the purpose of this document?

   f. Who was the audience for this document?

In His Own Words:
Richard Henry Lee on the Constitution

Letters from the Federal Farmer to the Republican

Note: *The* Letters from the Federal Farmer to the Republican *was a series of newspaper essays published anonymously in Virginia in 1787–1788 by an opponent of the Constitution. Some historians have claimed that Richard Henry Lee was the author of these letters, though this is still a matter of much debate. Nevertheless, the views of the Federal Farmer mirror Lee's own quite closely.*

Directions: *Consider whether each excerpt is (1) a statement of Lee's principles, or (2) a criticism of the proposed Constitution. Mark each excerpt with "principle" or "criticism" accordingly.*

A

The plan of government now proposed is evidently calculated totally to change, in time, our condition as a people. Instead of being thirteen republics, under a federal head, it is clearly designed to make us one consolidated government.

B

The essential parts of a free and good government are a full and equal representation of the people in the legislature, and the jury trial of the vicinage in the administration of justice.

C

There are certain inalienable and fundamental rights, which in forming the social compact, ought to be explicitly ascertained and fixed. . . . These rights should be made the basis of every constitution.

D

A wise and honest administration can make the people happy under any government; but necessity only can justify even our leaving open avenues to the abuse of power, by wicked, unthinking, or ambitious men.

E

By this plan there can be no doubt, but that the powers of congress will be complete as to all kinds of taxes whatever.

F

Liberty, in its genuine sense, is security to enjoy the effects of our honest industry and labors, in a free and mild government.

G

The supreme power is in the people, and rulers possess only that portion which is expressly given them.

H

The government [as proposed by the Constitution] will take every occasion to multiply laws, and officers to execute them, considering these as so many necessary props for its own support.

I

A virtuous people make just laws, and good laws tend to preserve unchanged a virtuous people.

J

Every man of reflection must see, that the change now proposed, is a transfer of power from the many to the few.

Source: Forrest McDonald, ed., *Empire and Nation: Letters from a Farmer in Pennsylvania by John Dickinson; Letters from the Federal Farmer to the Republican by Richard Henry Lee* (Indianapolis, Ind.: Liberty Fund, 1999), 92, 97–98, 100, 104, 111–113, 126, 139, and 146.

JAMES MADISON
(1751–1836)

T he essence of Government is power; and power, lodged as it must in human hands, will ever be liable to abuse.

—*James Madison, 1787*

Introduction

James Madison's slight stature and reserved personality gave little indication of the keen intellect and shrewd nature of the man. Perhaps no other person of the Founding generation had as much influence as he in crafting, ratifying, and interpreting the United States Constitution and the Bill of Rights. A skilled political tactician, Madison proved instrumental in determining the form of the early American republic.

Madison's political theory was founded upon a realistic view of human nature. He believed that men in society tended to form factions, defined as groups that promoted their own interest at the expense of the rest. Factions posed a special problem for democratic societies because a faction composed of the majority of the people could easily oppress the minority. To combat this, as he argued in *Federalist Paper No. 51*, power must be set against power, "ambition must be made to counteract ambition." Madison therefore favored the separation of powers within the central government and a division of power between the national and state governments. This latter concept, federalism, was a radical idea in the late eighteenth century. Few people at the time believed that power in a nation could be divided between two levels of government, each supreme in its own sphere.

Madison believed that safety lay in numbers. The more heterogeneous the society, the less chance there would be for any one group to combine with others to form a faction of the majority. Though ancient philosophers had argued that only small republics could survive for a long period of time, Madison believed the opposite. A large republic could encompass many different groups and different interests—economic, religious, and social—and thereby provide a safeguard against the tyranny of the majority.

Relevant Thematic Essays for James Madison

- Federalism
- Republican Government (Volume 2)
- Limited Government (Volume 2)

In His Own Words:
JAMES MADISON
ON THE PROBLEM OF FACTION

Overview

In this lesson, students will learn about James Madison. They should first read as background homework **Handout A—James Madison (1751–1836)** and answer the **Reading Comprehension Questions.** After discussing the answers to these questions in class, the teacher should have the students answer the **Critical Thinking Questions** as a class. Next, the teacher should introduce the students to the primary source activity, **Handout C—In His Own Words: James Madison on the Problem of Faction,** in which Madison addresses the problem of faction in a democratic society. As a preface, there is **Handout B—Vocabulary and Context Questions,** which will help the students understand the document.

In order for the students to understand the role of factions in everyday life, the teacher should divide the students into groups based on food preference and ask each group to design a menu for the school cafeteria that is acceptable to a majority of the class. There are **Follow-Up Homework Options** that ask the students to list real-life factions that exist in their school and consider how these groups may infringe on the rights of others. **Extensions** provides opportunity for thought as students are asked to consider the role of special-interest groups in modern America.

Objectives

Students will:
- explain why Madison is often called "The Father of the Constitution"
- understand Madison's view of the Bill of Rights
- explain what Madison meant by *faction*
- understand Madison's remedy for the problem of factions in a democratic republic
- analyze the role of factions in their school

Standards
  CCE (9–12): IIA1, IIC1, IIIA1, IIIA2
  NCHS (5–12): Era III, Standards 3A, 3B
  NCSS: Strands 2, 5, 6, and 10

Materials
Student Handouts
- Handout A—James Madison (1751–1836)
- Handout B—Vocabulary and Context Questions
- Handout C—In His Own Words: James Madison on the Problem of Faction

Additional Teacher Resource
- Answer Key

Recommended Time
One 45-minute class period. Additional time as needed for homework.

LESSON PLAN

I. Background Homework

Ask students to read **Handout A—James Madison (1751–1836)** and answer the Reading Comprehension Questions.

II. Warm-Up [10 minutes]

A. Review answers to homework questions.

B. Conduct a whole-class discussion to answer the Critical Thinking Questions.

C. Ask a student to summarize the historical significance of James Madison.

James Madison is often called "The Father of the Constitution." He was a leader in organizing the Constitutional Convention, and many of his ideas shaped the final document produced by the delegates. After the convention, Madison co-authored the Federalist Papers, a series of newspaper essays that defended the Constitution. He also took a leading role in support of the Constitution at the Virginia Ratifying Convention. As a member of the House of Representatives, he guided a bill of rights through Congress.

III. Context [5 minutes]

A. Briefly review with students the main issues involved in the debate between Federalists and Anti-Federalists. (The Federalists believed that the confederation would break up if the Constitution was not ratified. Anti-Federalists feared that a stronger central government would endanger the rights of the people.)

B. Remind the students that James Madison, Alexander Hamilton, and John Jay wrote the Federalist Papers as a series of newspaper essays to convince the people of New York of the need to ratify the Constitution. But the essays were read by many people across the country and played an influential role in the Federalist/Anti-Federalist debate.

IV. In His Own Words [25 minutes]

A. Distribute **Handout B—Vocabulary and Context Questions.**

B. Distribute **Handout C—In His Own Words: James Madison on the Problem of Faction.** Be sure that the students understand the vocabulary and the "who, what, where, and when" of the document.

C. Tell the students to imagine that they are in charge of determining the menu for the school cafeteria. Divide the class into two groups. The first group should consist of a clear majority of the class. Tell this group that they are meat eaters who do not mind having vegetarian dishes on the menu. The second group should consist of a clear minority of the class. Tell this group that they are vegetarians who desire to eliminate all meat from the cafeteria menu, despite the wishes of the meat-eating majority. Then have a student read Excerpt A to the entire class. Refer to the Answer Key for a scripted discussion of **Handout C.**

V. Wrap-Up Discussion [5 minutes]

Ask students if a larger school would reduce the problem of faction, as Madison would have predicted. If so, why? If not, why not?

Answers will vary.

VI. Follow-Up Homework Options

Have the students create a list of at least five factions at their school. They should also describe in one to three sentences how each faction infringes on or threatens the rights of other students/groups or undermines the ability of the school to educate students.

VII. Extensions

Some people today would argue that certain contemporary special-interest groups fulfill Madison's definition of a faction. Some groups are listed below.

Recording Industry Association of America
<http://www.riaa.com/news/newsletter/press2000/041100.asp>.

National Rifle Association **<http://www.nra.org/>**.

People for the Ethical Treatment of Animals **<http://www.peta.org/>**.

Americans United for the Separation of Church and State **<http://www.au.org/>**.

American Association of Retired Persons **<http://www.aarp.org/>**.

Christian Coalition **<http://www.cc.org/>**.

People for the American Way **<http://www.pfaw.org/pfaw/general/>**.

Suggestions:

A. Ask the students to research one of the special-interest groups above and list its goals. They could then list how each of these goals could infringe upon the rights of other individuals/groups or the common good.

B. Ask the students to make a list of other special-interest groups through Web searches. They could look for groups that promote similar interests, or they could find groups that are in opposition to each other.

LESSON PLAN

Resources

Print

Banning, Lance. *The Sacred Fire of Liberty: James Madison and the Founding of the Federal Republic.* Ithaca: Cornell University Press, 1995.

Ketcham, Ralph. *James Madison: A Biography.* Charlottesville: University of Virginia Press, 1990.

Matthews, Richard K. *If Men Were Angels: James Madison and the Heartless Empire of Reason.* Lawrence: University Press of Kansas, 1995.

McCoy, Drew. *The Last of the Fathers.* New York: Cambridge University Press, 1989.

Rakove, Jack N. *James Madison and the Creation of the American Republic.* Glenview, IL: Scott, Foresman, 1990.

Internet

"The Federalist Papers." The Avalon Project at Yale Law School. <**http://www.yale.edu/lawweb/avalon/federal/fed.htm**>.

The James Madison Center at James Madison University Home Page. <**http://www.jmu.edu/madison/**>.

James Madison's Montpelier. <**http://www.montpelier.org/**>.

"Notes of Debates in the Federal Convention of 1787." The Avalon Project at Yale Law School. <**http://www.yale.edu/lawweb/avalon/debates/debcont.htm**>.

The Papers of James Madison. <**http://www.virginia.edu/pjm/**>.

Selected Works by James Madison
- *Notes on Ancient and Modern Confederacies* (1786)
- *The Vices of the Political System of the United States* (1787)
- *Notes of Debates in the Federal Convention of 1787*
- *The Federalist Papers* [with Alexander Hamilton and John Jay] (1787–1788)
- *The Virginia Resolutions* (1798)

JAMES MADISON (1751–1836)

Place three individuals in a situation wherein the interest of each depends on the voice of the others, and give to two of them an interest opposed to the rights of the third.
Will the latter be secure? The prudence of every man would shun the danger.
The rules & forms of justice suppose & guard against it.
Will two thousand in a like situation be less likely to encroach on the rights of one thousand?

—James Madison, 1821

The short, thin figure dressed in black dismounted his horse and strode toward the front door of the white farmhouse in the rolling hills of Orange County, Virginia. The year was 1788, and James Madison was campaigning for a seat in the first Congress of the United States. But he would rather have been doing almost anything else this chilly Saturday afternoon. The shy and modest son of a wealthy planter, he despised the handshaking and self-promotion that democratic politics required. Madison was at heart a thinker, a student of history and government, not a politician. Yet he wanted to play a major role in shaping the new American nation, and so he knocked on this voter's door, as he had already done dozens of times on other doors that day.

Background

James Madison did not look the part of a nation builder. He was short (only five feet, six inches in height), thin, and introverted. In poor health throughout his life, he often believed that death was near. His favorite attire was black clothing, a fitting sign of his usual dark mood. But Madison's slight appearance and somber demeanor masked a brilliant and determined man.

Born on March 16, 1751, Madison was raised on his father's plantation, Montpelier, in Orange County, Virginia. At the age of nineteen, he entered the College of New Jersey (later Princeton University), graduating two years later. Madison then began studies for the Christian ministry.

In 1772, Madison returned to Virginia. Rejecting the idea of the ministry, he turned his attention to politics and embraced the patriot cause. In 1775, he was appointed to the Orange County Committee of Safety. Later he was elected to the Virginia convention.

The Articles of Confederation

Because of his poor health, Madison did not fight in the American Revolution. Instead, he continued his political career. During the 1780s, he served in the Virginia House of Delegates and the Continental Congress. As a member of Congress, he witnessed firsthand the inability of the government under the Articles of Confederation to address many of the problems among the states. Convinced that the Articles were too weak and needed to be altered or replaced, Madison set out on a determined campaign to organize a meeting of the states to discuss amending the Articles. He met with some success in regional meetings: the Mount Vernon Conference of 1785 and the Annapolis Convention of 1786. At Annapolis, Madison and other delegates began to organize a general meeting of all the states.

In 1786 and 1787, Madison began planning for this national convention by writing out his thoughts on government. He explored how nations with weak central governments tended to fall apart. He explained why the central government created by the Articles of Confederation was too weak to solve problems among and within the states.

Central to Madison's political theory was the idea that people tend to be guided by their "passions," defined as feelings of self-interest. People usually seek to advance their own interests at the expense of others. They then form groups with others who have the same goals. Madison called these groups "factions" and feared that in a democratic society a majority faction would oppress the minority.

"Father of the Constitution"

Madison was pleased when a meeting of all the states was set for the summer of 1787 in Philadelphia. (Rhode Island was the only state that failed to attend.) So eager was he that he arrived in the city eleven days early to prepare his plans.

Many of Madison's ideas were embodied in the Virginia Plan, which was proposed by the Virginia delegation early in the convention. This plan called for a national government with powers separated among the legislative, executive, and judicial branches. The legislature would be split into two houses, a concept called bicameralism. The executive and judicial branches would constitute a council of revision, which could veto acts passed by the legislature. Madison also included in the Virginia Plan a provision giving the federal government the power to veto state laws.

Madison believed that it was crucial to separate powers within the central government. The resulting system of checks and balances, he believed, would prevent any faction from seizing control of the government. Similarly, the proper division of power between the national and state governments, a novel concept called "federalism," would preclude the dangerous concentration of power in any one place. Madison thought that the Articles had not given the central government enough power to check the states, and therefore he supported a stronger central government.

Madison played a major role in the debates as the convention proceeded. He spoke often in support of his ideas and designed compromises to break gridlocks. He also took detailed notes on the debates at the end of each day. Because the debates were secret, Madison's notes provide a valuable record of what happened during the convention.

On September 17, 1787, after weeks of debate, the delegates approved the Constitution. This final version closely resembled the main outlines of the Virginia Plan.

The Federalist Papers

The Constitution was then sent to the states for ratification. But there was significant opposition to the document throughout the nation. Therefore, Madison joined with Alexander Hamilton and John Jay in composing a series of newspaper essays that defended the Constitution. Though intended for New York newspaper readers, the essays were also read in other states and helped to convince many to support the Constitution. They became known as the Federalist Papers. Madison wrote twenty-nine of the eighty-five essays, including two of the most famous, Nos. 10 and 51.

The Bill of Rights

Madison attended the ratification convention in his home state of Virginia. There he battled Anti-Federalist forces led by Patrick Henry, whose main objection to the Constitution was that it lacked a bill of rights. Madison at first opposed a bill of rights for several reasons: first, he argued that the rights of the people were already implied in the Constitution; second, he worried that any such listing of rights would surely omit some rights held by the people; and third, he believed that written lists of rights were not effective in protecting the liberty of the people. But Madison finally promised the Anti-Federalists that a bill of rights would be adopted after the new government went into effect.

During the debate, the Constitution went into effect when New Hampshire became the ninth state to ratify it on June 21, 1788. Four days later, Virginia also approved the Constitution, and New York did so on July 26.

Madison was elected to the United States House of Representatives in 1789. One of his first actions was to guide a bill of rights through Congress. Madison proposed a list of seventeen amendments, of which Congress approved twelve. Ten of the twelve were ratified by the states, and in 1791 the ten amendments known as the Bill of Rights were added to the Constitution.

"Mr. Madison's War"

Madison served eight years in the House of Representatives. During this time, he helped Thomas Jefferson organize the Democratic-Republican Party, which was formed to oppose the nationalist policies of Secretary of State Alexander Hamilton. Once in favor of a stronger central government, Madison now worried that the states could become the only strongholds against tyrannical federal power. In 1798, Madison wrote the Virginia Resolutions, which suggested that states could block unconstitutional federal laws.

In 1801, Thomas Jefferson became president. He appointed Madison as secretary of state. Madison succeeded Jefferson as president in 1809. His eight years as chief executive were troubled. The country sank into an economic depression. In 1812, the United States and Britain went to war. The United States was ill prepared. The White House itself was burned by British troops, and Madison and his wife, Dolley, were forced to flee the capital. In 1815, Britain and the United States signed the Treaty of Ghent, ending the war.

Retirement

After serving as president for two terms, Madison retired to his Montpelier home. At his estate, some 100 slaves continued to toil. Despite his opposition to slavery, Madison never freed any of his slaves, not even upon his death. He knew that blacks could not immediately prosper in American society and that, therefore, sudden emancipation would be a disaster for all.

Madison stayed involved with public life by helping President James Monroe with foreign policy. He also helped Jefferson found the University of Virginia and served as its rector from 1826–1836.

Several years after the states ratified the U.S. Constitution, an admirer of James Madison labeled him "the Father of the Constitution." Madison rejected the title, rightly claiming that the document was "the work of many heads & many hands." He died at his home on June 28, 1836, at the age of eighty-five, the last of the Founders to die. Madison himself was surely surprised to have lived so long.

James Madison   97

Reading Comprehension Questions

1. Why has Madison been called the "Father of the Constitution"?

2. Why did Madison want to separate the powers of the federal government between three branches and also divide power between the federal government and the states?

3. Why did Madison originally not want a bill of rights?

Critical Thinking Questions

4. How would Madison have felt if the Constitution had not been approved by the required nine states and had therefore not gone into effect?

5. Re-read the introductory quotation by Madison at the top of Handout A. Was Madison correct in believing that people always act out of self-interest at the expense of others? Can you think of a time when you acted out of self-interest at someone's expense? Can you think of a time when you put aside your own interest to help someone else?

VOCABULARY AND CONTEXT QUESTIONS

Excerpts from *Federalist Paper No. 10*

1. **Vocabulary:** *Use context clues to determine the meaning or significance of each of these words and write their definitions:*

   a. actuated

   b. adverse

   c. aggregate

   d. fallible

   e. latent

   f. inference

   g. sinister

   h. compass

   i. concert

   j. oppression

2. **Context:** *Answer the following questions.*

   a. When was this document written?

   b. Where was this document written?

   c. Who wrote this document?

   d. What type of document is this?

   e. What was the purpose of this document?

   f. Who was the audience for this document?

IN HIS OWN WORDS:
JAMES MADISON ON THE PROBLEM OF FACTION

Excerpts from *Federalist Paper No. 10*

A

By a faction, I understand a number of citizens, whether amounting to a majority or a minority of the whole, who are united and actuated by some common impulse of passion, or of interest, adverse to the rights of other citizens, or to the permanent and aggregate interests of the community. . . .

B

As long as the reason of man continues fallible, and he is at liberty to exercise it, different opinions will be formed. . . .

The latent causes of faction are thus sown in the nature of man. . . .

The inference to which we are brought is, that the *causes* of faction cannot be removed, and that relief is only to be sought in the means of controlling its *effects*.

C

If a faction consists of less than a majority, relief is supplied by the republican principle, which enables the majority to defeat its sinister views by regular vote. . . .

D

When a majority is included in a faction, the form of popular government, on the other hand, enables it to sacrifice to its ruling passion or interest both the public good and the rights of other citizens.

E

To secure the public good and private rights against the danger of such a faction, and at the same time to preserve the spirit and the form of popular government, is then the great object to which our inquiries are directed. . . .

F

The smaller the society, the fewer probably will be the distinct parties and interests composing it; the fewer the distinct parties and interests, the more frequently will a majority be found of the same party; and the smaller the number of individuals composing a majority, and the smaller the compass within which they are placed, the more easily will they concert and execute their plans of oppression. Extend the sphere, and you take in a greater variety of parties and interests; you make it less probable that a majority of the whole will have a common motive to invade the rights of other citizens; or if such a common motive exists, it will be more difficult for all who feel it to discover their own strength, and to act in unison with each other. . . .

Source: *Federalist Paper No. 10.* The Avalon Project at Yale Law School.
   <**http://www.yale.edu/lawweb/avalon/federal/fed10.htm**>.

GEORGE MASON
(1725–1792)

We claim Nothing but the Liberty & Privileges of Englishmen, in the same Degree, as if we had still continued among our Brethren in Great Britain: these Rights have not been forfeited by any Act of ours, we can not be deprived of them without our Consent, but by Violence & Injustice; We have received them from our Ancestors and, with God's Leave, we will transmit them, unimpaired to our Posterity.

—*George Mason, June 6, 1776*

Introduction

George Mason's ideas helped to shape the Founding documents of the United States, but few Americans remember him today. The words he used when writing the Virginia Declaration of Rights and the Virginia Constitution of 1776 inspired the nation's Declaration of Independence and Bill of Rights. Mason was an associate of fellow Virginians George Washington, James Madison, and Thomas Jefferson, the last of whom called Mason "a man of the first order of greatness."

Though he detested politics, Mason believed that it was his duty to protect the rights of his fellow citizens. He therefore entered public life and took an active role in shaping the governments of his state and nation. He was an eloquent advocate for individual freedom and states' rights. He also spoke out against the institution of slavery, though he owned hundreds of slaves who toiled on his Gunston Hall plantation.

Mason spent the last years of his life fighting to ensure that the newly minted Constitution would guarantee the rights of the people. Though the Bill of Rights was eventually approved, Mason was unsatisfied, believing that it failed to protect the people's rights adequately. Faithful to his principles, he retired to his plantation a defeated man, choosing not to serve as Virginia's first senator to avoid joining a government he feared could be the beginning of the end of liberty in the United States.

Relevant Thematic Essays for George Mason

- Slavery
- Freedom of Religion
- Liberty (Volume 2)

In His Own Words:
GEORGE MASON
ON LIBERTY

Overview

In this lesson, students will learn about statesman George Mason. They should first read as background homework **Handout A—George Mason (1725–1792)** and answer the **Reading Comprehension Questions.** After discussing the answers to these questions in class, the teacher should have the students answer the **Critical Thinking Questions** as a class. Next, the teacher should introduce the students to the primary source activity, **Handout C—In His Own Words: George Mason on Liberty.** As a preface, there is **Handout B—Context Questions,** which will help the students understand the document.

There are **Follow-Up Homework Options** that ask the students to compose either an essay comparing the Virginia Declaration of Rights with relevant clauses of the Constitution, or a two-paragraph speech that Mason could have made at the Virginia Ratifying Convention. **Extensions** provides an opportunity for thought as students are asked to consider whether liberty is more easily preserved in a small republic than in a large one.

Objectives

Students will:
- understand Mason's view of the rights of Virginians
- analyze Mason's objections to the Constitution
- evaluate the importance of Mason's contributions to the Founding
- appreciate Mason's devotion to personal liberty and states' rights

Standards

CCE (9–12): IIA1, IIC1, IIIA1, IIIA2
NCHS (5–12): Era III, Standards 3A, 3B
NCSS: Strands 2, 5, 6, and 10

Materials
Student Handouts
- Handout A—George Mason (1725–1792)
- Handout B—Context Questions
- Handout C—In His Own Words: George Mason on Liberty
- Handout D—Student Answer Bank
- Copy of the Declaration of Independence <http://www.billofrightsinstitute.org/sections.php?op=viewarticle&artid=50>
- Copy of the United States Constitution <http://www.billofrightsinstitute.org/sections.php?op=viewarticle&artid=44>

Additional Teacher Resource
- Answer Key

Recommended Time
One 45-minute class period. Additional time as needed for homework.

LESSON PLAN

I. Background Homework
Ask students to read **Handout A—George Mason (1725–1792)** and answer the Reading Comprehension Questions.

II. Warm-Up [10 minutes]
A. Review answers to homework questions.
B. Conduct a whole-class discussion to answer the Critical Thinking Questions.
C. Ask a student to summarize the historical significance of George Mason.

George Mason was a Virginian dedicated to the principles of individual liberty and states' rights. He was the primary author of the Virginia Declaration of Rights and the Virginia Constitution. These documents influenced the Declaration of Independence, the U.S. Constitution, and the Bill of Rights. He opposed the U.S. Constitution based on the fact that it did not adequately protect the rights of the people.

III. Context [10 minutes]
Briefly review with students the mounting crisis in the relationship between America and Great Britain between 1763 and 1776.

IV. In His Own Words [20 minutes]
A. Distribute **Handout B—Context Questions.** Be sure that the students understand the "who, what, where, and when" of the document.
B. Divide the class into equal groups. Assign each group one of the clauses of **Handout C—In His Own Words: George Mason on Liberty.** (For a small, advanced class, each clause may be assigned to one student.)
C. Give each group the job of paraphrasing its assigned clause in one to two sentences. At the bottom of each clause are vocabulary words that will help the students understand the document.
D. Once the groups believe that they understand their assigned clauses, give each group a copy of the first two paragraphs of the Declaration of Independence and a copy of the United States Constitution and the first ten amendments. Ask each group to match its assigned clause with a similar clause/section of one or more of these documents.
E. **Handout D—Student Answer Bank** can be used with this activity. **Handout D** lists specific clauses and amendments in which the students can find their matches. (Advanced students can probably find the appropriate matches without the answer bank.)

V. Wrap-Up Discussion [5 minutes]
Bring the class together as a whole and have each group share its responses to **Handout C.**

VI. Follow-Up Homework Options
A. Have the students assume Mason's persona and compose a one-page essay in which they compare one or more of the clauses of the Virginia Declaration of Rights with the relevant clauses of the Constitution. The students should accurately convey Mason's satisfaction or displeasure with each of the Constitution's clauses.
B. Have the students assume Mason's persona and compose and present a one-page speech that he could have made at the Virginia Ratifying Convention in opposition to the Constitution.

Lesson Plan

 VII. Extensions

Mason made the following comments at the Virginia Ratifying Convention:

> *Was there ever an instance of a general National Government extending over so extensive a country, abounding in such a variety of climates, &c. where the people retained their liberty? I solemnly declare, that no man is a greater friend to a firm Union of the American States than I am: But, Sir, if this great end can be obtained without hazarding the rights of the people, why should we recur to such dangerous principles?*

Suggestions:

A. Students could first paraphrase Mason's comments:

> *A country as large and diverse as the United States cannot be governed by a strong national government without compromising the people's liberty. I am in favor of a union of the states, under a plan that ensures the people's rights. But this plan risks those rights.*

B. At the time of the American Founding, most political thinkers shared Mason's belief that liberty was more easily preserved in a small republic than in a large one. (This was the belief of many ancient political philosophers.) Students can write an essay in which they take a stand on this issue and support their position with four or five points.

Resources

Print

Copeland, Pamela C., and Richard K. MacMaster. *The Five George Masons: Patriots and Planters of Virginia and Maryland.* Charlottesville: University Press of Virginia, 1975.

Miller, Helen Hill. *George Mason, Gentleman Revolutionary.* Chapel Hill: University of North Carolina Press, 1975.

Rutland, Robert A. *The Papers of George Mason.* Chapel Hill: University of North Carolina Press, 1970.

Rutland, Robert A. *George Mason: Reluctant Statesman.* New York: Holt, Rinehart, and Winston, 1961.

Tarter, Brent. "George Mason and the Conservation of Liberty." *Virginia Magazine of History and Biography* 99 (1991): 279–304.

Internet

"The Debates in the Federal Convention of 1787 reported by James Madison: July 11." The Avalon Project at Yale Law School. <**http://www.yale.edu/lawweb/avalon/debates/711.htm**>.

"George Mason, Remarks on Annual Elections for the Fairfax Independent Company." The Founders' Constitution Volume 1, Chapter 18, Document 5. <**http://press-pubs.uchicago.edu/founders/documents/v1ch18s5.html**>.

"George Mason, Virginia Ratifying Convention, 4 June 1788." The Founders' Constitution Volume 1, Chapter 8, Document 37. <**http://press-pubs.uchicago.edu/founders/documents/v1ch8s37.html**>.

Gunston Hall Plantation. <**http://gunstonhall.org/**>.

"Virginia Declaration of Rights." The Avalon Project at Yale Law School. <**http://www.yale.edu/lawweb/avalon/debates/virginia.htm**>.

Selected Works by George Mason
- **The Virginia Constitution** (1776)
- **The Virginia Declaration of Rights** (1776)
- *Objections to This Constitution of Government* (1787)

GEORGE MASON (1725–1792)

In all our associations; in all our agreements let us never lose sight of this fundamental maxim—that all power was originally lodged in, and consequently is derived from, the people. We should wear it as a breastplate, and buckle it on as our armour.

—*George Mason, 1775*

Dressed in black clothes, the elder statesman from Fairfax rose once again to speak to the members of the Virginia Ratifying Convention. George Mason was widely respected by his fellow delegates as the author of the state constitution and Declaration of Rights. But his staunch opposition to the U.S. Constitution had made him many enemies. Some even questioned his sanity. Mason feared that the new federal government would be too strong and would "annihilate totally the State Governments." As the sixty-two-year-old champion of liberty began to speak, all eyes were upon him.

Background

George Mason was born to a wealthy landowner in northern Virginia. His father died when George was ten. As a youth, Mason eagerly read many of the books in his uncle's large library. He became one of the most educated men in Virginia. Mason married at the age of twenty-five, and he eventually had nine children. His family lived on the great Virginia plantation he called Gunston Hall. About three hundred slaves also lived there. As Mason's reputation grew, Gunston Hall became a stopping place for political and business leaders.

Defender of American Liberty

George Mason took his place in local politics as a judge and town trustee. He did not like politics, but he believed it was his duty to protect the people's liberty. This, in his view, was the main role of government. When Virginia's liberty was threatened, Mason left home to join the battle. As George Washington's supply officer in the French and Indian War, he fought to protect his state against a foreign power. As a member of the Virginia House of Burgesses, Mason opposed attempts by Parliament to restrict American rights. When these threats passed, he returned to Gunston Hall, content to run his plantation.

In the 1770s, Parliament continued to pass laws attacking American liberty, and Mason responded. He joined the Virginia Committee of Correspondence. This body worked with other colonies to oppose Parliament's actions through "nonimportation agreements"—boycotts of British goods. Mason helped write the rules for the boycotts in Virginia. But Parliament refused to repeal the acts, instead passing more restrictions. George Mason then joined George Washington in writing the Fairfax Resolves in 1774. This document condemned Parliament's acts as illegal and a violation of American liberty. Mason gave Virginians a reason to resist British interference in their lives.

The Virginia Constitution and Declaration of Rights

When it became obvious that America would separate from Great Britain, Mason supported the cause. He also wanted to make sure that the new government of Virginia would guarantee the rights of individuals. Mason was elected to represent Fairfax County at the Virginia Convention, where the new government would be formed.

James Madison was also a delegate to that convention. Madison named Mason the "master builder"—the primary author—of the Virginia Declaration of Rights and the Virginia Constitution. The Declaration of Rights argued that mankind is "by nature equally free and independent, and has certain inherent rights," such as the rights to life, liberty, and happiness. It insisted that "a majority of the community" has the right to "reform, alter, or abolish" any government that endangers the liberty of the people. These rights were clearly not intended to apply to Virginia's slaves. Though Mason believed that "every master of slaves is a petty tyrant," he never freed any of his own slaves.

Mason's ideas about natural rights and liberty were based on the ideas of the English philosophers John Locke and Algernon Sidney. The Declaration of Rights in turn influenced Jefferson's Declaration of Independence, which was written shortly afterward. Mason listed several liberties in his Declaration, including freedom of the press, freedom of religion, and the right to a speedy trial by jury, which appeared later in the Bill of Rights. The Virginia Constitution influenced the U.S. Constitution in defining the separation of powers among the executive, legislative, and judicial branches. Virginia adopted both documents in June 1776.

Critic of the Constitution

After helping to create the new state government, Mason joined the House of Delegates and supported the war effort. He retired in 1781 due to illness and returned home. During the 1780s, many statesmen came to believe that the Articles of Confederation were a failure. At the age of sixty-two, George Mason was called on and agreed to serve Virginia once more at the Constitutional Convention in Philadelphia. James Madison admired Mason's dedication to his country and its people: "It could not be more inconvenient to any gentleman to remain absent from his private affairs, than it was for him."

Soon, however, Madison and Mason would become enemies. Though Mason agreed that the Articles of Confederation needed to be changed, he feared making the central government too strong. As the convention wore on, he became alarmed by several proposals aimed at reducing the power of the states. Mason believed that the states represented the people better than any national government ever could.

Mason also thought the new Constitution did not go far enough in protecting individual rights and local interests. He feared that the presidency was too powerful. His calls for a bill of rights and for an end to the importation of slaves were rejected. Mason therefore refused to sign the Constitution and spoke out against its approval. This opposition brought to an end his long friendship with George Washington. It also inspired attacks on his mental powers. One supporter of the Constitution accused him of having lost his wits in his old age. To this Mason responded: "Sir, when yours fail, nobody will ever discover it."

Ratification and the Bill of Rights

Immediately after the convention approved the Constitution, Mason wrote his *Objections to This Constitution of Government*, which was published by newspapers and in pamphlet form. In this essay, Mason warned that the new federal government would destroy the states. He argued that the Constitution gave "no security" to the "Declarations of Rights in the separate States."

Mason was elected to the Virginia Ratifying Convention that met in June 1788. There he joined Patrick Henry in the fight against ratification of the Constitution. Mason warned the members of the ratifying convention that all three branches of the federal government had been given too much power. The "necessary and proper" and "general welfare" clauses would give Congress unlimited power over the states. Mason demanded that the Constitution be changed so as to protect the people's rights.

Madison, who was also a member of the convention, tried to reassure Mason and his allies. Madison promised that a list of amendments would be introduced in the first Congress. Based on this pledge, Virginia approved the Constitution. Madison's twelve amendments were based on Mason's ideas. Ten of these, known as the Bill of Rights, would be ratified in 1791. But the ten amendments were not enough to satisfy Mason, who wished to see "two or three" more added. Mason retired from public life and returned to his beloved Gunston Hall to live out his few remaining days. Mason died less than a year after the Bill of Rights went into effect.

Reading Comprehension Questions

1. What did Mason believe to be the main role of government?

2. What two founding documents of Virginia did Mason author?

3. Why did Mason object to the Constitution?

Critical Thinking Questions

4. Why do you think Mason wore black clothes at the Virginia Ratifying Convention?

5. Mason hated politics, but he entered public life because he believed it to be his duty. Have you ever done something you did not like because of a sense of duty?

CONTEXT QUESTIONS

The Virginia Declaration of Rights

Answer the following questions.

1. When was this document written?

2. Where was this document written?

3. Who wrote this document?

4. What type of document is this?

5. What was the purpose of this document?

6. Who was the audience for this document?

In His Own Words:
George Mason on Liberty

The Virginia Declaration of Rights

The Virginia Declaration of Rights, which was drafted by George Mason, was adopted unanimously on June 12, 1776, by the Virginia Convention of Delegates. The sixteen clauses in the Virginia Declaration of Rights are shown below.

Directions:

1. Working in a group, paraphrase the clause assigned to your group in one or two sentences. Be sure to refer to the vocabulary words and their definitions below the clause for better understanding.

2. Match each clause with similar sections in the first two paragraphs of the Declaration of Independence, the U.S. Constitution, and/or the first ten amendments to the U.S. Constitution. Note that sections of these documents may match more than one clause. In some cases, there may not be an appropriate match.

1

That all men are by nature equally free and independent, and have certain inherent rights, of which, when they enter into a state of society, they cannot, by any compact, deprive or divest their posterity; namely, the enjoyment of life and liberty, with the means of acquiring and possessing property, and pursuing and obtaining happiness and safety.

Vocabulary:
inherent = natural
deprive/divest = take away from

2

That all power is vested in, and consequently derived from, the people; that magistrates are their trustees and servants, and at all times amenable to them.

Vocabulary:
vested = placed in
magistrates = government officials
amenable = answerable

3

That government is, or ought to be, instituted for the common benefit, protection, and security of the people, nation or community; of all the various modes and forms of government that is best, which is capable of producing the greatest degree of happiness and safety and is most effectually secured against the danger of maladministration; and that, whenever any government shall be found inadequate or contrary to these purposes, a majority of the community hath [has] an indubitable, unalienable, and indefeasible right to reform, alter or abolish it, in such manner as shall be judged most conducive to the public weal.

Vocabulary:
maladministration = poor operation
indubitable = undoubted
unalienable/indefeasible = not capable of being taken away/undone
public weal = general good

4

That no man, or set of men, are entitled to exclusive or separate emoluments or privileges from the community, but in consideration of public services; which, not being descendible, neither ought the offices of magistrate, legislator, or judge be hereditary.

Vocabulary:
emoluments = payments for holding an office
descendible/hereditary = passed from one generation to the next

---

5

That the legislative and executive powers of the state should be separate and distinct from the judicative; and, that the members of the two first may be restrained from oppression by feeling and participating the burthens of the people, they should, at fixed periods, be reduced to a private station, return into that body from which they were originally taken, and the vacancies be supplied by frequent, certain, and regular elections in which all, or any part of the former members, to be again eligible, or ineligible, as the laws shall direct.

Vocabulary:
oppression = tyranny, misrule
eligible = qualified

6

That elections of members to serve as representatives of the people in assembly ought to be free; and that all men, having sufficient evidence of permanent common interest with, and attachment to, the community have the right of suffrage and cannot be taxed or deprived of their property for public uses without their own consent or that of their representatives so elected, nor bound by any law to which they have not, in like manner, assented, for the public good.

Vocabulary:
suffrage = the ability to vote
assented = agreed to

7

That all power of suspending laws, or the execution of laws, by any authority without consent of the representatives of the people is injurious to their rights and ought not to be exercised.

Vocabulary:
injurious = harmful
exercised = carried out

8

That in all capital or criminal prosecutions a man hath a right to demand the cause and nature of his accusation to be confronted with the accusers and witnesses, to call for evidence in his favor, and to a speedy trial by an impartial jury of his vicinage, without whose unanimous consent he cannot be found guilty, nor can he be compelled to give evidence against himself; that no man be deprived of his liberty except by the law of the land or the judgement of his peers.

Vocabulary:
capital = punishable by death (crime)
vicinage = vicinity
unanimous = having the agreement and consent of all
peers = people of the same social rank

9

That excessive bail ought not to be required, nor excessive fines imposed; nor cruel and unusual punishments inflicted.

Vocabulary:
excessive = extreme/too much
inflicted = imposed

10

That general warrants, whereby any officer or messenger may be commanded to search suspected places without evidence of a fact committed, or to seize any person or persons not named, or whose offense is not particularly described and supported by evidence, are grievous and oppressive and ought not to be granted.

Vocabulary:
grievous = serious

11

That in controversies respecting property and in suits between man and man, the ancient trial by jury is preferable to any other and ought to be held sacred.

12

That the freedom of the press is one of the greatest bulwarks of liberty and can never be restrained but by despotic governments.

Vocabulary:
bulwarks = defenses
despotic = tyrannical, cruel

13

That a well regulated militia, composed of the body of the people, trained to arms, is the proper, natural, and safe defense of a free state; that standing [permanent] armies, in time of peace, should be avoided as dangerous to liberty; and that, in all cases, the military should be under strict subordination to, and be governed by, the civil power.

Vocabulary:
regulated = organized
subordination = subservience

14

That the people have a right to uniform government; and therefore, that no government separate from, or independent of, the government of Virginia, ought to be erected or established within the limits thereof.

Vocabulary:
uniform = consistent

15

That no free government, or the blessings of liberty, can be preserved to any people but by a firm adherence to justice, moderation, temperance, frugality, and virtue and by frequent recurrence to fundamental principles.

Vocabulary:
adherence = devotion
temperance = moderation
frugality = care in spending money
recurrence = repetition
fundamental = basic

16

That religion, or the duty which we owe to our Creator and the manner of discharging it, can be directed by reason and conviction, not by force or violence; and therefore, all men are equally entitled to the free exercise of religion, according to the dictates of conscience; and that it is the mutual duty of all to practice Christian forbearance, love, and charity towards each other.

Vocabulary:
discharging = fulfilling
dictates = orders
forbearance = patience

Source: "The Virginia Declaration of Rights." The Avalon Project at Yale University Law School.
<http://www.yale.edu/lawweb/avalon/virginia.htm>.

STUDENT ANSWER BANK

*You may use this answer bank with **Handout C.** The following is a list of specific paragraphs, clauses, and amendments that are similar to the clauses in the Virginia Declaration of Rights. Match your assigned clause to the documents below.*

- Declaration of Independence (Paragraphs 1 and 2)
- The Constitution: Articles I, II, III, and IV
- The Constitution: Article I, Section 2, Clause 1
- The Constitution: Article I, Section 9, Clause 2
- The Constitution: Article I, Section 9, Clause 8
- The Constitution: Article II, Section 2, Clause 1
- The Constitution: Article II, Section 3
- The Constitution: Article IV, Section 3
- First Amendment
- Second Amendment
- Fourth Amendment
- Fifth Amendment
- Sixth Amendment
- Seventh Amendment
- Eighth Amendment

ROBERT MORRIS
(1734–1806)

I t is the duty of every individual to act his part in whatever station his country may call him to in hours of difficulty, danger, and distress.

—*Robert Morris*

Introduction

Known as the "Financier of the Revolution," Robert Morris played a critical role in winning and securing American independence. As chairman of the Continental Congress's Finance Committee between 1775 and 1778, Morris traded flour and tobacco to France in exchange for war supplies such as guns, powder, and blankets. Morris risked his own ships in bringing these supplies past the fearsome British Navy. He was also the architect of the financial system of the early republic. As superintendent of finance under the Articles of Confederation, Morris almost single-handedly saved the United States from financial catastrophe in the 1780s. His plan to fund the national debt and to deposit federal money in a private bank foreshadowed the financial system that Secretary of the Treasury Alexander Hamilton would implement in the 1790s.

Though Morris risked much of his personal wealth in service to his country, he was criticized by some for profiting from public service. During his chairmanship of Congress' Finance Committee, Morris' company was paid by the American government a commission of two percent on each shipment of supplies the company brought into the country. This compensation was in lieu of the salary that most public officials received. Nevertheless, Morris's enemies seized upon the appearance of impropriety and charged him with malfeasance. But investigations of Morris's conduct failed to turn up evidence of wrongdoing. Some of the accusations against him were motivated by jealousy, as Morris became perhaps the richest man in America in the 1780s.

Morris signed all three of the nation's principal documents: the Declaration of Independence, the Articles of Confederation, and the Constitution. He was indeed a leading supporter of the Constitution, believing it imperative that the national government be empowered to deal with the country's financial problems. Despite his genius for money, however, Morris fell on hard times in the 1790s. The man who was largely responsible for the nation's emerging prosperity ironically spent his final years in poverty.

Relevant Thematic Essay for Robert Morris
- Commerce

In His Own Words:
ROBERT MORRIS
ON STATES' RESPONSIBILITIES

Overview

In this lesson, students will learn about Robert Morris. They should first read as background homework **Handout A—Robert Morris (1734–1806)** and answer the **Reading Comprehension Questions.** After discussing the answers to these questions in class, the teacher should have the students answer the **Critical Thinking Questions** as a class. Next, the teacher should introduce the students to the primary source activity, **Handout C—In His Own Words: Robert Morris on States' Responsibilities,** in which Morris tries to persuade the governors of the states to fulfill their quotas of money and supplies. As a preface, there is **Handout B—Vocabulary and Context Questions,** which will help the students understand the document.

There are **Follow-Up Homework Options** that ask the students to compare the Articles of Confederation to the United States Constitution or to revise one part of the Articles as Morris would have liked it to read. **Extensions** provides opportunity for thought as students are asked to compose a letter of supplication using techniques employed by Morris in his *Circular to the Governors of the States.*

Objectives

Students will:
- appreciate Morris' role as a leader of the American opposition to British tyranny
- explain Morris' role in stabilizing the finances of the United States
- analyze the reasons for Morris's support of the Constitution
- understand how Morris accumulated and then lost his wealth

Standards
  CCE (9–12): IIA1, IIC1, IIIA1, IIIA2
  NCHS (5–12): Era III, Standards 3A, 3B
  NCSS: Strands 2, 5, 6, and 10

Materials
Student Handouts
- Handout A—Robert Morris (1734–1806)
- Handout B—Vocabulary and Context Questions
- Handout C—In His Own Words: Robert Morris on States' Responsibilities

Additional Teacher Resource
- Answer Key

Recommended Time
  One 45-minute class period. Additional time as needed for homework.

LESSON PLAN

I. Background Homework
Ask students to read **Handout A—Robert Morris (1734–1806)** and answer the Reading Comprehension Questions.

II. Warm-Up [10 minutes]
A. Review answers to homework questions.
B. Conduct a whole-class discussion to answer the Critical Thinking Questions.
C. Ask a student to summarize the historical significance of Robert Morris.

> *Robert Morris was a successful Philadelphia merchant. In the 1760s and 1770s, he became a leader of American resistance to British rule. During the Revolution, he held the post of chairman of the Continental Congress's Finance Committee. After the Articles of Confederation were adopted, he became superintendent of finance, the highest-ranking office under the Articles. Morris had broad powers, which he used to stabilize the nation's financial system. Morris made money from public service. Some people at the time criticized Morris for profiting at the expense of the country, but a congressional committee found him innocent of any wrongdoing. Morris was a proponent of a strong central government and supported the Constitution, which he signed as a delegate to the Philadelphia Convention of 1787. Morris became a United States senator in the first federal Congress. In the 1790s, he had financial trouble and was put into debtor's prison. The man who had once been called "the richest man in America" died in poverty in 1806 at the age of seventy-three.*

III. Context [5 minutes]
Explain to the students that the national Congress created by the Articles of Confederation (which went into effect in 1781) had few powers and could not force the individual states to comply with its requests. As superintendent of finance, Robert Morris was forced to rely on his persuasive powers in order to get the states to fulfill quotas of money and supplies that Congress asked them to contribute to the national government.

IV. In His Own Words [20 minutes]
A. Distribute **Handout B—Vocabulary and Context Questions.**
B. Distribute **Handout C—In His Own Words: Robert Morris on States' Responsibilities.** Be sure that the students understand the vocabulary and the "who, what, where, and when" of the document.
C. Have the students read the document aloud, taking turns every sentence or so. After each sentence, have a volunteer paraphrase Morris's words.

V. Wrap-Up Discussion [10 minutes]
Ask the students to consider the tone of Morris' letter. What is Morris' attitude toward the governors? Have students underline/circle words and phrases that reflect this tone. What does this letter reveal about the relationship between the central government and the states under the Articles of Confederation?
See Answer Key.

VI. Follow-Up Homework Options
A. Students could compare the powers given to Congress by Article IX of the Articles of Confederation to the powers given to Congress by Article I, Section 8 of the Constitution.

LESSON PLAN

B. Students could assume the identity of Robert Morris and revise Article IX of the Articles of Confederation as he would have liked it to read.

The Articles of Confederation can be found at:
<http://www.yale.edu/lawweb/avalon/artconf.htm>

The Constitution can be found at:
<http://www.billofrightsinstitute.org/sections.php?op=viewarticle&artid=44>

 VII. Extensions

Suggestions:

Students could compose a letter of supplication to someone over whom they have no authority. They can use the techniques of persuasion employed by Morris. Possibilities for the letter include the following:

A. a letter to a parent asking permission to go on an overnight trip with friends
B. a cover letter for a job application
C. a letter inviting a speaker to address a student group
D. a letter pleading with a school official to reduce a punishment for an infraction committed by the student
E. a letter to be published in a student newspaper asking students to contribute to a charitable fund

Resources

Print

Catanzariti, John, and James E. Ferguson (ed). *The Papers of Robert Morris, 1781–1784.* 9 vols. Pittsburgh: University of Pittsburgh Press, 1973–1999.

Cook, Frank Gaylord. "Robert Morris." *The Atlantic Monthly* 66, (November 1890): 607–618.

Oberholtzer, Ellis P. *Robert Morris: Patriot and Financier.* New York: Burt Franklin, 1969.

Sumner, William Graham. *Robert Morris, The Financier and the Finances of the American Revolution.* 2 vols. Reprint. Frederick, MD: Beard, 2000.

Ver Steeg, Clarence L. *Robert Morris: Revolutionary Financier.* New York: Octagon Books, 1972.

Internet

"Robert Morris." U.S. Army Center of Military History. **<http://www.army.mil/cmh-pg/books/revwar/ss/morris.htm>**.

"Robert Morris, Circular to the Governors of the States." The University of Chicago Press. **<http://press-pubs.uchicago.edu/founders/documents/v1ch5s3.html>**.

"Robert Morris, Pennsylvania." U.S. National Archives & Records Administration. **<http://www.archives.gov/exhibit_hall/charters_of_freedom/constitution/pennsylvania.html#morris_R>**.

"Robert Morris to the President of Congress." The University of Chicago Press. **<http://press-pubs.uchicago.edu/founders/documents/v1ch5s7.html>**.

"Sen. Robert Morris of Pennsylvania to Governeur Morris, March 4, 1789." First Federal Congress Project, The George Washington University. **<http://www.gwu.edu/~ffcp/exhibit/p1/p1_5.html>**.

CD-ROM

Robert Morris, 1734–1806, Revolutionary. Created by Robert Morris VIII. Self-published, © 2003.

Selected Works by Robert Morris
• *Circular to the Governors of the States* (1781)

ROBERT MORRIS (1734–1806)

For my part I considered this Subject [independence] early & fixed on principles the part I should take in the unhappy Contest. I sided with this Country because their claims are founded in Justice and I wish every Friend to the American Cause may act on the same principle.

—*Robert Morris, 1776*

The group of soldiers huddled around a small fire in front of their tent as darkness fell on the encampment of the Continental Army at Valley Forge, Pennsylvania. It was a cold December night in 1777, and the American army had been fighting the British for two years. The men were downhearted, having little food and thin, ragged uniforms. Some lacked boots or footwear of any kind. In addition, the prospects for the American cause seemed bleak after the military setbacks of the summer and fall. As the soldiers warmed themselves at the fire, one of them called his comrades' attention to two men on horseback heading in their direction. As the riders drew closer, the men recognized one as their commander, General George Washington. The soldiers quickly snapped to attention and gave a salute as their tall, solemn leader passed. They did not recognize his companion. He was shorter than Washington, heavy-set, and lacked the aura of the great Virginian. He did not look like a leader of men. In fact, Robert Morris's appearance gave little indication of the crucial role he was to play during the next few years in keeping this army alive—a role second in importance only to the man with whom he rode that night.

Background

Morris was born in Liverpool, England, in 1734. His father, a merchant, immigrated to Maryland and soon brought his son across the Atlantic to join him. Morris was sent to Philadelphia for an education, but his father was dissatisfied with his progress. He asked his son why he had learned so little from his tutor. "Sir," the young Morris replied, "I have learned all that he can teach me." When Morris was sixteen years old, his father was accidentally shot and killed. The boy then became an apprentice at the shipping and banking firm of Willing and Company. In 1757, at the age of twenty-three, Morris became a partner in the renamed firm of Willing, Morris, and Company.

Morris became a leading citizen in Philadelphia. He founded the London Coffee House, which was a predecessor of the Philadelphia Stock Exchange. The Coffee House was a center of trade and political discussion. His company traded in a variety of products, including tobacco, flour, rum, molasses, and wheat. Morris's company also transported European indentured servants to America and, for a brief time, African slaves.

Resistance to British Rule

Morris took a leading role in opposing British policies in the 1760s. He believed that the new taxes imposed by Parliament during this decade violated the colonists' rights as English citizens. In 1765, Morris served on a local committee formed to oppose the Stamp Act. The next year, in response to the Townshend duties, he led local merchants in a campaign to close the port of Philadelphia to imported goods from England. One result of this action was the end of the slave trade in Philadelphia.

After the bloodshed at Lexington and Concord in 1775, Morris again assumed a prominent role in the resistance to British oppression. He served on Pennsylvania's Committee of Correspondence as well as its Council of Safety, and he was appointed warden of the port of Philadelphia. Morris also was elected a member of the Pennsylvania legislature and was chosen to represent the colony at the Continental Congress.

In Congress, Morris served on the Marine Committee. He took charge of building a sixteen-ship American navy, selling some of his own ships to Congress. Morris was also a member of the Secret Committee for the Procurement of Munitions. In this role, he obtained from Europe weapons and ammunition for American forces.

Independence

Until 1776, Morris hoped that America and Great Britain could reach a settlement and avoid war. Morris even initially voted against independence in the Continental Congress, but he changed his mind and signed the Declaration of Independence. Morris also signed the Articles of Confederation on behalf of Pennsylvania in 1778.

In that same year Morris became chairman of Congress's Finance Committee. In this position, he persuaded reluctant states to contribute funds to the continental system and the army, and he obtained loans from wealthy businessmen. Morris also obtained war supplies, such as guns, powder, and blankets, from Europe, risking his own ships in bringing these supplies past the powerful British navy. The Continental Army would likely have disintegrated if not for Morris's efforts.

Morris' company was paid by the American government a commission of two percent on each shipment of supplies the company brought into the country. But Morris did not receive a salary for his work as chairman of the Finance Committee. Some people at the time criticized Morris for profiting at the expense of the country. There were even whispers that Morris had taken more money than he was entitled to. Congress appointed a committee to look into these charges. The committee found Morris innocent of any wrongdoing, concluding that he had "acted with fidelity and integrity and an honorable zeal for the happiness of his country." John Adams, who was a member of the Continental Congress at the time, also defended Morris, saying that the Pennsylvanian was "an excellent Member of our Body."

Superintendent of Finance

Morris left Congress in 1778. He served again in the Pennsylvania legislature until 1781. In that year, the Articles of Confederation went into effect. Morris accepted an appointment as superintendent of finance in the new government. This was the highest-ranking office under the Articles. Morris had broad powers, which he used to stabilize the nation's financial system. He cut spending, streamlined accounting procedures, and cajoled the states into meeting their quotas of money and supplies. Morris risked his own money and credit to help keep the government afloat, putting up more than one million dollars of his own fortune to finance the decisive Battle of Yorktown that assured America's victory in the war.

Morris believed it was essential that the United States be placed on firm financial footing. He knew that the government must honor its debts. To this end, he urged Congress to adopt an impost, a tax on imports that would serve to provide the government with funds. But the impost amendment failed to win the approval of all thirteen states as required by the Articles of Confederation.

Morris next decided to try to pay the country's debts by enticing the wealthy to invest in United States bonds. He promised investors a six percent return on their money, which was guaranteed by the government. To further this plan, Morris established the Bank of North America, which opened its doors in 1782. The bank handled the nation's money as well as Morris's own financial affairs. This unusual arrangement generated renewed criticism from his enemies. Some again leveled the charge of corruption. When in 1783 the states again failed to approve an impost, Morris's frustration boiled over. "At the moment," he complained, "I fill the most powerful position of the new government and I am trying to get rid of it."

The Constitutional Convention

Morris resigned his position as superintendent of finance in 1783. Returning home, he was once more elected to the Pennsylvania legislature. Though he participated in state politics, he also remained concerned about national affairs. His disputes with the states had convinced him of the need for a stronger national government. Morris therefore supported the movement to revise the Articles of Confederation. He attended the Annapolis Convention of 1786 and the following year was elected to the Constitutional Convention.

No orator or student of political theory, Morris rarely spoke at the convention. "The science of law is entirely out of my line," he commented. But Morris made no secret of his strong nationalist sentiments. He was pleased with the final document produced by the convention and eagerly affixed his name to the Constitution. Morris declined George Washington's offer to be the first secretary of the treasury. Instead, he accepted his state's offer of a senate seat in the first Congress of the United States.

Later Years

During his years as a senator, Morris got himself into financial trouble. He speculated in Western land, buying vast tracts of land cheaply in the hope of selling them later at a high price. This gamble and several other new business ventures failed. During the 1790s, Morris also invested an enormous amount of money into the construction of an extravagant mansion in Philadelphia. In 1797 he was bankrupt, and the following year he was arrested for failure to pay his debts. Morris was put into debtor's prison. He was released in 1801 because of a new federal bankruptcy law. But by then his health had deteriorated, and he was unable to revive his businesses. The man who had once been called "the richest man in America" died in poverty in 1806 at the age of seventy-three.

Reading Comprehension Questions

1. What three important American documents did Morris sign?

2. What led Morris to favor a strong central government?

3. How did Morris end up in poverty at the end of his life?

Critical Thinking Questions

4. The introduction to this essay suggests that Morris's role in the establishment of the United States may have been second in importance only to that of George Washington. How can this statement be supported?

5. Do you think it is proper for government officials to profit from public service as Morris did?

VOCABULARY AND CONTEXT QUESTIONS

Excerpts from *Circular to the Governors of the States*

1. **Vocabulary:** *Use context clues to determine the meaning or significance of each of these words and write their definitions:*

   a. pernicious

   b. prevalent

   c. listless

   d. languor

   e. strenuous

   f. consequence

   g. magistrate

   h. extracted

   i. entreat

   j. assessing

   k. levying

2. **Context:** *Answer the following questions.*

   a. When was this document written?

   b. Where was this document written?

   c. Who wrote this document?

   d. What type of document is this?

   e. What was the purpose of this document?

   f. Who was the audience for this document?

In His Own Words:
Robert Morris on States' Responsibilities

Excerpts from *Circular to the Governors of the States*

Directions: *Robert Morris wrote this letter from Philadelphia, soon after assuming the office of superintendent of finance under the Articles of Confederation. Underline/circle words and phrases that reveal Morris' attitude toward the governors.*

Note: Capitalization, spelling, and punctuation have been modernized.

July 25, 1781

It gives me very great pain to learn that there is a pernicious idea prevalent among some of the States that their accounts are not to be adjusted with the Continent; such an idea cannot fail to spread a listless languor over all our operations. To suppose this expensive war can be carried on without joint and strenuous efforts is beneath the wisdom of those who are called to the high offices of legislation. . . . I shall never permit a doubt that the States will do what is right; neither will I ever believe that any one of them can expect to derive any advantage from doing what is wrong. It is by being just to individuals, to each other, to the Union, to all; by generous grants of solid revenue, and by adopting energetic measures to collect that revenue . . . that these States must expect to establish their independence and rise into power, consequence, and grandeur. . . .

I enclose you an account of the specific supplies demanded of your State as extracted from the Journals of Congress. . . . I am further to entreat Sir that I may be favored with copies of the several acts passed in your State since the 18th March 1780 for the collection of taxes and furnishing supplies or other aids to the United States. . . . I must also pray to be informed of so much of the internal police of your state as relates to the laying, assessing, levying and collecting of taxes. I beg leave to assure your Excellency that I am not prompted by an idle curiosity or by any wish to discover what prudence would dictate to conceal. It is necessary I should be informed of these things and I take the plain, open, candid method of acquiring information. . . .

I entreat your Excellency to undertake one more task which perhaps is far from being the least difficult. It is Sir that you write very fully as to the amount of the several paper currencies now circulating in your State. . . .

I know that I give you a great deal of trouble but I also know it will be pleasing to you because the time and the labour will be expended in the service of your country.

Source: "Robert Morris, Circular to the Governors of the States." The University of Chicago Press.
    <**http://press-pubs.uchicago.edu/founders/documents/v1ch5s3.html**>.

CHARLES PINCKNEY
(1757–1824)

They [Africans] certainly must have been created with less intellectual power than the whites, and were most probably intended to serve them, and be the instruments of their cultivation.

—*Charles Pinckney, Debate about the Missouri Compromise, 1821*

Introduction

Born near Charles Town (now Charleston), South Carolina, Charles Pinckney was the child of a wealthy family. He received a first-rate education and became an accomplished lawyer. Pinckney joined the state militia during the American Revolution and fought the British at Savannah and Charles Town. After the war, he became a member of the Confederation Congress and then a delegate to the Philadelphia Convention, which was convened for the purpose of revising the Articles. A moderate whose wartime experience caused him to see the necessity for a stronger central government, Pinckney nevertheless was jealous of the rights of the South in general and his native state in particular.

Pinckney was most sensitive to infringements upon the South's right to preserve slavery and the slave trade. Like most Americans of his time—in both North and South—Pinckney held what modern people would call "racist" views. Pinckney saw slavery as a positive good and could not imagine blacks as equals. He therefore fought for the protection of the slave trade at the Constitutional Convention and, thirty years later, opposed the Missouri Compromise because it set the dangerous precedent of allowing the federal Congress to outlaw slavery in the territories.

Relevant Thematic Essay for Charles Pinckney
- Slavery

In His Own Words:
CHARLES PINCKNEY
AND THE ISSUE OF SLAVERY

Overview

In this lesson, students will learn about statesman Charles Pinckney. They should first read as background homework **Handout A—Charles Pinckney (1757–1824)** and answer the **Reading Comprehension Questions.** After discussing the answers to these questions in class, the teacher should have the students answer the **Critical Thinking Questions** as a class. Next, the teacher should introduce the students to the primary source activity, **Handout C—In His Own Words: Charles Pinckney and the Issue of Slavery, 1787,** in which Pinckney and other Founders debate Article 1, Section 9, Clause 1 of the Constitution (the "Slave Trade Clause"). As a preface, there is **Handout B—Vocabulary and Context Questions,** which will help the students understand the document.

Next, ten students will assume the roles of the delegates and read the document in a dramatic presentation. The students will then complete **Handout D—Analysis: Debate about Article I, Section 9, Clause 1,** which analyzes and summarizes the views of the delegates in table form. There are **Follow-Up Homework Options** that ask the students to summarize the views of a particular delegate or create a diary entry for him. **Extensions** provides opportunity for thought as students are asked to examine Pinckney's views about slavery thirty years later during the debate about the Missouri Compromise.

Objectives
Students will:
* evaluate the importance of Pinckney's contributions to the Founding
* understand Pinckney's views on the Articles of Confederation and the Constitution
* analyze Pinckney's role in the Constitutional Convention
* understand the arguments about Article I, Section 9, Clause 1
* appreciate the passions and the interests of both pro- and antislavery proponents

Standards
CCE (9–12): IC2, IIB1, IIIA2
NCHS (5–12): Era III, Standard 3A; Era IV, Standard 3B
NCSS: Strands 1, 2, 5, 6, and 10

Materials
Student Handouts
* Handout A—Charles Pinckney (1757–1824)
* Handout B—Vocabulary and Context Questions
* Handout C—In His Own Words: Charles Pinckney and the Issue of Slavery
* Handout D—Analysis: Debate about Article I, Section 9, Clause 1

Additional Teacher Resource
* Answer Key

Recommended Time
One 45-minute class period. Additional time as needed for homework.

LESSON PLAN

I. Background Homework

Ask students to read **Handout A—Charles Pinckney (1756–1824)** and answer the Reading Comprehension Questions.

II. Warm-Up [10 minutes]

A. Review answers to homework questions.

B. Conduct a whole-class discussion to answer the Critical Thinking Questions.

C. Ask a student to summarize the historical significance of Charles Pinckney.

Charles Pinckney was a southern landowner who was one of the most active participants in the Constitutional Convention. Speaking more than 100 times, he contributed ideas about the role of the executive branch, the powers of the federal government, and the place of slavery in the new nation. In later years, he was one of the key figures in the debate about the extension of slavery into the territories.

III. Context [10 minutes]

A. Briefly review with students the controversial discussions of slavery at the Constitutional Convention. One of the most heated discussions revolved around what would eventually become Article I, Section 9, Clause 1. Write the following on the board or overhead:

The migration or importation of such persons as any of the states now existing shall think proper to admit, shall not be prohibited by the Congress prior to the year one thousand eight hundred and eight, but a tax or duty may be imposed on such importation, not exceeding ten dollars for each person.

B. Help the students (as a large group) paraphrase this excerpt. Answers will vary, but the paraphrasing should be similar to the following:

Congress will not prohibit the importation of slaves [such persons] before 1808 and Congress may tax each imported slave at a rate of $10 each.

Explain to the students that they will listen to and analyze the arguments offered during the debate about this clause at the Constitutional Convention.

IV. In His Own Words [20 minutes]

A. Distribute **Handout B—Vocabulary and Context Questions.**

B. Distribute **Handout C—In His Own Words: Charles Pinckney and the Issue of Slavery.** Be sure that the students understand the vocabulary and the "who, what, where, and when" of the document.

C. Choose ten students who are good dramatic readers to read the parts of the ten delegates to the Convention. Give the students a couple of minutes to review the parts, and encourage them to read with fervor.

D. Give the students **Handout D—Analysis: Debate about Article I, Section 9, Clause 1.** Divide the class into groups, one group for each of the delegates. Have each group complete the appropriate sections of **Handout D.** It might be helpful to have a brief discussion of the differences between moral, economic, and political arguments for and against slavery.

V. Wrap-Up Discussion [5 minutes]

Have the students share their answers to **Handout D.** Ask them to consider which delegates defended slavery and which opposed it. Did any delegates take a middle ground in regard to slavery?

Answers will vary.

LESSON PLAN

VI. Follow-Up Homework Options

A. Have the students summarize in a short essay the arguments of one delegate, based on **Handouts C** and **D.** Be sure to assign each delegate to at least one student.

B. Have the students assume the identity of one of the delegates and write a diary entry that describes his thoughts and feelings as he spends a day at the convention. Again, be sure to assign each delegate to at least one student.

VII. Extensions

Mr. Madison. At the conclusion of the debate about Article I, Section 9, Clause 1, James Madison made the following comment:

"Twenty years will produce all the mischief that can be apprehended from the liberty to import slaves. So long a term will be more dishonorable to the National character than to say nothing about it in the Constitution."

The Debate Continues. Thirty years after the Constitutional Convention, Charles Pinckney, then a member of the House of Representatives, participated in the debates regarding the admission of Maine and Missouri to the Union. Both states were admitted, Maine as a free state and Missouri as a slave state, along with the added proviso that slavery would be prohibited north of 36°30' latitude. This arrangement is known as the Missouri Compromise. Pinckney's comments included the following:

In considering this article, I will detail, as far as at this distant period is possible, what was the intention of the Convention that formed the Constitution in this article. The intention was, to give Congress a power, after the year 1808, to prevent the importation of slaves either by land or water from other countries. The word import, includes both, and applies wholly to slaves. Without this limitation, Congress might have stopped it sooner under their general power to regulate commerce; and it was an agreed point, a solemnly understood compact, that, on the Southern States consenting to shut their ports against the importation of Africans, no power was to be delegated to Congress, nor were they ever to be authorized to touch the question of slavery; that the property of the Southern States in slaves was to be as sacredly preserved, and protected to them, as that of land, or any other kind of property in the Eastern States were to be to their citizens. (14 February, 1820)

I perfectly knew that there did not then exist such a thing in the Union as a black or colored citizen, nor could I then have conceived it possible such a thing could have ever existed in it; nor, notwithstanding all that has been said on the subject, do I now believe one does exist in it. (13 February, 1821)

Sources: "Charles Pinckney, House of Representatives, 14 February 1820." The Founders' Constitution. **<http://press-pubs.uchicago.edu/founders/documents/a1_9_1s23.html>**.

"Missouri Compromise (1820)." Our Documents. National Archives and Records Administration. **<http://www.ourdocuments.gov/doc.php?doc=22>**.

Suggestions:

A. Students could write a brief paper in which they use historical evidence to prove that Madison's prediction was right (or wrong).

B. Students could compare Pinckney's views with those expressed by him (and others) thirty years earlier at the Constitutional Convention.

C. Students could consider why Pinckney and his fellow Southerners were so deeply committed to slavery as an institution.

D. Pinckney's words about the inferiority of Africans, quoted at the beginning of this lesson, could serve as a starting point for a discussion about racial attitudes in eighteenth-century America.

Resources

Print

Broussard, James H. *The Southern Federalists, 1800–1816.* Baton Rouge: Louisiana State University Press, 1978.

Singer, Charles Gregg. *South Carolina in the Confederation.* Philadelphia: Porcupine Press, 1976.

Weir, Robert M. "South Carolinians and the Adoption of the United States Constitution." *South Carolina Historical Magazine* 89 (April 1988): 73–89.

Williams, Frances Leigh. *A Founding Family: The Pinckneys of South Carolina.* New York: Harcourt Brace Jovanovich, 1978.

Zahnhiser, Marvin R. *Charles Cotesworth Pinckney, Founding Father.* Chapel Hill: University of North Carolina Press, 1967.

Internet

Annals of Congress, 16th Congress, 2nd Session. <**http://memory.loc.gov/ammem/amlaw/lwac.html**>.

"Charles Pinckney and the U.S. Constitution." The Charleston Multimedia Project. <**http://www.ccpl.org/ ccl/cpinckney.html**>.

"Charles Pinckney, South Carolina." U.S. National Archives and Records Administration. <**http://www.archives.gov/exhibit_hall/charters_of_freedom/constitution/south_carolina.html #Pinckney**>.

"The Debates in the Federal Convention of 1787 reported by James Madison: August 22." The Avalon Project at Yale Law School. <**http://www.yale.edu/lawweb/avalon/debates/822.htm**>.

"The Plan of Charles Pinckney (South Carolina), Presented to the Federal Convention, May 29, 1787." The Avalon Project at Yale Law School. <**http://www.yale.edu/lawweb/avalon/const/pinckney.htm**>.

Selected Works by Charles Pinckney
- ***The Plan Presented to the Federal Convention*** (1787)

CHARLES PINCKNEY (1757–1824)

We may congratulate ourselves with living under the blessings of a mild and equal government, which knows no distinctions but those of merits or talents—under a government whose honors and offices are equally open to the exertions of all her citizens, and which adopts virtue and worth for her own, wheresoever she can find them.

—*Charles Pinckney, May 14, 1788, at the South Carolina Ratifying Convention*

The room fell silent as the president of the Constitutional Convention called the delegates to order. A new article was read. Almost immediately, a familiar voice filled the hall. Charles Pinckney was, once again, sharing his opinion. He had a view on everything, as the delegates knew well. Many at the Convention distrusted Pinckney, thinking he was too young, too proud, and too ambitious. No one, however, would deny his contributions to the Constitution or to the continuing debate about slavery.

Background

Charles Pinckney was born on October 26, 1757, near Charles Town (now Charleston), South Carolina. His father was a well-known lawyer and slaveholding planter whose wealth made it possible for young Pinckney to study languages and the law from local tutors. Pinckney had hoped to continue his studies in England, as his cousins Thomas and Charles Cotesworth Pinckney had, but the American Revolution changed his plans.

Forced to remain in South Carolina, Pinckney studied in his father's office and was admitted to the bar in 1779. Election to the South Carolina Assembly quickly followed. At the same time, he joined the militia and fought in losing battles against the British in Savannah and Charleston. When his city surrendered, he became a prisoner of war but was released in the summer of 1781, a few months prior to the great American victory at Yorktown.

Representative Pinckney

By 1784, Pinckney was back in Philadelphia. For the next two years, he sat as a representative of South Carolina in the new Confederation Congress. He soon became convinced that the Articles of Confederation were flawed. He saw firsthand their weaknesses and concluded that the growing nation needed a strong central government. Without one, he believed that established foreign powers would not give financial or political credit to the new country.

In May 1786, Pinckney suggested revising the Articles. He was named to a new committee for revision and drafted most of the amendments proposed. But Pinckney then went further and advocated a "general convention of the states for the purposes of increasing the powers of the federal government and rendering it more adequate for the ends for which it was ratified." By the fall of 1787, however, he acknowledged the need to create a completely new form of government.

Constitution Charlie

When the Constitutional Convention was organized in Philadelphia in 1787, South Carolina sent Pinckney as one of her four delegates. Twenty-nine years of age, he was one of the youngest men there. Many considered him too vain and ambitious. Nevertheless, he was one of the most active participants in the proceedings, speaking more than one hundred times. Pinckney was eager to contribute and make a name for himself. In his later years, those who knew him playfully referred to him as "Constitution Charlie" because he often referred to his contributions at Philadelphia.

Early in the debates, Pinckney gave a celebrated speech in which he trumpeted the uniqueness of America. "Our true situation," he declared, "appears to me to be this—a new extensive Country containing within itself the materials for forming a Government capable of extending to its citizens all the blessings of civil & religious liberty." At the convention, Pinckney championed civil liberties, and though the safeguards he suggested were not incorporated into the new Constitution, many of them were later included in the Bill of Rights.

Some of Pinckney's ideas did, however, make their way into the Constitution. He is credited, for example, for being the first to use the term *Senate*. He worked to prohibit religious qualifications for public office. He also pushed for a "vigorous Executive," but with limitations. He feared that if the executive had too much power in the realms of war and peace, then the system "would render the Executive a Monarchy, of the worst kind, to wit an elective one." Despite his fear of an overzealous ruler, he supported a single executive, with the title President, instead of a governing body. These ideas were part of the plan of government he introduced at Philadelphia—a plan similar to the Virginia Plan, which was offered the same day and which resembled closely the final version of the Constitution.

An advocate of elitist government, he proposed high property qualifications for federal office, arguing that "the Legislature, the Executive, and the judges should be possessed of competent property to make them independent and respectable." He encouraged the selection of representatives by state legislatures and wanted the legislature, not the executive, to choose justices for the Supreme Court. Pinckney also favored a federal veto over state laws and backed an effort to establish a national university. But these two proposals failed to pass.

Pinckney did not back away from difficult issues. As a large slaveholder, he was steadfast in his support of the institution of black slavery and defended the slave trade, a practice that even many of his fellow southerners found revolting. He deemed the trade in human flesh to be "in the interest of the whole Union," and he warned that "South Carolina can never receive the plan [of the new national government] if it prohibits the slave trade." In the end, however, believing the Constitution to be on the whole a worthy document, he was ready to compromise on the issue, agreeing to the clause that prohibited Congress's interference with the practice for twenty years. He reassured antislavery delegates by suggesting, "if the States be all left at liberty on this subject, South Carolina may perhaps by degrees do of herself what is wished [banning the importation of slaves], as Virginia and Maryland have already done."

The debates at Philadelphia ended, compromises were made, the vote was taken, and the Constitution was sent to the states. Pinckney diligently pursued its ratification in South Carolina, making passionate speeches in support of the new government. He told his fellow South Carolinians that they should be "astonishingly pleased" that a government "so perfect could have been formed from such discordant and unpromising material." On May 23, 1788, South Carolina became the eighth state to ratify the Constitution.

The Question of Slavery Continued

In the years that followed, Pinckney continued to be active in state and national politics, initially as an ally of those who formed the Federalist Party. He was elected governor of South Carolina four times, served as senator two terms, and sat as a member of the House of Representatives for one term. In the early 1800s, Pinckney, like most Southerners, became uncomfortable with Federalist policies and embraced the Jeffersonian Republicans instead. Pinckney served as ambassador to Spain for the Jefferson Administration.

Thereafter, Pinckney returned to the national arena only once before his death in 1824. To prevent the election of a Federalist, he ran for and was elected to the House of Representatives in 1819. In the House, he participated in the debates about the western expansion of slavery, opposing the Missouri Compromise, which proposed to ban slavery in the rest of the Louisiana Territory above 36°30' latitude. In the debate about the extension of slavery, "Constitution Charlie" relied heavily on his personal experience at the Philadelphia Convention, arguing that Congress was never "authorized to touch the question of slavery." Had Southerners known that Northerners intended to meddle with the institution, Pinckney declared, "no Constitution would have been achieved." But the Missouri Compromise passed, the balance between slave and free states in the Union was preserved, and the resolution of the slavery question was left for another day. For the nation, it was the beginning of heightened sectional discord. For Charles Pinckney, it was the end of an era.

Reading Comprehension Questions

1. What were Pinckney's contributions to the Constitution?

2. Which provisions supported by Pinckney never made it into the final version of the Constitution?

Critical Thinking Questions

3. Explain how Pinckney was consistent when he supported the slave trade at the Constitutional Convention and later opposed the Missouri Compromise.

4. You are young Charles Pinckney attending the first day of the Constitutional Convention. You have your plan for the government in hand and you are preparing to speak, when the Virginia Plan is introduced. You've been "beaten to the punch"! How do you deal with the situation?

5. Describe a time in your own life when someone beat you to the punch. How did you deal with it?

VOCABULARY AND CONTEXT QUESTIONS

Excerpt from *Notes of Debates in the Federal Convention of 1787*
(reported by James Madison)

1. **Vocabulary:** *Use context clues to determine the meaning or significance of each of these words and write their definitions:*

    a. apportionment

    b. apprehensive

    c. insurrections

    d. exempt

    e. commodities

    f. meddle

    g. meddling

    h. expedient

    i. dispatching

    j. render

    k. provision

    l. sanction

    m. avail

    n. assent

    o. contend

    p. consumption

    q. revenue

    r. impeded

    s. sagacity

    t. traffic

2. **Context:** *Answer the following questions.*

    a. When was this document written?

    b. Where was this document written?

    c. Who wrote this document?

    d. What type of document is this?

    e. What was the purpose of this document?

    f. Who was the audience for this document?

IN HIS OWN WORDS:
CHARLES PINCKNEY AND THE ISSUE OF SLAVERY

**Excerpt from *Notes of Debates in the Federal Convention of 1787*
(reported by James Madison)**

Note: *Before reading the following excerpt, please note that it is taken from the debate about Article I, Section 9, Clause 1, with two major changes. The dialogue is now conveyed in the **present** tense, and from the **first person point of view** ("I" rather than "he"). Also, capitalization, punctuation, and spelling have been modernized.*

August 22, 1787

Luther Martin (Maryland): I propose . . . to allow a prohibition or tax on the importation of slaves as five slaves are to be counted as 3 free men in the apportionment of Representatives; such a clause would leave an encouragement to this traffic. Slaves weaken one part of the Union, which the other parts are bound to protect: the privilege of importing them is therefore unreasonable. It is inconsistent with the principles of the revolution and dishonorable to the American character to have such a feature in the Constitution.

John Rutledge (South Carolina): I am not apprehensive of insurrections and would readily exempt the other states from the obligation to protect the southern against them. Religion and humanity have nothing to do with this question. Interest alone is the governing principle with nations. The true question at present is whether the southern states shall or shall not be parties to the Union. If the northern states consult their interest, they will not oppose the increase of slaves, which will increase the commodities of which they will become the carriers.

Oliver Ellsworth (Connecticut): I believe we should leave the clause as it stands. Let every state import what it pleases. The morality or wisdom of slavery are considerations belonging to the states themselves. What enriches a part enriches the whole, and the states are the best judges of their particular interest. The old confederation did not meddle with this point, and I do not see any greater necessity for bringing it within the policy of the new one.

Charles Pinckney (South Carolina): South Carolina can never receive the plan [the Constitution] if it prohibits the slave trade. In every proposed extension of the powers of the Congress, that state has expressly and watchfully excepted that of meddling with the importation of negroes. If the states be all left at liberty on this subject, South Carolina may perhaps by degrees do of herself what is wished, as Virginia and Maryland have already done.

Roger Sherman (Connecticut): I disapprove of the slave trade; yet as the states were now possessed of the right to import slaves, as the public good did not require it to be taken from them, and as it was expedient to have as few objections as possible to the proposed scheme of government, I think it best to leave the matter as we find it. The abolition of slavery seems to be going on in the U.S., and the good sense of the several states will probably by degrees complete it. I urge on the Convention the necessity of dispatching its business.

George Mason (Virginia): The present question concerns not the importing states alone but the whole Union. . . . Maryland and Virginia have already prohibited the importation of slaves expressly. North Carolina has done the same in substance. All this will be in vain if South Carolina and Georgia are at liberty to import. The western people are already calling out for slaves for their new lands, and will fill that country with slaves if they can be got through South Carolina and Georgia. Slavery discourages arts and manufactures. The poor despise labor when performed by slaves. They prevent the immigration of whites, who really enrich and strengthen a country. They produce the most pernicious effect on manners. Every master of slaves is born a petty tyrant. They bring the judgment of heaven on a country. As nations cannot be rewarded or punished in the next world they must be in this. By an inevitable chain of causes and effects providence punishes national sins, by national calamities. I lament that some of our eastern brethren have from a lust of gain embarked in this nefarious traffic. As to the states being in possession of the right to import, this is the case with many other rights, now to be properly given up. I hold it essential in every point of view that the general government should have power to prevent the increase of slavery.

Oliver Ellsworth (Connecticut): Since I have never owned a slave, I cannot judge of the effects of slavery on character: However, if it is to be considered in a moral light we ought to go farther and free those already in the country. . . . As population increases, poor laborers will be so plenty as to render slaves useless. Slavery in time will not be a speck in our country. Provision is already made in Connecticut for abolishing it. And the abolition has already taken place in Massachusetts.

Charles Pinckney (South Carolina): If slavery be wrong, it is justified by the example of all the world. I cite the case of Greece, Rome, and other ancient states; the sanction given by France, England, Holland, and other modern states. In all ages one half of mankind have been slaves. If the southern states were let alone they will probably of themselves stop importations. I would myself as a citizen of South Carolina vote for it. An attempt to take away the right as proposed will produce serious objections to the Constitution which I wish to see adopted.

Charles Cotesworth Pinckney [second cousin of Charles Pinckney] (South Carolina): I declare it to be my firm opinion that if I and all my colleagues were to sign the Constitution and use our personal influence, it would be of no avail towards obtaining the assent of our constituents. South Carolina and Georgia cannot do without slaves. As to Virginia she will gain by stopping the importations. Her slaves will rise in value, and she has more than she wants. It would be unequal to require South Carolina and Georgia to confederate on such unequal terms. . . . I contend that the importation of slaves would be for the interest of the whole Union. The more slaves, the more produce to employ the carrying trade; the more consumption also, and the more of this, the more of revenue for the common treasury. I admit it to be reasonable that slaves should be duties like other imports, but should consider a rejection of the clause as an exclusion of South Carolina from the Union.

John Dickinson (Delaware): I consider it inadmissible on every principle of honor and safety that the importation of slaves should be authorized to the states by the Constitution. The true question was whether the national happiness would be promoted or impeded by the importation, and this question ought to be left to the national government, not to the states particularly interested.

Rufus King (Massachusetts): I think the subject should be considered in a political light only. If two states will not agree to the Constitution as stated on one side, I can affirm with equal belief on the other, that great and equal opposition would be experienced from the other states. I believe that the exemption of slaves from duty whilst every other import was subjected to it, as an inequality that could not fail to strike the commercial sagacity of the northern and middle states.

John Langdon (New Hampshire): We must give this power to the general government. I cannot with a good conscience leave it with the states who could then go on with the traffic, without being restrained by the opinions here given that they will themselves cease to import slaves.

Charles Cotesworth Pinckney (South Carolina): I am bound to declare candidly that I do not think South Carolina will stop her importations of slaves in any short time, but only stop them occasionally as she now does.

Source: "The Debates in the Federal Convention of 1787 reported by James Madison: August 22." The Avalon Project at Yale University Law School. <**http://www.yale.edu/lawweb/avalon/debates/822.htm**>.

ANALYSIS:
DEBATE ABOUT ARTICLE I, SECTION 9, CLAUSE 1

Directions: *In each of the Statements columns, mark Y (Yes) if the statement applies; mark N (No) if it does not apply; mark X if you cannot determine the position from the document excerpt. In the appropriate columns labeled Moral, Economic, and Political, summarize or paraphrase the arguments of each speaker (not every speaker uses all three types of argument). Please remember that several of the speakers have more than one passage.*

SPEAKER	STATEMENTS			ARGUMENTS		
	1. He supports slavery.	2. He supports some federal regulation of slavery.	3. He supports taxation on slaves as imported property.	Moral	Economic	Political
Martin						
Rutledge						
Ellsworth						
Pinckney						
Sherman						
Mason						
Genl. Pinckney						
Dickinson						
King						
Langdon						

ROGER SHERMAN
(1721–1793)

Government is instituted for those who live under it.

—*Roger Sherman, 1787*

Introduction

Although not the most charismatic or eloquent Founder, Roger Sherman was highly esteemed by his contemporaries. At Sherman's death, Ezra Stiles, president of Yale College, wrote, "He was an extraordinary man—a venerable uncorrupted patriot." A talented politician, Sherman was also a man of deep religious faith who approached life seriously. Thomas Jefferson once claimed that the Connecticut statesman "never said a foolish thing in his life." A self-made man with the power of common sense and the ability to compromise, Sherman was completely dedicated to public service at both the state and national levels. He had a hand in the creation of the Declaration of Independence, the Articles of Confederation, and the Constitution.

Sherman was an early champion of union first among the colonies and then among the states. He understood the benefits of having a central government that could address national needs and handle international affairs. Sherman jealously guarded the rights of the people of America in general and of Connecticut in particular against encroachments by, first, the government of Great Britain, and, after independence, the government of the United States. A leader of American opposition to British tyranny in the 1760s and 1770s, he served in the First and Second Continental Congresses and was a member of the committee that drafted the Declaration of Independence. At the Constitutional Convention of 1787, he fought to protect the rights of the states, thereby lending support to the principle of federalism that was crucial to the American system of government.

Relevant Thematic Essay for Roger Sherman
- Federalism

In His Own Words:
ROGER SHERMAN
ON THE ROLE OF GOVERNMENT

Overview

In this lesson, students will learn about Roger Sherman. They should first read as background homework **Handout A—Roger Sherman (1721–1793)** and answer the **Reading Comprehension Questions.** After discussing the answers to these questions in class, the teacher should have the students answer the **Critical Thinking Questions** as a class. Next, the teacher should introduce the students to the primary source activity, **Handout C—In His Own Words: Roger Sherman on the Role of Government,** in which students consider how government affects their everyday life and compare Sherman's view of the role of government with the reality of today. As a preface, there is **Handout B—Context Questions,** which will help the students understand the document.

There are **Follow-Up Homework Options** that ask the students to find a news article that illustrates the federal government either fulfilling one of the roles of which Sherman approved, or fulfilling a role of which he disapproved. The students will then write a one-paragraph essay from Sherman's point of view, explaining how the government is properly fulfilling, or exceeding, its role. **Extensions** provides opportunity for thought as students are asked to research how a contemporary problem has been addressed by government.

Objectives

Students will:

- understand Sherman's contributions to public service
- appreciate Sherman's role as a leader of the American opposition to British tyranny
- analyze Sherman's view of the proper division of power between the states and the national government
- understand the reasons for Sherman's initial opposition to a bill of rights
- explain Sherman's view of the role of government

Standards
  CCE (9–12): IIA1, IIC1, IIIA1, IIIA2
  NCHS (5–12): Era III, Standards 3A, 3B
  NCSS: Strands 2, 5, 6, and 10

Materials
Student Handouts
- Handout A—Roger Sherman (1721–1793)
- Handout B—Context Questions
- Handout C—In His Own Words: Roger Sherman on the Role of Government

Additional Teacher Resource
- Answer Key

Recommended Time
  One 45-minute class period. Additional time as needed for homework.

LESSON PLAN

I. **Background Homework**
    Ask students to read **Handout A—Roger Sherman (1721–1793)** and answer the Reading Comprehension Questions.

II. **Warm-Up** [10 minutes]
    A. Review answers to homework questions.
    B. Conduct a whole-class discussion to answer the Critical Thinking Questions.
    C. Ask a student to summarize the historical significance of Roger Sherman.

    Roger Sherman was a leader of American opposition to British tyranny in the 1760s and 1770s. He served in the First and Second Continental Congresses and was a member of the committee that drafted the Declaration of Independence. At the Constitutional Convention of 1787, he fought to protect the rights of the states, championing the principle of federalism that was crucial to the American system of government. Sherman had a hand in the creation of the Declaration of Independence, the Articles of Confederation, and the Constitution. He initially opposed adding a bill of rights to the Constitution but later changed his mind and worked to win the approval of Connecticut for the Bill of Rights.

III. **Context** [5 minutes]
    A. Briefly review with students the idea of federalism, an invention of the American Founders. (In a federal system, government power is divided between central and local governments, each of which is supreme in its sphere.)
    B. Also review with students the main issues involved in the debate between Federalists and Anti-Federalists. (The Federalists asserted the need for a stronger central government and believed that the confederation of the states would break up if the Constitution was not ratified. Anti-Federalists feared that a stronger central government would endanger the rights of the people and the states.)

IV. **In His Own Words** [20 minutes]
    A. Ask the students to brainstorm ways in which government touches their lives on a daily basis. (See the Answer Key for possible responses.) Write their answers on the board. Then ask them to label each example according to which level of government—federal, state, and/or local—is involved. Place an *F* next to the item for federal, an *S* next to state, and an *L* next to local. (Many examples will be labeled more than once.)
    B. Ask the students to consider which of the activities on the list are legitimate functions of government at some level. Place stars next to these activities. Place lines through those activities that are not legitimate activities of government at any level.
    C. Distribute **Handout B—Context Questions.** Be sure that the students understand the "who, what, where, and when" of the document.
    D. Distribute **Handout C—In His Own Words: Roger Sherman on the Role of Government.**
    E. Ask a student to read the excerpt from the speech by Sherman to the class.

LESSON PLAN

V. Wrap-Up Discussion [10 minutes]
Conduct a whole-class discussion about Sherman's view of the role of government.
A. In 1787, what did he say about the roles of the federal and state governments?
B. Today, what would Sherman say about the roles of government listed on the board?
C. Why do you think the role of government has expanded since 1787?
See Answer Key.

VI. Follow-Up Homework Options
A. Have the students find a news article that illustrates the federal government fulfilling a role of which Sherman approved. Have the students write a one-paragraph essay from Sherman's point of view, explaining how the government is properly fulfilling this role.
B. Have the students find a news article that illustrates the federal government fulfilling a role of which Sherman might have disapproved. Have the students write a one-paragraph essay from Sherman's point of view, explaining how the government is exceeding its proper role.

VII. Extensions
Have the students select a contemporary problem and research how the federal, state, or local government responded to that problem. Then have them write a two- to three-page paper in which they (1) recommend which level of government—if any—should address that problem and (2) state how the problem should be addressed. Topics for research could include the following:
- Pollution
- Lack of medical care
- Failing schools
- Crime
- Terrorism

LESSON PLAN

Resources

Print

Bradford, M. E. *Founding Fathers: Brief Lives of the Framers of the United States Constitution.* Lawrence: University Press of Kansas, 1994.

Collier, Christopher. *Roger Sherman's Connecticut: Yankee Politics and the American Revolution.* Middletown, CT: Wesleyan University Press, 1971.

Kurland, Philip B., and Ralph Lerner. *The Founders' Constitution.* 5 vols. Indianapolis: Liberty Fund, 1987.

McDonald, Forrest. *E Pluribus Unum: The Formation of the American Republic, 1776–1790.* Reprint. Indianapolis: Liberty Fund, 1979.

Rommel, John G. *Connecticut's Yankee Patriot: Roger Sherman.* Hartford: American Revolution Bicentennial Commission of Connecticut, 1980.

Internet

"The Charters of Freedom: America's Founding Fathers." The National Archives and Records Administration. <**http://www.archives.gov/exhibit_hall/charters_of_freedom/constitution/connecticut.html**>.

"The Debates in the Federal Convention of 1787 reported by James Madison." The Avalon Project at Yale University Law School. <**http://www.yale.edu/lawweb/avalon/debates/debcont.htm**>.

"Roger Sherman." New Milford Historical Society. <**http://www.nmhistorical.org/learningzone/sherman.htm**>.

"Roger Sherman, 1721–1793." Colonial Hall. <**http://www.colonialhall.com/sherman/sherman.asp**>.

"Sherman, Roger." Biographical Directory of the United States Congress. <**http://bioguide.congress.gov/scripts/biodisplay.pl?index=S000349**>.

Selected Works by Roger Sherman
- Letter to John Adams, July 20, 1789

ROGER SHERMAN (1721–1793)

The Constitution should lay as few temptations as is possible in the way of those in power.

—*Roger Sherman, 1787*

Philadelphia was hot and still as darkness descended on the evening of June 22, 1787. The city was the site of the Constitutional Convention, which had begun a month earlier. Its purpose was to fashion a new system of government for the young American republic. Inside the rented quarters of a small house near Convention Hall, Roger Sherman, the tall, stern, plainly dressed delegate from Connecticut, was having dinner with a delegate from South Carolina. Sherman was engaged in one of his favorite activities: hard-nosed political bargaining. He was hoping to obtain the South Carolina delegate's support for Connecticut's claim to western lands in return for supporting protection of the slave trade and a prohibition against the taxing of exported goods. Sixty-six years of age and a devout Calvinist, "Father Sherman," as many of the delegates called him, had a well-deserved reputation for honesty. The delegate from South Carolina had no doubt that Sherman would live up to any bargain the two men struck. And he also knew that he could trust the elder statesman to keep their dinner meeting a secret.

Background

Roger Sherman was born in 1721 in Newton, Massachusetts, the son of a farmer. When he was two years old, his family moved to Stoughton. There Sherman attended the common school and learned the practice of shoemaking from his father. He spent his spare time studying theology, mathematics, history, and law. In 1743, two years after his father's death, Sherman and his family joined his older brother in New Milford, Connecticut.

In New Milford, Sherman opened a shoemaker—or "cobbler"—shop and earned a position as the county surveyor in 1745. The income from this office enabled him to buy land and to earn a favorable reputation throughout the county. Sherman published a series of almanacs between 1750 and 1761. He also studied law on his own, passing the bar in 1754.

During the next few years, Sherman served in the General Assembly, as a justice of the peace, and as a justice of the county court. In 1761, he gave up practicing law and moved to New Haven, Connecticut. There he opened a large general store and later served as treasurer of Yale College.

During the 1760s, Sherman became a leader of American resistance to British tyranny. Ever moderate and practical, however, he initially favored peaceful forms of protest, such as boycotts and petitions. In order to devote more time to public affairs, he retired from business in 1772. Two years later, Connecticut sent him as a representative to the First Continental Congress.

Continental Congress and the Declaration of Independence

While in Philadelphia, Sherman established himself as a peer among the most respected and well-educated men of the colonies. He voiced his opinions with clarity, if without eloquence. The Continental Congress passed the Articles of Association, which established a nonimportation and nonexportation policy in the colonies. The colonies vowed to boycott goods coming from Great Britain and to refrain from delivering goods to the mother country.

In 1775, Sherman returned for the Second Continental Congress, where he served on various committees dealing with foreign trade and military supply and planning. That same year, fighting broke out between colonial and British forces, and so the issue of formally creating an independent nation soon arose. When the time came to pick a committee to draft a declaration of independence, Sherman was chosen along with John Adams, Robert Livingston, Benjamin Franklin, and Thomas Jefferson. They were known as the Committee of Five.

The committee outlined the declaration and chose Jefferson to write the actual document. Jefferson presented his draft to Sherman and the other members of the committee, who made revisions. In June 1776, the committee agreed upon a final draft, which was presented to Congress. Once the delegates approved the document, Roger Sherman signed his name to the Declaration of Independence.

Sherman kept busy in committees throughout the Second Continental Congress. The military committees were soon organized into the Board of War. Sherman's business background qualified him to handle purchasing and distribution of supplies. He also dealt with military correspondence and served on committees that handled economic issues and Indian affairs.

Articles of Confederation

In June 1776, Congress appointed Sherman to the committee that drafted a plan of union for the colonies. The Articles of Confederation were approved by Congress the next year. But concerns about representation and taxation delayed ratification of the document by the states until 1781.

While debate about the Articles of Confederation continued in the states, Sherman maintained his devotion to public service and Connecticut politics. He served in the state senate, on the Council of Safety, and as judge of the superior court. In 1783, he returned to Congress to approve the Treaty of Paris. The next year he was elected the first mayor of New Haven.

Constitution of the United States

In 1787, at the age of sixty-six, Sherman was chosen as one of Connecticut's delegates to a convention whose purpose was to revise the Articles of Confederation. Soon after the convention began in Philadelphia, it became clear that most of the delegates wanted to create an entirely new government.

Sherman consented to the writing of a new constitution, but he was afraid of making the central government too strong. During the convention, therefore, he worked to guard the power of the states against the national government. He believed that the authority of the national government should be carefully restricted to a few areas. "All other matters civil & criminal," Sherman proclaimed on June 6, 1787, "would be much better in the hands of the States."

In order to protect the people's liberty, Sherman also argued for placing the balance of the national government's power in the legislature. He asserted that the executive was "nothing more than an institution for carrying the will of the Legislature into effect." To this end, Sherman proposed that the president be chosen by Congress and serve at its pleasure.

© The Bill of Rights Institute

Sherman spoke at least one hundred thirty-eight times during the convention on a variety of subjects. He consistently argued for the careful limiting of government power. He also proposed the Great Compromise, which decided the method of representation in the Congress. By this agreement, the Congress would be divided into two houses. In the Senate, each state would have an equal vote. In the House of Representatives, each state would be represented according to its population. The Great Compromise settled the most difficult issue dividing the large and small states.

Sherman opposed listing the people's rights in the Constitution. He feared that such a bill of rights would give the federal government the authority to intervene in state affairs. Also, any such list would surely omit certain rights held by the people. This could be used by tyrants to take away the people's rights.

Ratification and the First Congress

Sherman was not entirely happy with the final version of the Constitution. But he supported ratification of the document. He played an important role in Connecticut's decision to approve the Constitution.

In 1789, Sherman took a seat in the new House of Representatives. In the first Congress, he supported James Madison's effort to add a bill of rights to the Constitution. Ever flexible, Sherman had changed his mind on this issue. He came to favor a bill of rights because the people of Connecticut supported one. In 1791, the seventy-year-old Sherman was appointed to the United States Senate, where he served until his death in July 1793.

Reading Comprehension Questions

1. Which important founding documents did Roger Sherman help to create?

2. What was Sherman's attitude toward the power of the national government at the Constitutional Convention?

3. What important dispute between the large and small states at the Constitutional Convention did Sherman help to resolve?

Critical Thinking Questions

4. Ezra Stiles, the president of Yale College, described Roger Sherman as "an extraordinary man." Why do you think Sherman deserved such high praise?

5. Historian Forrest McDonald writes that Sherman "combined incorruptible moral rectitude with wily political talent." Do you think it is possible for a person to have both good morals and good political skills? Why or why not?

CONTEXT QUESTIONS

From a speech by Roger Sherman, June 6, 1787, at the Constitutional Convention

Answer the following questions. Note that some of these answers must be inferred.

   a.   When was this document written?

   b.   Where was this document written?

   c.   Who wrote this document?

   d.   What type of document is this?

   e.   What was the purpose of this document?

   f.   Who was the audience for this document?

IN HIS OWN WORDS:
ROGER SHERMAN ON THE ROLE OF GOVERNMENT

Note: *Before reading the following excerpt, please note that it is taken from* Madison's Notes of Debates in the Federal Convention, *with a few changes. The dialogue is now conveyed in the **present** tense, and from the **first person point of view** ("I" rather than "he"). Also, punctuation, capitalization, spelling, formatting, and abbreviations have been changed for the sake of clarity.*

From a speech by Roger Sherman, June 6, 1787, at the Constitutional Convention

The objects of the Union are few:
1. defense against foreign danger.
2. [defense] against internal disputes and a resort to force.
3. treaties with foreign nations.
4. regulating foreign commerce, and drawing revenue from it.

These and perhaps a few lesser objects alone render a Confederation of the States necessary. All other matters civil and criminal would be much better in the hands of the States. . . . I am for giving the General Government power to legislate and execute [the laws] within a defined province.

Source: "The Debates in the Federal Convention of 1787 Reported by James Madison: June 6." The Avalon Project at Yale Law School. <**http://www.yale.edu/lawweb/avalon/debates/606.htm**>.

Discussion Questions

1. In 1787, what did Sherman say about the roles of the federal and state governments?

2. Today, what would Sherman say about the roles of government listed on the board?

3. Why do you think the role of government has expanded since 1787?

JOHN WITHERSPOON
(1723–1794)

Nothing is more certain than that a general profligacy and corruption of manners make a people ripe for destruction. A good form of government may hold the rotten materials together for some time, but beyond a certain pitch, even the best constitution will be ineffectual, and slavery must ensue.

—*John Witherspoon*

Introduction

John Witherspoon, a Scottish immigrant to America, was a minister, member of the Continental Congresses, and signer of the Declaration of Independence. He made his most important contribution to the causes of American independence and liberty, however, in his role as an educator. Witherspoon was president of the College of New Jersey (later, Princeton University) for twenty-six years, between 1768 and 1794. His ideas about religion, education, and free enterprise had a significant impact on his contemporaries. Witherspoon himself taught one president (James Madison) and one vice president (Aaron Burr). He also instructed nine cabinet officers, twenty-one senators, thirty-nine congressmen, three justices of the Supreme Court, and twelve state governors. Five of the fifty-five members of the Constitutional Convention were his former students.

Witherspoon's impact on the ministry of the Presbyterian Church was also significant. Of the one hundred seventy-seven ministers in America in 1777, fifty-two of them had been Witherspoon's students. As a clergyman active in public affairs, Witherspoon resented the clause in Georgia's new constitution of 1777 that expressly forbade clergymen of any denomination from sitting in the legislature. He wrote a letter protesting this exclusion, but the clause was not removed until 1798, four years after Witherspoon's death.

Relevant Thematic Essays for John Witherspoon
- Freedom of Religion
- Limited Government (Volume 2)

In His Own Words:
JOHN WITHERSPOON
ON THE CLERGY IN POLITICS

Overview

In this lesson, students will learn about John Witherspoon. They should first read as background homework **Handout A—John Witherspoon (1723–1794)** and answer the **Reading Comprehension Questions.** After discussing the answers to these questions in class, the teacher should have the students answer the **Critical Thinking Questions** as a class. The teacher should then review what the Constitution (in Article VI) says about a religious test for office. Next, the teacher should introduce the students to the primary source activity, **Handout C—In His Own Words: John Witherspoon on the Clergy in Politics,** in which Witherspoon offers his ironic commentary on the role of the clergy in politics. As a preface, there is **Handout B—Vocabulary and Context Questions,** which will help the students understand the document, and, as a follow-up, there is **Handout D—Discussion Questions.**

There are **Follow-Up Homework Options** that ask the students to analyze and reflect upon the role of the clergy in politics today. **Extensions** provides opportunity for thought as students are asked to compare religious liberty in the United States today with the role of religion in other historical or cultural environments.

Objectives

Students will:
- understand the significance of Article VI, Section 3 of the Constitution
- compare and contrast the statements about religion in the Georgia Constitution of 1777 with those in the federal Constitution
- analyze the concept of a "religious test" for public office and apply that concept to contemporary society
- appreciate the ironic humor of John Witherspoon

Standards
CCE (9–12): IIA1, IIC1, IIIA1, IIIA2
NCHS (5–12): Era III, Standards 3A, 3B
NCSS: Strands 2, 5, 6, and 10

Materials
Student Handouts
- Handout A—John Witherspoon (1723–1794)
- Handout B—Vocabulary and Context Questions
- Handout C—In His Own Words: John Witherspoon on the Clergy in Politics
- Handout D—Discussion Questions

Additional Teacher Resource
- Answer Key

Recommended Time
One 45-minute class period. Additional time as needed for homework.

LESSON PLAN

I. Background Homework

Ask students to read **Handout A—John Witherspoon (1723–1794)** and answer the Reading Comprehension Questions.

II. Warm-Up [10 minutes]

A. Review answers to homework questions.

B. Conduct a whole-class discussion to answer the Critical Thinking Questions.

C. Ask a student to summarize the historical significance of John Witherspoon.

John Witherspoon was a minister, college president, member of the Continental Congresses, and signer of the Declaration of Independence. His ideas about religion, education, and free enterprise had a significant impact on his contemporaries.

III. Context [5 minutes]

A. Explain to the students that the Constitution explicitly prohibits religious tests for office at the federal level. Write on the board (or distribute copies of) Article VI, Section 3 of the Constitution:

The Senators and Representatives before mentioned, and the members of the several state legislatures, and all executive and judicial Officers, both of the United States and of the several States, shall be bound by Oath or Affirmation, to support this Constitution; but no religious Test shall ever be required as a Qualification to any Office of public Trust under the United States.

B. Point out to the students that many of the Founders did not object to religious tests for office at the state level. Indeed, at the time the Constitution was adopted, several state constitutions included religious tests for office, for voting, or both. The Constitution indirectly acknowledges the validity of such religious tests for voting. Article I, Section 1 declares that each state's voting qualifications for its lower house shall be the voting qualifications for the United States House of Representatives:

The House of Representatives shall be composed of members chosen every second year by the people of the several States, and the elector in each State shall have the qualifications requisite for electors of the most numerous branch of the State Legislature.

C. Explain to the students that the Founders did not intend for the liberties and rights guaranteed by the first ten amendments to apply to the states. The idea that the amendments to the Constitution should apply to the states came much later, in the "incorporation" decisions issued by the Supreme Court. The establishment clause of the First Amendment, therefore, was binding only on the federal government:

Congress shall make no law respecting an establishment of religion, or prohibiting the free exercise thereof.

IV. In His Own Words [20 minutes]

A. Distribute **Handout B—Vocabulary and Context Questions.**

B. Distribute **Handout C—In His Own Words: John Witherspoon on the Clergy in Politics** and **Handout D—Discussion Questions.** Give students a few minutes to review the questions.

C. Read the letter aloud to students, emphasizing the irony and sarcasm of Witherspoon's writing. (Students sometimes find it difficult to determine the tone of a passage when reading it on their own.)

D. Ask students to pair up with partners to answer the discussion questions in **Handout D.**

E. Bring the class back together for large-group sharing.

V. Wrap-Up Discussion [10 minutes]

Ask the students to answer these questions:

A. What is a "religious test" for office?

A "religious test" for office means that a person must belong to a certain religious domination or adhere to certain religious beliefs in order to serve in elected office. This was a practice in England and in some of the American colonies.

B. Why does the Constitution prohibit such a test?

Because of the multiplicity of religious sects in America, the Founders determined that the official establishment of a particular religion at the federal level was both impractical and unjust.

VI. Follow-Up Homework Options

Students could answer the following questions in a class discussion or for homework:

A. Was the Georgia prohibition on ministers in public office a type of religious test?

B. Should members of the clergy (e.g., rabbis, ministers, priests, imams) be elected to public office? Why or why not?

VII. Extensions

Suggestions:

Students could compare and contrast the constitutional freedom of religion in the United States today with the role of religion in these societies:

A. seventeenth-century Massachusetts

B. eighteenth-century Virginia

C. contemporary Iran or Saudi Arabia

D. Afghanistan under the Taliban

LESSON PLAN

Resources

Print

Miller, Thomas, ed. *Selected Writings of John Witherspoon.* Carbondale: Southern Illinois University Press, 1990.

Morrison, Jeffrey Hays. "John Witherspoon and 'The Public Interest of Religion.'" *Journal of Church and State* 41 (Summer 1999): 551–574.

Noll, M. *Princeton and the Republic, 1768–1822.* Princeton: Princeton University Press, 1989.

Stohlman, Martha Lou Lemmon. *John Witherspoon: Parson, Politician, Patriot.* Louisville: John Knox Press, 1989.

Trait, L. Gordon. *The Piety of John Witherspoon: Pew, Pulpit, and Public Forum.* Louisville: Geneva Press, 2001.

Internet

Bearce, Robert G. "John Witherspoon: Disciple of Freedom." *The Freeman,* May 1977, Vol. 27, No. 5, <**http://www.libertyhaven.com/thinkers/johnwitherspoon/johnwitherspoon.html**>.

"John Witherspoon." Princeton University. <**http://www.princeton.edu/pr/facts/presidents/07.htm#witherspoon**>.

"John Witherspoon." U.S. History.org. <**http://www.ushistory.org/declaration/signers/witherspoon.htm**>.

Peterson, Robert A. "John Witherspoon: 'Animated Son of Liberty'." *The Freeman,* December 1985, Vol. 35, No. 12, <**http://www.libertyhaven.com/thinkers/johnwitherspoon/johnson.shtml**>.

"Should Christians—or Ministers—Run for Office?" Wallbuilders. <**http://www.wallbuilders.com/resources/search/detail.php?ResourceID=59**>.

Selected Works by John Witherspoon
- *Lectures on Moral Philosophy*

JOHN WITHERSPOON (1723–1794)

I willingly embrace the opportunity of declaring my opinion without any hesitation,
that the cause in which America is now in arms,
is the cause of justice, of liberty, and of human nature.

—John Witherspoon, 1776

He was a father figure to America's Founding Fathers. A renowned theologian from Scotland, John Witherspoon educated many young men who became prominent leaders of the Founding generation. He went on to embrace the revolutionary cause. He signed the Declaration of Independence, participated in the Continental Congress, and served in positions of influence in New Jersey state government. Yet Witherspoon's greatest legacy remains that of educator. Dozens of his students went on to leadership positions in the emerging United States. He had challenged them in their youth to read widely and think deeply about theology, economics, natural science, and political philosophy. By so doing, Witherspoon provided intellectual training in the battle for individual liberty.

Background

John Witherspoon was born in Gifford, Scotland, in 1723. His father served as the Presbyterian minister for the parish, and Witherspoon eventually followed in his footsteps. He received a Master of Arts degree from the University of Edinburgh and attended divinity school. At age twenty, he took a position at a parish in Beith, Scotland. For the next twenty years, he worked diligently and wrote widely admired theological works.

Witherspoon developed a positive reputation and a persuasive speaking style. Six feet tall, with bushy eyebrows, a prominent nose, and large ears, he was a formidable presence in his Scottish parish. Dr. Benjamin Rush, an American living in Scotland at the time, described Witherspoon's sermons as "loaded with good sense and adorned with elegance and beauty." Witherspoon memorized his sermons. He never carried notes to the pulpit, but his delivery did not seem rigid or rehearsed. He refrained from using dramatic gestures or elaborate language. Instead, his well-reasoned arguments conveyed his message and increased his renown.

President of the College of New Jersey

Witherspoon's reputation as a theologian spread. In 1766, the College of New Jersey (later renamed Princeton University) proposed that he leave Scotland and become the college's sixth president. He considered the opportunity. His wife, however, hesitated because of the treacherous transatlantic journey. Dr. Rush, a graduate of the College, convinced Witherspoon and his wife to move. In August of 1768, they arrived in Princeton with their five children and more than three hundred books.

A small colonial college, the College of New Jersey was ailing. It urgently needed funds to keep its doors open. Enrollment was low. The curriculum and instruction needed improvement. Incoming students were poorly prepared for college. As the lead instructor, college president, and fund-raiser, Witherspoon shouldered all of these challenges.

Fund-raising proved difficult. In the 1770s, conflict with Great Britain was intensifying, and many colonists wanted to hold on to their money. But Witherspoon was persuasive. He traveled extensively, preaching and soliciting contributions. Those who heard him speak described him as "a profound theologian . . . a universal scholar acquainted with human nature; a grave, dignified, solemn speaker." His trips to New York, Boston, and Virginia were successes. Contributions increased.

Enrollment presented a different challenge. To attract students, Witherspoon added to the curriculum. The college changed its exclusive focus on spiritual studies. Under Witherspoon, the college offered more comprehensive courses. He expanded the library to include contemporary philosophical writings. He did not limit students' exposure to new ideas. Instead, he encouraged them to read various perspectives. He preferred to allow reason and faith to guide their opinions. As a result of these changes, enrollment increased steadily. The graduating class of 1768 had only eleven students, but there were twenty-nine in the class of 1773.

The founders of the college wanted to educate men who would be "ornaments of the State as well as the Church." Witherspoon himself taught one president (James Madison) and one vice president (Aaron Burr). He also instructed nine cabinet officers, twenty-one senators, thirty-nine congressmen, three justices of the Supreme Court, and twelve state governors. Five of the fifty-five members of the Constitutional Convention were his former students. Witherspoon's impact on the ministry of the Presbyterian Church was also significant. Of the one hundred seventy-seven ministers in America in 1777, fifty-two of them had been Witherspoon's students.

With the Revolutionary War unfolding on its doorstep, the College of New Jersey suffered. Most students left to fight. Witherspoon was forced to shut down the school. He assisted in the safe evacuation of the students in November of 1776. During the war, both British and American troops at one time or another used the college's buildings as barracks and hospital facilities. American troops even fired into the college's main building, Nassau Hall, during the Battle of Princeton in January 1777. Their hope was to persuade the British troops camped inside to surrender. After the war, Witherspoon worked to restore the college's appearance, reputation, and finances. He served as its president until his death in 1794.

Service to the Colonies

Over a period of years, Witherspoon gradually became an ardent supporter of revolution. He joined his state's Committees of Correspondence and Safety in 1774. Once the war began, he represented New Jersey in the Continental Congress from 1776–1782. In 1776, when a fellow delegate questioned whether or not the colonies were ripe for independence, Witherspoon replied, "Sir, in my judgment, the country is not only ripe for the measure, but we are in danger of rotting for want of it." Witherspoon was the only active clergyman to sign the Declaration of Independence. He was liked for his sense of humor and pleasant personality and respected for his intellect. Witherspoon served on more than one hundred congressional committees during his six years in office. Following the Constitutional Convention in 1787, Witherspoon supported ratification at the New Jersey convention.

Witherspoon was a traditional Christian who was firmly committed to religious liberty. He feared that the Anglican Church would send a resident bishop to America who could then encroach on religious liberties. He also did not hesitate to address political issues from the pulpit. In his "Dominion of Providence" sermon in the spring of 1776, Witherspoon declared that "the cause in which America is now in arms, is the cause of justice, of liberty, and of human nature."

Witherspoon signed the Declaration of Independence, shepherded the College of New Jersey for three decades, and championed political and religious liberty. His most significant legacy, however, has been handed down through the work of his students. Witherspoon helped nurture a generation of revolutionary thinkers and religious leaders. Their efforts, in turn, produced the Constitution and the Bill of Rights. John Witherspoon ought to be remembered, in the words of John Adams, "as high a Son of Liberty as any Man in America."

Reading Comprehension Questions

1. What were the characteristics of Witherspoon's speaking style?

2. What changes did Witherspoon make in the curriculum of the College of New Jersey?

3. What national and state offices did Witherspoon hold during his career in public service?

Critical Thinking Questions

4. What is the significance of Witherspoon's role in educating members of the Founding generation?

5. John Adams declared that Witherspoon ought to be remembered "as high a Son of Liberty as any Man in America." Do you agree?

VOCABULARY AND CONTEXT QUESTIONS

Letter on the Clergy in Politics

1. **Vocabulary:** *Use context clues to determine the meaning or significance of each of these words and write their definitions:*

    a. denomination

    b. ascertain

    c. freeholders

    d. exclusion

    e. ecclesiastical

    f. indelible

    g. injurious

    h. wholly

    i. apprehended

    j. clerical

    k. relinquished

    l. litigation

    m. ambiguous

    n. alterations

    o. deposition

2. **Context:** *Answer the following questions. Note that some of the answers must be inferred.*

    a. When was this document written?

    b. Where was this document written?

    c. Who wrote this document?

    d. What type of document is this?

    e. What was the purpose of this document?

    f. Who was the audience for this document?

In His Own Words:
John Witherspoon on the Clergy in Politics

Letter on the Clergy in Politics

The 1777 Georgia state constitution included a provision that "No clergyman of any denomination shall be a member of the General Assembly." John Witherspoon wrote the following letter commenting upon that statement.

Sir,

In your paper of Saturday last, you have given us the new Constitution of Georgia, in which I find the following resolution, "No clergyman of any denomination shall be a member of the General Assembly." I would be very well satisfied that some of the gentlemen who have made that an essential article of this constitution, or who have inserted and approve it in other constitutions, would be pleased to explain a little the principles, as well as to ascertain the meaning of it.

Perhaps we understand pretty generally, what is meant by a clergyman, viz. [namely] a person regularly called and set apart to the ministry of the gospel, and authorized to preach and administer the sacraments of the Christian religion. Now suffer me to ask this question: Before any man among us was ordained a minister, was he not a citizen of the United States, and if being in Georgia, a citizen of the state of Georgia? Had he not then a right to be elected a member of the assembly, if qualified in point of property? How then has he lost, or why is he deprived of this right? Is it by offence or disqualification? Is it a sin against the public to become a minister? Does it merit that the person, who is guilty of it should be immediately deprived of one of his most important rights as a citizen? Is not this inflicting a penalty which always supposes an offence? Is a minister then disqualified for the office of a senator or representative? Does this calling and profession render him stupid or ignorant? I am inclined to form a very high opinion of the natural understanding of the freemen and freeholders of the state of Georgia, as well as of their improvement and culture by education, and yet I am not able to conceive, but that some of those equally qualified, may enter into the clerical order: and then it must not be unfitness, but some other reason that produces the exclusion. Perhaps it may be thought that they are excluded from civil authority, that they may be more fully and constantly employed in their spiritual functions. If this had been the ground of it, how much more properly would it have appeared, as an order of an ecclesiastical body with respect to their own members. In that case I should not only have forgiven but approved and justified it; but in the way in which it now stands, it is evidently a punishment by loss of privilege, inflicted on those, who go into the office of the ministry; for which, perhaps, the gentlemen of Georgia may have good reasons, though I have not been able to discover them.

But besides the uncertainty of the principle on which this resolution is founded, there seems to me much uncertainty as to the meaning of it. How are we to determine who is or is not a clergyman? Is he only a clergyman who has received ordination from those who have derived the right by an uninterrupted succession from the apostles? Or is he also a clergyman, who is set apart by the imposition of hands of a body of other clergymen, by joint authority? Or is he also a clergyman who is set a part [sic] by the church members of his own society, without any imposition of hands at all? Or is he also a clergyman who has exhorted in a Methodist society, or spoken in a Quaker meeting, or any other religious assembly met for public worship? There are still greater difficulties behind: Is the clerical character indelible? There are some who have been ordained who occasionally perform some clerical functions, but have no pastoral charge at all. There are some who finding public speaking injurious to health, or from other reasons easily conceived, have resigned their pastoral charge, and wholly discontinued all acts and exercises of that kind; and there are some, particularly in New England, who having exercised the clerical office some time, and finding it less suitable to their talents than they apprehended, have voluntarily relinquished it, and taken to some other profession. . . . Do these all continue clergymen, or do they cease to be clergymen, and by that cessation return to, or recover the honorable privileges of laymen?

I cannot help thinking that these difficulties are very considerable, and may occasion much litigation, if the article of the constitution stands in the loose, ambiguous form in which it now appears; and therefore I would recommend the following alterations, which I think will make every thing definite and unexceptionable.

"No clergyman, of any denomination, shall be capable of being elected a member of the Senate or House of Representatives, because {here insert the grounds of offensive disqualification, which I have not been able to discover} Provided always, and it is the true intent and meaning of this part of the constitution, that if at any time he shall be completely deprived of the clerical character by those by whom he was invested with it, as by deposition for cursing and swearing, drunkenness or uncleanness, he shall then be fully restored to all the privileges of a free citizen; his offence shall no more be remembered against him; but he may be chosen either to the Senate or House of Representatives, and shall be treated with all the respect due to his brethren, the other members of Assembly."

Source: John Witherspoon, *The Works of John Witherspoon* (Edinburgh: J. Ogle, Parliament-Square, 1815), Vol. IX, 220–223, as found in "Should Christians—or Ministers—Run for Office?" Wallbuilders. **<http://www.wallbuilders.com/resources/search/detail.php?ResourceID=59>**.

DISCUSSION QUESTIONS

Letter on the Clergy in Politics

1. Why is Witherspoon writing this letter?

2. Why is Witherspoon concerned about the Georgia constitution's position on clergy in the legislature?

3. Does Witherspoon think that there are valid reasons for excluding the clergy from the legislature?

4. What does Witherspoon mean by the phrase "a punishment by loss of privilege"?

5. What possible definitions does Witherspoon give for the word "clergyman"?

6. What possible problems does Witherspoon foresee about excluding members of the clergy?

7. What specific changes does Witherspoon recommend for the Georgia Constitution?

8. Does Witherspoon want his suggestions taken seriously?

Charles Carroll

Handout A—Charles Carroll (1737–1832)

1. Carroll denied the governor's right to impose the fee scale for public officials. He also defended the right of Catholics to participate in public affairs.

2. Carroll believed that the Protestant majority simply wanted to exclude Catholics from positions of power. Religious belief was merely an excuse to deny political influence to men like Carroll.

3. He became the last surviving signer of the Declaration of Independence.

4. If Britain won the war, Carroll would certainly lose his family estate and perhaps even his life. Victory, however, could bring both political and religious liberty.

5. Answers will vary. Students should mention that Catholics in this period had earned the right to vote and hold office and practice their religion openly. America had also established its independence.

Handout B—Vocabulary and Context Questions

1. Vocabulary
   a. prohibited/disqualifications
   b. declaration, law, or rule
   c. theoretical
   d. approval
   e. Roman Catholic
   f. people of bad character
   g. religious groups
   h. desire to cause pain
   i. lowest

2. Context
   a. The documents were written in 1773.
   b. The documents were written in Maryland.
   c. Charles Carroll and Daniel Dulany wrote the documents.
   d. The documents are a series of newspaper essays.

   e. Carroll's purpose was to convince the people of Maryland about the illegality of the fees imposed by the governor and about his right as a Catholic to comment on public affairs. Dulany's purpose is to question the right of Carroll in particular, and, by implication, Catholics in general, to engage in political debate. Dulany's other purpose is to defend the legality of the governor's proclamation setting officials' fees.

   f. The audience for these documents was the people of Maryland.

Handout C—In His Own Words: Charles Carroll on Religious Liberty

Answers will vary, but these are the main points of the dialogue between Dulany and Carroll:

Antilon's Third Letter
Dulany argues that Carroll should not be allowed to comment on public affairs because he is a Catholic, and that the law rightly prohibits Carroll from voting and holding office because Catholic beliefs pose a danger to society.

First Citizen's Third Letter
Carroll argues that his religious views should not be the issue, as they have nothing to do with his political beliefs.

Antilon's Fourth Letter
Dulany again points out that Maryland law rightly bars Carroll and all Catholics from interfering in political and religious affairs. (The "established religion" is Protestantism.)

First Citizen's Fourth Letter
Carroll expresses his devotion to the idea of religious tolerance. He argues that, though a Catholic, he should be allowed to comment on public affairs. Carroll accuses Dulany of trying to deny him freedom of thought and speech and of having evil purposes.

BENJAMIN FRANKLIN

Handout A—Benjamin Franklin (1706–1790)

1. Franklin improved lives in all these ways:
   a. He made scientific inventions.
   b. He refused to accept patent protection for his famous stove.
   c. He promoted public virtues through his many writings.
   d. He formed a secret society, the Junto, to promote beneficial ideas.
   e. He helped to create the American Philosophical Society to advance the cause of science in the New World.
   f. He played a major role in building the first fire department, the first public library, and the first hospital in Philadelphia.
   g. He served in many public offices.

2. In 1754, the prospect of war with the French led several of the royal governors to call for a congress of all the colonies. One purpose of the meeting was to plan war operations against the French. Another purpose was to prepare some plan of confederation among the colonies. Only seven colonies sent commissioners to this congress, which met in Albany, New York. At Albany, Franklin drafted and introduced the first formal proposal for a permanent union of the thirteen colonies. This became known as the Albany Plan. It was similar to the decentralized system of government that would later emerge under the Articles of Confederation. There would be a union of the colonies under a single central government, though each colony would preserve its local independence.

3. Franklin favored giving the lower house of Congress the sole power to propose money and tax bills. He successfully opposed property requirements for voting and financial tests for holders of federal office. He desired a clear listing of the powers of the federal government. He also supported an executive council instead of a single president. When this idea failed, Franklin seconded the call for an advisory council to the president. He believed that the president should be limited to only one term in office, so that no one man should gain too much power. He also opposed giving the executive absolute veto power over the Congress.

4. As the oldest member of the convention, and as someone who had a long record of accomplishment and public service, Franklin was certainly viewed with respect by most delegates. Perhaps some thought his day had passed. He was seen as a centrist on the issue of the power of the central government. Southern delegates surely resented his antislavery views.

5. Answers will vary but could include the following: Franklin believed that the survival of the republic depended not only on the form of government but also on the virtue of the people; the people have the responsibility of preserving the Constitution.

Handout B—Vocabulary and Context Questions

1. Vocabulary
   a. calm, peace
   b. descendants
   c. enact
   d. given
   e. individual, particular
   f. placed
   g. agreement
   h. required
   i. been created
   j. approval
   k. agree
   l. permission
   m. diplomats
   n. impose, place upon
   o. taxes on imported goods
   p. taxes on ships bringing goods from foreign countries
   q. taxes on domestic goods

2. Context
    a. The document was written in 1754.
    b. It was written in Albany, New York.
    c. Benjamin Franklin wrote the document.
    d. The document is a primary source—a plan of government.
    e. Franklin wrote the plan to propose a design of union of the colonies.
    f. The American colonists and the British government were the audience for the plan.

Handout C—Benjamin Franklin and the Albany Plan of Union

1: *Similarities:* Both documents propose a stronger union of the colonies in a federal system. The colonies/states retain certain powers in each system.
Differences: The Albany Plan creates a central government among the colonies for the first time, whereas the Constitution aims to strengthen the existing general government ("to form a more perfect Union").

2. *Similarities:* Both documents create an executive and a legislative branch. Under the Albany Plan, the members of the Grand Council, like the members of the Senate created by the Constitution, are chosen by the colonial/state legislatures.
Differences: The Albany Plan creates a unicameral (one-house) legislature, elected every three years. The Constitution creates a bicameral (two-house) legislature, the House members being chosen every two years and the senators every six. House members are elected directly by the people, unlike the members of the Grand Council, who are chosen by the colonial assemblies.

3. *Similarities:* Both legislatures meet at least once a year. Under both plans, the executive and legislature have a role in the lawmaking process. The president (or president-general) must execute the laws.
Differences: Under the Albany Plan, the president-general has an absolute veto (i.e., acts of the Grand Council cannot become law without his approval). Under the Constitution, the president has a limited veto (i.e., even if the president disapproves of the measure, the Congress can still enact a bill into law by a two-thirds vote of each house).

4. *Similarities:* Both the president and the president-general make treaties with the advice of the legislature. They also appoint military officers with the consent of the legislature.
Differences: Under the Albany Plan, the president-general does not need the approval of the Grand Council to make war and treaties. Under the Constitution, the president needs two thirds of the senators to approve a treaty he has made. The Congress is given the power to declare war, though the President is commander-in-chief of the armed forces of the United States.

5. *Similarities:* Both central governments are given the power to tax. Taxes should be just.
Differences: There are no significant differences here.

ELBRIDGE GERRY

Handout A—Elbridge Gerry (1744–1814)

1. Gerry signed the Declaration of Independence and the Articles of Confederation.
2. Gerry announced that he could not sign the Constitution. He believed it would create a too-powerful central government. Despite his refusal to approve the document, Gerry did not speak against it. He believed the Constitution was necessary to prevent the union of the states from falling apart. During the ratification debates in Massachusetts, he argued

that the state should approve the Constitution only on the condition that amendments would be added as soon as possible.

3. During his second term as governor of Massachusetts, Gerry approved a redistricting plan that gave an electoral advantage to Republicans. One of the districts resembled a salamander, so Federalists termed the practice "gerrymandering."

4. Answers will vary. Students could mention the X, Y, Z Affair and Gerry's decision to stay behind in France after he and his fellow delegates were asked to bribe French officials. This led to criticism of him by Federalists. Students could also mention Governor Gerry's attempt to ensure the election of Republicans to the state senate through the tactic of "gerrymandering." The unpopularity of this tactic contributed to Gerry's defeat in the next election for governor.

5. Answers will vary. In regard to politics, students should mention that Gerry was active in the patriot movement and sympathetic to the idea of independence. In regard to personality, students should mention that Gerry was a stubborn and difficult man who lacked a sense of humor and seemed to enjoy arguing.

Handout B—By His Own Hand: Elbridge Gerry and Gerrymandering

Below are two examples of how students could draw district boundaries so as to favor one party.

Example A: Republicans are favored in 7 out of 10 districts.
- Federalist Districts = 1, 2, 3
- Republican Districts = 4, 5, 6, 7, 8, 9, 10

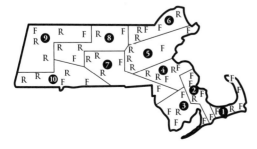

Example B: Federalists are favored in 8 out of 10 districts.
- Federalist Districts = 1, 2, 3, 4, 5, 6, 7, 9
- Republican Districts = 8, 10

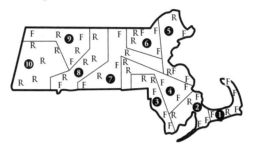

PATRICK HENRY

Handout A—Patrick Henry (1736–1799)

1. Saying he "smelled a rat," Henry feared that the meeting was a plot by the powerful to construct a strong central government of which they would be the masters.

2. Henry warned that the new Constitution would create a "consolidated" government in which power would be concentrated in the hands of a few. The document did not provide for adequate checks and balances and therefore did not protect the people against evil rulers. It gave the central government the dangerous power of direct taxation. It created a standing army, which a power-hungry president could use to awe the people into submission. It also lacked a bill of rights.

3. He disliked Thomas Jefferson and James Madison, the founders of the party. Also, as a devout Christian, Henry was disgusted by the party's approval of the atheistic French Revolution.

4. In both cases, Henry questioned the right of the British government to interfere in Virginia's affairs. In the Parson's Cause, Henry denounced the king's repeal of the Two-Penny Act as "an instance of misrule" and perhaps tyranny. During the Stamp Act Crisis, Henry asserted that "the General Assembly of this

Colony have the only and sole exclusive Right & Power to lay . . . taxes upon the Inhabitants of this Colony."

5. Answers will vary, but students should recognize that Henry's speech was a defiant call for armed resistance to British forces. He declared that war, in effect, had already begun.

Handout B—Context Questions

a. The document was written in 1788.
b. It was written in Virginia.
c. Patrick Henry wrote the document.
d. The document is a speech.
e. Henry wrote the speech to convince the Virginia delegates to oppose ratification of the Constitution.
f. The audience for this speech was the Virginia delegates in particular, but also the people of all the states.

Handout C—In His Own Words: Patrick Henry on the Constitution

Main idea of each passage:

1. Majority Rule: Henry favors majority rule and democratic government. He argues that under the new Constitution, a small minority of Americans could thwart the will of the majority by refusing to ratify a proposed amendment. For example, four small states—such as New Jersey, Rhode Island, Connecticut, and New Hampshire—containing only five to ten percent of the total population of the country could block approval of an amendment favored by the remaining nine more populous states.

2. A Standing Army: Henry argues that the Constitution will create a standing army that the government will use to crush any opposition to its exercise of power. The militia will be powerless to stop it. Henry warns that the seat of government will become an armed fortress used by this army.

3. Liberty vs. Empire: Henry laments the fact that Americans seem to favor the building of a great empire, which will come at the expense of their liberty.

4. Good and Bad Rulers: Henry argues that the Constitution does not include sufficient safeguards against the abuse of power by evil officeholders.

5. The President, a Tyrant: Henry cautions that the presidency is poorly designed and that a power-hungry occupant of that office will be able to use the standing army and the militia to establish tyranny.

THOMAS JEFFERSON

Handout A—Thomas Jefferson (1743–1826)

1. Jefferson had mixed feelings about slavery. He warned that slavery might one day tear the Union apart. He condemned the slave trade and proposed a plan for ending it. But Jefferson owned more than 200 slaves who lived on and near his great plantation of Monticello, and he freed none of them while he lived. He did provide in his will for the emancipation of seven of his slaves, including Sally Hemings (the slave with whom Jefferson is alleged to have had a sexual relationship), her five children, and her nephew.

2. While he was president, Jefferson reduced the number of public employees, cut military spending, and lowered the national debt.

3. Jefferson championed the right to bear arms, religious freedom, the rights of people accused of crimes, and the right to property.

4. Answers will vary. Some students will point out the contradictions between Jefferson's opinions and his actions. For example, he condemned the slave trade, warned that slavery might one day tear the Union apart, and proposed a plan for ending slavery in the United States. But he owned more than 200 slaves who

lived on and near his great plantation of Monticello, and he freed few of them while he lived. Also, despite his opposition to powerful government, he purchased the Louisiana Territory from Napoleon for $15 million. And though he advocated the rights of individuals, Jefferson violated the civil liberties of many Americans when enforcing the Embargo Act. Students may argue that these facts are proof that Jefferson did indeed violate his principles at times. Other students, however, may say that Jefferson was sometimes forced to choose between competing principles. In purchasing Louisiana, for instance, he hoped to provide for the happiness of America. By harshly enforcing the Embargo Act, he wished to keep the United States out of European wars.

5. Jefferson believed that these achievements were the high points of a life dedicated to the promotion of human freedom. Education, he held, freed the mind from ignorance. Tolerance freed the will from coercion. And the assertion of human liberty and equality freed the body from the chains of tyranny.

6. Jefferson was trying to unite the nation after the bitterness of the 1800 presidential contest. His words implied that all Americans shared certain philosophical principles—those embodied by the terms "federalism" and "republicanism"—that superseded petty political differences between the Federalist and Republican Parties.

Handout B—Vocabulary and Context Questions
1. Vocabulary
   a. impose, charge
   b. leaving out
   c. errors in reasoning
   d. businesses that dominate a sector of the economy
   e. undying
   f. constant

g. the requirement that the government must show good cause in order to hold a person in jail
h. to have a right to
i. leaving behind
j. official

2. Context
   a. The document was written on December 20, 1787.
   b. It was written in Paris, France.
   c. Thomas Jefferson wrote the document.
   d. The document is a personal letter.
   e. Jefferson wrote the letter to respond to Madison's previous letter and to inform him of Jefferson's opinion of the Constitution.
   f. The audience for the letter was James Madison and, by extension, the other members of Congress he would be addressing on the issue.

Handout D—Analysis: Thomas Jefferson on the Constitution
A. Jefferson approved of this separation of powers.
B. He approved of the House—whose members are chosen by the people—possessing the taxing power.
C. He approved of voting in the legislature being done by individual members and not by state delegations.
D. He approved of the president's veto power, although he wanted the judicial branch to have a veto power also.
E. He wanted the right of habeas corpus to be more firmly established in a bill of rights.
F. He wanted the right to a trial by jury to be more firmly established in a bill of rights.
G. He approved of Congress' oversight of the military forces but wanted protection against a standing army to be more firmly established in a bill of rights.

H. He was troubled by the lack of limitation on how many terms the president could serve.

RICHARD HENRY LEE

Handout A—Richard Henry Lee (1732–1794)

1. Lee was an outspoken opponent of the international slave trade. His first official act in the Virginia House of Burgesses was to introduce a bill that proposed "to lay so heavy a duty on the importation of slaves as to put an end to that iniquitous and disgraceful traffic within the colony of Virginia." Lee also condemned the institution of slavery itself. Blacks, Lee declared, were "equally entitled to liberty and freedom by the great law of nature." He warned that slaves would rebel if they "observed their masters possessed of a liberty denied to them." Nevertheless, Lee did not free any of his slaves. He simply could not afford to do so.

2. On June 7, 1776, Lee introduced a resolution that declared "that these United Colonies are, and of right ought to be, free and independent States." This led to the drafting of the Declaration of Independence. Lee's resolution was adopted by Congress on July 2, 1776.

3. In the *Federal Farmer*, Lee criticized the Constitution's centralization of powers in the federal government and its lack of a bill of rights. He warned that the Constitution would destroy the states and create a "consolidated" government in which all power was dangerously concentrated in one place. Lee wished instead to preserve a federal system, in which power is divided between the national and state governments.

4. Answers will vary. Some students may say that Lee did not want anyone to know he was the author of the *Federal Farmer*. Anonymous authorship was a common tactic of political pamphleteers at the time. This was a way to keep people focused on the arguments and not the author of the pamphlet. Some students may suggest that the pseudonym "Federal Farmer" reflects Lee's identity as a plantation owner who favored the principle of federalism. Lee probably also wished to imply that the views expressed in the pamphlet were held by all virtuous farmers of America.

5. Answers will vary. Some students may agree with Lee that no constitutional procedures or laws can stop corrupt office-holders from doing evil. Others may disagree with Lee and argue that a well-designed constitution can reign in evil-doers by pitting the interest of one against the other. (Madison famously expressed this latter idea in *Federalist No. 51*, in which he argued that "ambition must be made to counteract ambition.")

Handout B—Vocabulary and Context Questions

1. Vocabulary
   a. united
   b. vicinity
   c. incapable of being taken away
   d. openly, clearly
   e. discovered, found out
   f. determined
   g. supports, buttresses

2. Context
   a. The document was written in 1787–1788.
   b. The document was written in Virginia.
   c. Richard Henry Lee is the author of the document.
   d. The document is a series of essays/letters.
   e. The purpose of the document was to convince Americans not to ratify the Constitution.
   f. The audience was Americans in every state.

Handout C—In His Own Words: Richard Henry Lee on the Constitution

a. Statements of Lee's principles: Excerpts B, C, D, F, G, I
b. Criticisms of the proposed Constitution: Excerpts A, E, H, J

Topic/main idea of each excerpt:

A   The Constitution will place too much power in the central government.
B   The two ingredients for good government are representation of the people and trial by jury.
C   People's rights cannot be taken away and should be the foundation of the Constitution.
D   "Wise and honest" administration of government is more important than the form of government; constitutions should not give men the opportunity to do evil.
E   The Constitution gives Congress unlimited power to tax.
F   Liberty is the freedom to enjoy life and work without too many restrictions by the government.
G   All power lies with the people.
H   The proposed government will grow too large and too powerful.
I   Virtue and good laws are mutually supportive.
J   The proposed government will be run by a few men.

James Madison

Handout A—James Madison (1751–1836)

1. Madison pressed for a meeting of the states to discuss amending the Articles of Confederation. He prepared his ideas for a new Constitution even before the states met. Many of Madison's ideas were embodied in the Virginia Plan, which the final version of the constitution closely resembled. Madison played a major role in the debates as the convention proceeded. He spoke often in support of his ideas and designed compromises to break gridlocks. After the convention, Madison joined with Alexander Hamilton and John Jay in composing the *Federalist Papers,* a series of newspaper essays that defended the Constitution. He also took a leading role in support of the Constitution at the Virginia Ratifying Convention. As a member of the House of Representatives, he guided a bill of rights through Congress.

2. Madison believed that it was crucial to separate power within the central government. This system of checks and balances would prevent any faction from seizing control of the government. Similarly, the proper division of power between the national and state governments, a novel concept called "federalism," would preclude the dangerous concentration of power in any one place.

3. First, he argued that the rights of the people were already implied in the Constitution; second, he worried that any such listing of rights would surely omit some rights held by the people; and third, he believed that written lists of rights were not effective in protecting the liberty of the people.

4. Madison would have been deeply disappointed because he had worked so hard to fashion a new constitution for the United States. He likely would have been concerned that the nation was in danger of collapse. Perhaps he would have tried to organize another convention or at least would have tried to have the Articles of Confederation amended.

5. Answers will vary.

Handout B—Vocabulary and Context Questions

1. Vocabulary
    a. motivated
    b. contrary, opposed

   c. total
   d. flawed
   e. underlying, not seen
   f. conclusion
   g. evil
   h. area
   i. cooperate
   j. tyranny, cruelty
2. Context
   a. The document was written in 1787.
   b. It was written in Virginia.
   c. James Madison wrote the document.
   d. The document is a newspaper essay.
   e. Madison wrote the essay to convince the people of New York to support ratification of the Constitution.
   f. The audience for this letter was the people of New York in particular, but also the people of all the states.

Handout C—In His Own Words: James Madison on the Problem of Faction—Scripted Discussion

Teacher: Ask the students which of the two food preference groups meets Madison's definition of a faction. Now ask the meat eaters if they would be willing to become vegetarians. Then ask the vegetarians if they would be willing to become meat eaters.

Answer: The vegetarian group is a faction. Students should recognize that changing their opinions is not an acceptable solution to most people in a free society. People are unlikely to change their opinions/ preferences in order to achieve harmony.

Teacher: Have a student read Excerpt B to the class.

- - - - - - - - - - - - - - - - - -

Teacher: Ask the students what Madison suggests as a solution since it is impossible

to prevent the formation of factions within a society.

Answer: Madison suggests that the effects of faction must be controlled.

Teacher: Tell the students that the cafeteria menu will be determined by majority vote. Ask the students to predict the result of such a vote.

Answer: The minority vegetarian faction will be defeated, and meat will be on the menu, though vegetarian dishes will be allowed.

Teacher: Tell the class that the defeat of the minority faction through majority vote is the solution Madison favored. Then have a student read Excerpt C to the class.

- - - - - - - - - - - - - - - - - -

Teacher: Ask the students to imagine that, in retaliation, the majority group of meat eaters now wants to ban all vegetarian dishes from the cafeteria menu. Once again, the menu will be decided by majority vote. Ask the students what Madison would now call the meat eating group.

Answer: Madison would call the meat eaters a majority faction.

Teacher: Tell the students that Madison was particularly concerned about majority factions in democratic societies. Have a student read Excerpt D to the class.

- - - - - - - - - - - - - - - - - -

Teacher: Ask the meat eaters what their "ruling passion" is. How did they sacrifice "both the public good and the rights of other citizens" in the last example?

Answer: Their ruling passion is meat eating. They deprived the vegetarians of their right to eat only vegetarian food and thereby harmed the public good.

Teacher: Ask the class what is the central problem, according to Madison, with governments based on majority rule.

Answer: Madison thought that the danger of a majority faction was the central problem with governments based on majority rule.

Teacher: Tell the class that they will now read what Madison had to say about the great danger faced by popular governments. Have a student read Excerpt E to the class.

- - - - - - - - - - - - - - - - -

Teacher: Now divide the class into seven groups relatively even in number: meat eaters, meat eaters who eat only white meat, vegetarians, vegetarians who also eat fish, vegans, pizza eaters, and those who eat only Chinese food. Have each group come up with a standard menu of three items that could win the approval of a majority of the class in a popular vote. Allow them five minutes to do this. Then ask one member of each group to write the group's menu on the blackboard. Next, have the class vote up or down on each menu separately. Ask the whole class to comment on why certain menus were approved and others were not approved.

The students will likely recognize that they had to compromise to win the support of other groups in order to form a majority. Ask the students in which model—the two-group society or the seven-group society—was the common good better achieved.

Answer: In the multigroup society each group was forced to seek the common good and respect the rights of the minority. The more groups there are, the more the common good is served.

Teacher: Ask the class what this says about the relationship between the size of a society and the achievement of the common good.

Answer: A larger society will include more groups and thereby better serve the common good.

Teacher: Have a student read Excerpt F to the class.

GEORGE MASON

Handout A—George Mason (1725–1792)

1. George Mason believed the main role of government was to protect the liberty of the people.
2. Mason wrote the Virginia Declaration of Rights and the Virginia Constitution.
3. He became alarmed by several proposals aimed at reducing the power of the states. Mason also thought the new Constitution did not go far enough in protecting individual rights and local interests. He feared that the presidency was too powerful. His calls for a bill of rights and for an end to the importation of slaves were rejected. Mason warned that the new federal government would destroy the states. He argued that the Constitution gave "no security" to the "Declarations of Rights in the separate States." He believed that all three branches of the federal government had been given too much power.
4. Mason wore the clothes as a symbol of the death of liberty if the Constitution were to be approved.
5. Answers will vary.

Handout B—Context Questions

1. The document was written in 1776.
2. The document was written in Virginia.
3. The document was written by George Mason.
4. The document is a statement of principles of government and the rights of the people of Virginia.
5. The purpose of the document was to proclaim these principles and rights.
6. The audience for this document was the people of Virginia and, in a broader sense, the people of America.

Handout C—In His Own Words: George Mason on Liberty

1. All people are born free with certain natural rights, namely the rights to life, liberty, property, happiness, and safety. These rights cannot be taken away.
   - Declaration of Independence (Paragraph 2)

2. All power comes from the people. Government officials, therefore, are answerable to the people.
   - Declaration of Independence (Paragraph 2)

3. The role of government is to protect and benefit the people. When a government fails to fulfill this role, it is the right of a majority of the people to change it or get rid of it.
   - Declaration of Independence (Paragraph 2)

4. No one has a special claim to offices or benefits from the rest of the community. No office should be given to anyone on the basis of bloodlines.
   - The Constitution: Article I, Section 9, Clause 8

5. Government should be separated into three branches: the legislative, executive, and judicial. There should be frequent elections so that no one stays in office too long and forgets what it is like to be an ordinary citizen.
   - The Constitution: Articles I, II, and III (separation of powers)
   - The Constitution: Article I, Section 2, Clause 1 (Elections for the House of Representatives are to be held every two years.)

6. Elections should be free. People who have a stake in society have the right to vote and should not be taxed or deprived of their property without their consent.
   - The Constitution: Article I, Section 2, Clause 1 (similar: qualifications for members based on state qualifications)
   - Fifth Amendment (the "due process" clause)

7. Laws must be enforced unless the representatives of the people agree to suspend them.
   - Article I, Section 9, Clause 2 (suspension of habeas corpus)
   - Article II, Section 3 (president to ensure "that the laws be faithfully executed")

8. A person accused of a crime has certain rights: the right to know the charges, the right to present evidence in his favor, the right to confront his accusers and witnesses, the right not to be forced to testify against himself, and the right to a fair and speedy trial by jury in the areas in which he lives. No one may be deprived of his liberty except by the law or a jury trial.
   - Fifth Amendment
   - Sixth Amendment

9. Excessive bail, excessive fines, and cruel and unusual punishments are prohibited.
   - Eighth Amendment

10. Search warrants can be granted only if there is evidence of a crime. They must also specifically name the people who are to be arrested.
    - Fourth Amendment

11. Trial by a jury should be used in cases involving property and in lawsuits between people.
    - Seventh Amendment

12. The freedom of the press should not be limited by government.
    - First Amendment

13. Professional, permanent armies endanger liberty, so the nation should rely instead upon the militia (citizen-soldiers). The civil authorities should always be in control of the military.
    - Constitution, Article II, Section 2, Clause 1
    - Second Amendment

14. Government should be the same throughout the state.
    - Constitution, Article IV, Section 3

15. In order for liberty to be preserved, people must act with certain virtues and must keep in mind the basic principles of a free society.
    - No matches
16. People should be able to practice their religion freely. It is everyone's duty to practice Christian virtues when dealing with others.
    - First Amendment

ROBERT MORRIS

Handout A—Robert Morris (1734–1806)

1. Morris signed the Declaration of Independence, the Articles of Confederation, and the Constitution.
2. Morris's difficulties with the states during his tenure as chairman of the Continental Congress's Finance Committee and as superintendent of finance under the Articles convinced him of the need for a stronger national government. He often had to badger the states to fulfill their quotas of money and supplies. He was particularly disappointed that the impost amendment failed to win the approval of all thirteen states as required by the Articles of Confederation.
3. He speculated in Western land, buying vast tracts of land cheaply in the hope of selling them later at a high price. This gamble and several other new business ventures failed. During the 1790s, Morris also sunk an enormous amount of money into the construction of an extravagant mansion in Philadelphia.
4. As chairman of the Continental Congress's Finance Committee and as superintendent of finance under the Articles, Morris worked hard to stabilize the nation's financial system. He cut spending, streamlined accounting procedures, and cajoled the states into meeting their quotas of money and supplies. Morris risked his own money and credit to help keep the government afloat. The Con-

tinental Army would likely have disintegrated if not for Morris's efforts.
5. Answers will vary.

Handout B—Vocabulary and Context Questions

1. Vocabulary
   a. destructive
   b. widespread
   c. lacking energy
   d. laziness/complacency
   e. exhausting
   f. importance
   g. government official
   h. taken
   i. beg
   j. determining
   k. charging
2. Context:
   a. The document was written in 1781.
   b. The document was written in Philadelphia.
   c. Robert Morris is the author of the document.
   d. The document is a letter to the governors of the states.
   e. The purpose of the document was to urge the governors to fulfill their quotas of money and supplies.
   f. The audience was the governors of the states.

Handout C—In His Own Words: Robert Morris on States' Responsibilities

Document Paraphrase
Paragraph One:
I am upset that many state officials think that their states don't have to fulfill their obligations to the national Congress; this idea makes everyone complacent. You wise governors should know that this war cannot be carried on without everyone's cooperation. I know that the states will do what is right. They know that they cannot gain by doing wrong. If the states

cooperate and give the money they owe to the Congress, then the United States will become powerful and great.

Paragraph Two:
I am enclosing in this letter a list of what you owe Congress. I also need to know the following information: all the laws passed in your state regarding how you will collect the money and supplies you owe the Congress; how your state is going to levy and collect taxes from your citizens; when your legislature is going to meet. I am not asking about these things because I am curious or nosy; I simply need to know these things, and I wish to ask you directly about them.

Paragraph Three:
I also need to know what types of money are used in your state.

Paragraph Four:
I know this is a lot of trouble, but I think that you will answer my questions happily because this is for the good of your country.

V. Wrap-Up Discussion

Tone of the Document
Morris' tone is one of supplication/ persuasion/flattery. He has no power to force the governors to comply with his requests, so he must employ tactics of persuasion. The following words and phrases indicate this tone.

Paragraph One:
- "is beneath the wisdom": Morris suggests that noncooperation with his requests would be unwise.
- "I shall never permit a doubt that the States will do what is right": Morris flatters the states and simultaneously puts them on the spot.
- "that these States must expect to establish their independence and rise into power, consequence, and grandeur": Morris suggests that the reward for cooperation with his request will be national power and glory.

Paragraph Two:
- Morris uses several verbs of supplication in this paragraph: "entreat," "pray," and "beg leave."

Paragraph Three:
- Morris uses the verb "entreat" once again.

Paragraph Four:
- "I know that I give you a great deal of trouble but I also know it will be pleasing to you because the time and the labour will be expended in the service of your country": Morris suggests that by complying with his requests, the governors will be doing their patriotic duty. The language is calculated to put the governors on the spot: Could it be possible, Morris implicitly asks, that they would be unwilling to devote time and labor in the service of their country?

CHARLES PINCKNEY

Handout A—Charles Pinckney (1757–1824)

1. Pinckney was the first to use the term *Senate*. He worked to prohibit religious qualifications for public office. He also pushed for a "vigorous Executive," but with limitations. He feared if the executive had too much power in the realms of war and peace, then the system "would render the Executive a Monarchy, of the worst kind, to wit an elective one." Despite his fear of an overzealous ruler, he supported a single executive, with the title President, instead of a governing body. These ideas were part of the plan of government he introduced at Philadelphia.

2. The following are Pinckney's proposals that failed to pass: He supported an elitist government. He wanted high property qualifications for federal offices and said that "the Legislature, the Executive, and the judges should be possessed of competent property to make them independent and respectable." He also

encouraged the selection of representatives by state legislatures and increased Congressional power. He wanted the Legislature, not the Executive, to choose justices for the Supreme Court. He thought the federal government should have more power over state governments, suggesting a federal veto over state laws. He backed an effort to establish a national university.

3. Students should recognize that, as a Southern planter and representative, Pinckney had a vested political and economic interest in slavery. He wanted to make sure that the federal government was not given power to touch slavery in any way. Therefore, during the convention, he opposed federal interference with the slave trade, though he was willing to compromise and agreed to the clause prohibiting Congress from interfering with the slave trade for twenty years. In the debate on the Missouri Compromise, he continued to oppose the federal government's right to interfere with slavery.

4. Answers will vary.
5. Answers will vary.

Handout B—Vocabulary and Context Questions

1. Vocabulary
   a. distribution
   b. concerned about
   c. rebellions
   d. free
   e. products
   f. interfere
   g. make
   h. arrangement
   i. interfering
   j. approval
   k. useful
   l. taking care of
   m. use
   n. agreement
   o. believe
   p. purchases
   q. money
   r. restricted
   s. perception
   t. slave trade

2. Context
   a. The document was written in 1787.
   b. It was written in Philadelphia.
   c. James Madison wrote the document.
   d. The document is a primary source—a journal.
   e. The journal was written to record the debates.
   f. Madison said that he wrote his notes for "the people of the United States" and "all those who take an interest in the progress of political science and the cause of true liberty."

Handout D—Analysis: Debate about Article I, Section 9, Clause 1

Martin: *N, Y, Y;* Slavery is dishonorable. / No Argument / Slavery weakens the Union.

Rutledge: *Y, N, X;* No Argument / Slavery produces goods for Northern consumption. / The South will only join the Union if slavery is allowed.

Ellsworth: *X, N, N;* Slavery is a moral question that should be decided by each state. / If the South benefits economically from slavery, the North also benefits. / The South may not join the Union if slavery is regulated by the federal government.

Pinckney: *Y, N, N;* History provides a moral justification for slavery. / No Argument / South Carolina will not accept the Constitution if it prohibits slavery.

Sherman: *N, N, N;* Abolition is already happening in the states. / There is no economic benefit to removing slaves. / Slavery is a divisive issue; we should minimize objections.

Mason: *N, Y, X;* Slavery is pernicious and sinful; it creates tyrants; and the slave trade is nefarious. / Slavery discourages manufacturing and white immigration. / All states should surrender the right to regulate slavery.

General Pinckney: *Y, Y, Y;* No Argument / More slaves results in more goods, which results in more revenue. / South Carolina will not join the Union if the clause is rejected.

Dickinson: *N, Y, X;* No Argument / No Argument / The question of slavery should be decided by the federal government.

King: *X, X, Y;* No Argument / Not taxing slaves would be an unfair economic burden on the North. / The North and the South disagree on this issue.

Langdon: *N, Y, X;* No Argument / No Argument / The question of slavery should be decided by the federal government.

ROGER SHERMAN

Handout A—Roger Sherman (1721–1793)

1. Sherman had a hand in the creation of the Declaration of Independence, the Articles of Confederation, and the Constitution.

2. He worked to guard the power of the states against the national government. He believed that the authority of the national government should be carefully restricted to a few areas. In order to protect the people's liberty, Sherman also argued for placing the balance of the national government's power in the legislature.

3. He proposed the Great Compromise, which decided the method of representation in the Congress. By this agreement, the Congress would be divided into two houses. In the Senate, each state would have an equal vote. In the House of Representatives, each state would be represented according to its population.

4. Answers will vary. Some students could argue that Sherman was a dedicated public servant but far from extraordinary. He was not a great speaker or deep thinker; he was not a leader; he did not change the course of history in a significant way. Other students will say that Sherman was extraordinary. He had a hand in creating the Declaration of Independence, Articles of Confederation, and United States Constitution. At the Philadelphia Convention, he spoke 138 times and proposed the Great Compromise, which solved the issue of representation in the national legislature. He helped to persuade the Connecticut Ratifying Convention to approve the Constitution, and he served in the first Congress. Few Americans of the time were as involved in public affairs for as long as Sherman was.

5. Answers will vary. Some students will say that this is not possible: in order to be a successful politician, one must be dishonest at times. These students may name as examples people who have served in public office during the last few years. Others will say that there are many examples of people who were skilled at politics but who also led good moral lives. George Washington, Abraham Lincoln, and Jimmy Carter are three examples.

Handout B—Context Questions

a. The document was written in 1787.
b. It was written in Philadelphia.
c. Roger Sherman wrote the document.
d. The document is an excerpt from a speech.
e. Sherman wrote the speech to persuade the delegates that the central government should not be too strong.
f. The audience for the document was the delegates to the Federal Convention of 1787.

ANSWER KEY

Handout C—In His Own Words: Roger Sherman on the Role of Government

A. Some examples of how government affects a student's life in a typical day include:

- Waking up to the clock radio: The Federal Communications Commission (FCC) regulates content of programs transmitted over the airwaves. (F)
- Using toothpaste and cosmetics: The federal Food and Drug Administration (FDA) enforces regulations on health aids and cosmetics. (F)
- Using the bathroom: Water purity and water content is regulated by the federal and local governments. (F,L)
- Use of electrical devices, such as a hair dryer or razor: Electricity is regulated by federal and state governments; electrical devices are checked for safety by federal agencies. (F,S)
- Getting dressed: Federal child-labor laws, safety standards, labor legislation, and international treaties regulate who makes clothes sold in the United States and how they are made. (F)
- Eating breakfast: Food is regulated by the FDA. Some states set safety standards for certain foods. (F,S)
- Putting out the garbage: Local government operates sanitation trucks. (L)
- Making phone calls: The Federal Trade Commission (FTC) and the FCC regulate use of phone lines. (F)
- Watching morning television: The FCC regulates program content. (F)
- Driving a car to school: A person must obtain a state license and may be required by the state to purchase insurance. Insurance companies are regulated by the federal government. Cars must usually pass a state inspection. Local traffic laws must be obeyed. Roads are funded by local, state, and federal governments. (F,S,L)
- Going to a public school: Local governments operate the schools, and state governments have authority over them. Students in these schools must meet state academic standards. Many programs in public schools are funded by the federal government. The safety of the workplace is monitored by the federal Occupational Safety and Health Administration (OSHA). (F,S,L)
- Going to a job after school: The safety of the workplace is monitored by OSHA. Federal, state, and local taxes are taken out of people's paychecks. (F,S,L)

B. Answers will vary. Some students, who believe that an activist government promotes the good of all, will approve of most or all of the roles of government listed. Others who see a danger in giving too much power to government will disapprove of many or most of the listed activities.

C. No answer is necessary.

D. No answer is necessary.

E. No answer is necessary.

V. Wrap-Up Discussion

1. Sherman limited the role of the federal government to four areas. He argued that states should legislate in all other areas.

2. Answers will vary. Sherman would probably disapprove of many of the roles that the federal government fulfills today because he believed that the federal government's power should be limited to only four areas.

3. Answers will vary. Students could refer to three historical benchmarks that propelled the growth of the federal government:
   • the Civil War, 1861–1865 (The federal government emerged supreme over the states, and the Supreme Court began to apply the Bill of Rights to the states.)
   • the New Deal, 1933–1945 (The federal government took direct responsibility for the economic welfare of individual Americans.)
   • the Great Society, 1960s (The federal government greatly expanded its efforts to help the poor, sick, and elderly.)

JOHN WITHERSPOON

Handout A—John Witherspoon (1723–1794)

1. Witherspoon's speaking style had the following characteristics:
   a. graceful and elegant
   b. filled with good sense
   c. memorized but natural
   d. no dramatic gestures
   e. simple language
   f. thoughtfully reasoned
2. Witherspoon improved the curriculum by offering more comprehensive courses, expanding the library, encouraging students to read a variety of sources, and encouraging students to consider various opinions while using reason and faith.
3. He held the following offices:
   a. member of Committees of Correspondence and Safety
   b. delegate to the Continental Congress (1776–1782)
   c. signer of the Declaration of Independence
   d. member of the New Jersey state ratifying convention

4. Witherspoon encouraged his students to be thinkers who could consider a wide range of viewpoints and then use their intellects to choose the best options. The deliberations of the Continental Congresses and at the Constitution Convention reflected this rational approach to decision making.
5. Answers will vary.

Handout B—Vocabulary and Context Questions

1. Vocabulary
   a. religious group
   b. determine
   c. property owners
   d. leaving out
   e. church-related
   f. permanent
   g. harmful
   h. completely
   i. anticipated
   j. relating to clergy
   k. given up
   l. controversy
   m. unclear
   n. changes
   o. removal
2. Context
   a. The document was written in 1777.
   b. The document is about a provision in the Constitution of Georgia, but there is no indication that the document was written or published in Georgia.
   c. John Witherspoon wrote the document.
   d. It is a letter to the editor of a newspaper.
   e. Witherspoon's purpose was to persuade those who were writing the Georgia state constitution to reconsider their prohibition on clergy serving in the legislature and to entertain his readers

through his ironic commentary on this prohibition.

f. The audience for this document was the general public, the readers of the newspaper, and the authors of the Georgia state constitution ("some of the gentlemen who have made that an essential article of this constitution").

Handout D—Discussion Questions

1. Witherspoon says that he is confused by the decision of the resolution in the Georgia Constitution that prohibits clergymen from serving in the state legislature.

2. Witherspoon believes that a person is a citizen before becoming a clergyman and therefore should, like all other citizens, have the right to serve in elected office. He asks the rhetorical question: "Is it a sin against the public to become a minister?" The implied answer is "no."

3. He believes that the responsibilities of the clergy could prevent them from serving in the legislature. However, he also believes that the churches and the clergy—not the constitution—should make this decision.

4. The proposed constitution punishes members of the clergy by taking away their privilege to serve in the state legislature.

5. Witherspoon gives several possible definitions for "clergyman":
   - one who has been ordained by a superior ("those who have derived the right by an uninterrupted succession from the apostles")
   - one who has been ordained by another clergyman
   - one who is not ordained but "set a part [sic]" by members of the congregation
   - one who has spoken at a religious assembly

6. He wonders whether the clerical character is indelible; i.e., if a person is once a member of the clergy, are they always a member and so are always excluded from public office? Or could they be excluded at one point and then included later? He raises the following examples:
   - an ordained minister who performs no religious functions
   - a retired minister
   - an ordained minister who leaves the ministry for another profession

7. Witherspoon suggests several changes for the Georgia Constitution:
   - insert the reasons for the disqualification of clergy (which he has been unable to determine)
   - remove from the ministry those clergymen who are guilty of cursing, swearing, drunkenness, and uncleanness
   - allow such people to be elected to the Georgia Senate or House of Representatives and be treated with the same respect as other members of the legislature

8. No, Witherspoon does *not* want his suggestions taken seriously. He is offering an ironic commentary about prohibiting clergymen from serving in the legislature.

Visual Assessment

1. **Founders Posters**—Have students create posters for either an individual Founder, a group of Founders, or an event. Ask them to include at least one quotation (different from classroom posters that accompany this volume) and one image.

2. **Coat of Arms**—Draw a coat of arms template and divide into 6 quadrants (see example). Photocopy and hand out to the class. Ask them to create a coat of arms for a particular Founder with a different criterion for each quadrant (e.g., occupation, key contribution, etc.). Include in the assignment an explanation sheet in which they describe why they chose certain colors, images, and symbols.

3. **Individual Illustrated Timeline**—Ask each student to create a visual timeline of at least ten key points in the life of a particular Founder. In class, put the students in groups and have them discuss the intersections and juxtapositions in each of their timelines.

4. **Full Class Illustrated Timeline**—Along a full classroom wall, tape poster paper in one long line. Draw in a middle line and years (i.e., 1760, 1770, 1780, etc.). Put students in pairs and assign each pair one Founder. Ask them to put together ten key points in the life of the Founder. Have each pair draw in the key points on the master timeline.

5. **Political Cartoon**—Provide students with examples of good political cartoons, contemporary or historical. A good resource for finding historical cartoons on the Web is <**http://www.boondocksnet.com/gallery/political_cartoons.html**>. Ask them to create a political cartoon based on an event or idea in the Founding period.

Performance Assessments

1. **Meeting of the Minds**—Divide the class into five groups and assign a Founder to each group. Ask the group to discuss the Founder's views on a variety of pre-determined topics. Then, have a representative from each group come to the front of the classroom and role-play as the Founder, dialoguing with Founders from other groups. The teacher will act as moderator, reading aloud topic questions (based on the pre-determined topics given to the groups) and encouraging discussion from the students in character. At the teacher's discretion, questioning can be opened up to the class as a whole. For advanced students, do not provide a list of topics—ask them to know their character well enough to present him properly on all topics.

2. **Create a Song or Rap**—Individually or in groups, have students create a song or rap about a Founder based on a familiar song, incorporating at least five key events or ideas of the Founder in their project. Have students perform their song in class. (Optional: Ask the students to bring in a recording of the song for background music.)

Web/Technology Assessments

1. **Founders PowerPoint Presentation**—Divide students into groups. Have each group create a PowerPoint presentation about a Founder or event. Determine the number of slides, and assign a theme to each slide (e.g., basic biographic information, major contributions, political philosophy, quotations, repercussions of the event, participants in the event, etc.). Have them hand out copies of the slides and give the presentation to the class. You may also ask for a copy of the

presentation to give you the opportunity to combine all the presentations into an end-of-semester review.

2. **Evaluate Web sites**—Have students search the Web for three sites related to a Founder or the Founding period (you may provide them with a "start list" from the resource list at the end of each lesson). Create a Web site evaluation sheet that includes such questions as: Are the facts on this site correct in comparison to other sites? What sources does this site draw on to produce its information? Who are the main contributors to this site? When was the site last updated? Ask students to grade the site according to the evaluation sheet and give it a grade for reliability, accuracy, etc. They should write a 2–3 sentence explanation for their grade.

3. **Web Quest**—Choose a Web site(s) on the Constitution, Founders, or Founding period. (See suggestions below.) Go to the Web site(s) and create a list of questions taken from various pages within the site. Provide students with the Web address and list of questions, and ask them to find answers to the questions on the site, documenting on which page they found their answer. Web site suggestions:

   - The Avalon Project <**http://www.yale.edu/lawweb/avalon/avalon.htm**>
   - The Founders' Constitution <**http://press-pubs.uchicago.edu/founders/**>
   - Founding.com <**http://www.founding.com/**>
   - National Archives Charters of Freedom <**http://www.archives.gov/national_archives_experience/charters.html**>
   - The Library of Congress American Memory Page <**http://memory.loc.gov/**>
   - Our Documents <**http://www.ourdocuments.gov/**>
   - Teaching American History <**http://www.teachingamericanhistory.org/**>

   A good site to help you construct the Web Quest is: <**http://trackstar.hprtec.org**>

Verbal Assessments

1. **Contingency in History**—In a one-to-two page essay, have students answer the question, "How would history have been different if [Founder] had not been born?" They should consider repercussions for later events in the political world.

2. **Letters Between Founders**—Ask students to each choose a "Correspondence Partner" and decide which two Founders they will be representing. Have them read the appropriate Founders essays and primary source activities. Over a period of time, the pair should then write at least three letters back and forth (with a copy being given to the teacher for review and feedback). Instruct them to be mindful of their Founders' tone and writing style, life experience, and political views in constructing the letters.

3. **Categorize the Founders**—Create five categories for the Founders (e.g., slaveholders vs. non-slaveholders, northern vs. southern, opponents of the Constitution vs. proponents of the Constitution, etc.) and a list of Founders studied. Ask students to place each Founder in the appropriate category. For advanced students, ask them to create the five categories in addition to categorizing the Founders.

4. **Obituaries and Gravestones**—Have students write a short obituary or gravestone engraving that captures the major accomplishments of a Founder (e.g., Thomas Jefferson's gravestone). Ask them to consider for what the Founder wished to be remembered.

5. **"I Am" Poem**—Instruct students to select a Founder and write a poem that refers to specific historical events in his life (number of lines at the teacher's discretion).

Each line of the poem must begin with "I" (i.e., "I am…," "I wonder…," "I see…," etc.). Have them present their poem with an illustration of the Founder.

6. **Founder's Journal**—Have students construct a journal of a Founder at a certain period in time. Ask them to pick out at least five important days. In the journal entry, make sure they include the major events of the day, the Founder's feelings about the events, and any other pertinent facts (e.g., when writing a journal about the winter at Valley Forge, Washington may have included information about the troops' morale, supplies, etc.).

7. **Résumé for a Founder**—Ask students to create a resume for a particular Founder. Make sure they include standard resume information (e.g., work experience, education, skills, accomplishments/honors, etc.). You can also have them research and bring in a writing sample (primary source) to accompany the resume.

8. **Cast of Characters**—Choose an event in the Founding Period (e.g., the signing of the Declaration of Independence, the debate about the Constitution in a state ratifying convention, etc.) and make a list of individuals related to the incident. Tell students that they are working for a major film studio in Hollywood that has decided to make a movie about this event. They have been hired to cast actors for each part. Have students fill in your list of individuals with actors/actresses (past or present) with an explanation of why that particular actor/actress was chosen for the role. (Ask the students to focus on personality traits, previous roles, etc.)

Review Activities

1. **Founders Jeopardy**—Create a Jeopardy board on an overhead sheet or handout (six columns and five rows). Label the column heads with categories and fill in all other squares with a dollar amount. Make a sheet that corresponds to the Jeopardy board with the answers that you will be revealing to the class. (Be sure to include Daily Doubles.)

   a. Possible categories may include:
   - Thomas Jefferson (or the name of any Founder)
   - Revolutionary Quirks (fun Founders facts)
   - Potpourri (miscellaneous)
   - Pen is Mightier (writings of the Founders)

   b. Example answers:
   - This Founder drafted and introduced the first formal proposal for a permanent union of the thirteen colonies. *Question: Who is Benjamin Franklin?*
   - This Founder was the only Roman Catholic to sign the Declaration of Independence. *Question: Who is Charles Carroll?*

2. **Who Am I?**—For homework, give each student a different Founder essay. Ask each student to compile a list of five-to-ten facts about his/her Founder. In class, ask individuals to come to the front of the classroom and read off the facts one at a time, prompting the rest of the class to guess the appropriate Founder.

3. **Around the World**—Develop a list of questions about the Founders and plot a "travel route" around the classroom in preparation for this game. Ask one student to volunteer to go first. The student will get up from his/her desk and "travel" along the route plotted to an adjacent student's desk, standing next to it. Read a question aloud, and the first student of the two to answer correctly advances to the next stop on the travel route. Have the students keep track of how many places they advance. Whoever advances the furthest wins.

A NOTE ON STANDARDS

The following national standards are referenced in this publication:

CCE   Center for Civic Education, National Standards for Civics and Government
NCHS National Center for History in the Schools, National History Standards
NCSS National Council for the Social Studies

❦ TEACHER NOTES ❦